BECOMING KEROUAC

BECOMING KEROUAC

A Writer in His Time

PAUL MAHER JR.

Essex, Connecticut

An imprint of Globe Pequot, the trade division of
The Rowman & Littlefield Publishing Group, Inc.
4501 Forbes Blvd., Ste. 200
Lanham, MD 20706
www.rowman.com

Distributed by NATIONAL BOOK NETWORK

British Library Cataloguing in Publication Information available

Library of Congress Cataloging-in-Publication Data
Names: Maher, Paul, 1963- author.
Title: Becoming Kerouac : a writer in his time / Paul Maher Jr.
Description: Essex, Connecticut : Lyons Press, [2023] | Includes bibliographical references and
    index.
Identifiers: LCCN 2023023794 (print) | LCCN 2023023795 (ebook) | ISBN 9781589796874
    (cloth) | ISBN 9781589796881 (epub)
Subjects: LCSH: Kerouac, Jack, 1922-1969. | Authors, American—20th century—Biography.
Classification: LCC PS3521.E735 Z7678 2023 (print) | LCC PS3521.E735 (ebook) | DDC
    813/.54 [B]—dc23/eng/20230607
LC record available at https://lccn.loc.gov/2023023794
LC ebook record available at https://lccn.loc.gov/2023023795

♾™ The paper used in this publication meets the minimum requirements of American National
Standard for Information Sciences—Permanence of Paper for Printed Library Materials, ANSI/
NISO Z39.48-1992.

Dedicated to Rachel Leigh and Chloe Jane Maher

Contents

Introduction

The year 2024 will mark the twentieth anniversary of *Kerouac: The Definitive Biography*. For this anniversary, I wanted to overhaul the book rather than reprint it as is. Since 2004, a flood of posthumous Kerouac titles have been published that I could not take advantage of the first time around, including several of the writer's apprentice works (*The Sea Is My Brother*, *The Haunted Life*); a spiritual biography of Buddha (*Wake Up*); and an original draft of *On the Road* (*On the Road: The Original Scroll*) among other works. I began expanding and revising a draft of my biography as these books became available. As I wrote it, it became clear to me that I was barely scratching the surface of the "real" Jack Kerouac, that even the deepest scrutiny of his letters, notebooks, and manuscripts would only achieve a surface construct of the man and the writer.

Becoming Kerouac: A Writer in His Time, then, follows the man and artist on his creative trajectory to a fully evolved author of his era. To accomplish this, I decided to eliminate the early Lowell years from my book, as well as anything from September 1957 through his death in October 1969. Much of this information is now common knowledge and eliminating it left room for new discoveries in research. The Kerouac archives had opened not only in New York, but also in Kerouac's (and my) hometown of Lowell thanks to a changing of the guard in the Kerouac Estate. This access made it infinitely easier for scholars to better study the evolution of Kerouac. I could proceed without caution.

Much of the quoted writing to be found in this book will be published by Sal Paradise Press/Rare Bird Books in a companion volume titled *Self-Portrait*.

—Paul Maher Jr.
February 2023
Lubec, Maine

CHAPTER ONE

The Show of Things

By October 1959, Jack Kerouac had maintained little contact with associates, friends, media, and readers. All that comprised Jack's world by this point was his mother, Gabrielle. With and through her, he retreated into dreams, visions, and stories of his childhood. She was there as a living ambassador of his former life in Lowell; Jack was confident enough in her memories to use them as material for a slew of Lowell novels. One day he fed a long taped-together paper roll into his loyal Underwood, the same that his father worked on all those years ago in 1930s Lowell, and began typing:

"I was born in 1922 in March in Lowell Mass. at five oclock in the afternoon, they tell me, when the sun was red in a sudden thaw and the river was high. The first four years of my life was spent playing with my older brother Gerard, who had rheumatic fever."[1]

It was a novel he had been thinking about for the past year and a half. He would title this "childhood halo" *Memory Babe*, an epithet ascribed to his fabled prodigious memory. Except, lately, he was not remembering much at all. Battling alcohol abuse, various head traumas, and reckless experimentation with various narcotics had diminished this capacity to remember. Instead he was embroiled within his fevered imagination manifested through a plethora of dreams, visions, tics, and "pomes."

He was Laocoön writhing in the folds of serpents.

By this time, Allen Ginsberg had fully embraced the ethos of the Beat Generation and was its eager spokesman. William S. Burroughs had warned Allen about becoming too political in light of his assuming the altar as High Priest of the Beats; Allen followed his advice and embraced the mystical, eager to place himself in the ranks of William Blake and less in the current political crises of the time. Yet, within the following two decades, Allen would place himself squarely into the covenant of the New Left, embracing such political hot-irons as gay rights, drug policy reforms, environmentalism, and gender roles.

In the fall of 1959, Allen swallowed yage[2] and experienced the "whole fucking Cosmos"[3] breaking loose around him. It was an experience comparable to his infamous Blakean vision he experienced in a New York City hotel room in 1948. Allen had ingested it to confront a fear of death, his "Shroudy Stranger." Life was empty. The "death-fear" of death was mere vanity. What it accomplished for Allen was a way to explore his consciousness through psychedelics, to open his world up fully within the cloak of his poetry. He had found his place in the emerging drug consciousness that came to define Youth America during the 1960s.

Burroughs was goaded to write by the coaxing of an invader, the "ugly spirit," a wrathful entity prompted by the death of his wife, Joan Vollmer Burroughs, by his hand in the fall of 1951. Now, this same October, he was in Paris during the aftermath of an obscenity charge lobbed at his novel, *Naked Lunch* (1959). He had written "Deposition: Testimony Concerning a Sickness" in response to the negative reception by critics and readers. In October 1959, Bill appeared at trial before three judges. After his lawyer read to the court the full text of Burroughs's "Deposition," the exiled author was handed a suspended sentence and fined $80. It was a comfort. In 1950s America, the notion was that a dope fiend was a step lower than a killer. He had avoided drug charges in Texas and New Orleans, and was charged with reckless homicide in Mexico. Now, at forty-five years old, Burroughs opted for the life of a quiet Parisian exile. He was Nero watching Rome burn. *Naked Lunch* was his fiddle.[4]

Ultimately, Ginsberg and Burroughs assumed an air of near-secular respectability. They were the High Priests of the Beats. The same cannot be said for Jack Kerouac.

In October 1959, Jack Kerouac was living with his mother, Gabrielle, in a three-bedroom suburban home at 49 Earl Avenue, Northport, Long Island. They bickered like husband and wife, as if Jack had assumed the place of long-dead father and husband, Leo.[5] Gabe thought Jack drank too much (he did), though she imbibed gin martini "hi-balls" drink-for-drink with her son. She was aging (sixty-five), yet hearty. She was gregarious: a chatterbox with a sturdy frame, ruddied cheeks, graying hair, pinched no-nonsense lips, and shrewd brown eyes magnified under her eyeglasses. To her eleven-year-old grandson, she was Mémère (French-Canadian moniker for "grandmother") and so she was called this by the entire family in her grandson's presence. She was a living room fixture, guarding the front door against Jack's encroachers like Cerberus. She gave him little privacy and forbade the presence of most women. Subsequently, Jack found it difficult to sneak them into his bedroom without her knowledge ("nothing gets past me but the wind," she was fond of saying). This day, he was alone, and so he removed himself into his basement for isolation. She did not follow because she would not chance falling down the stairs. He wanted to trip in privacy. He popped a hallucinogen in the form of a "big red pill" into his mouth; it was mescaline.[6]

Within an hour he was nauseous and trembling on his couch. Chills swept through his body. By 7:00 p.m., he fumbled his way upstairs to the living-room couch like a reclining Siddhartha. A Will Rogers movie flickered on the black-and-white television. Gabe was drunk and blank-faced watching it. She told Jack to eat if he was drinking and fed him rice and ragout as he lay on his side. Jack took several bites, and felt better. Then the television screen blew out white. Flashes. Crackles. He said "goodnight" to his mother and retired upstairs. He carried the thought of her with him. He got in bed with his jeans and shirt still on. He closed his eyes; the next wave hit him harder. His heartbeat accelerated. Flashes of light blinded him. It was late dusk. He lifted the window to let the cool autumn air flow in. The moon had risen, silhouetting the backyard trees. He closed his eyes. The "Show began."

The Show of Things.

Trees shaped like women waved their heads in an oscillating dance. Many-armed Mother Kali danced before him. Goddess of sex and death. He fixated on her nakedness: "and I kneel in front of all the assembled saints of the world and start sucking on her beautiful cunt which snaps at me and wants to eat me back and as it does take back everything in the world."

Mother Earth. Father Sky.

A woman in a shroud in her grave. Jack reached out to touch her eyelid and poked through "ever so softly into clean soft gray dust."

"I must stop THINKING AND JUST LOOK," he thought.

A headless torso adorned in purple turned to him: "the body of a Buddha." Snapping "cunts" danced around like a witch's coven. A golden light. Images of gods flew by at 100 miles per hour. Jesus's soft kiss. Father Light from Heaven. Witches skulking in Jack's moonlit yard. Neal Cassady became Archangel Michael. Gregory Corso became Archangel Raphael who morphed into the Errol Flynn of his dreams. Adoring angels. Dancing devils. The Virgin Mary in heaven rising to a lineage of mothers leading to Gabe who transformed into a beautiful brunette "with a snapping cunt." Gabe was King Kong climbing the Empire State Building. He hallucinated the structure; she climbed his cock in his incestuous hallucination. He had an erection. His vision flickered from birth mother to Mother Earth to Mother Kali: "In thinking of eating cunt suddenly i was eating one that got all juicy and smoshy and started to disgust me and almost suck and snap me on, my mouth all flopped with shperm and i cried in my thoughts mother earth gets too juicy sometimes and now i realized why men die to fuck and suck and the next minute suddenly vacantly forget about it!"

After three hours the high had passed. He began typing in unflinching detail[7]: "in dreams the long mountains and long caves, the skyscrapers, all the huge landscape is simply as James Joyce knew the very body of someone, yourself or a girl's—so that everything is alright not because the communists believe in a better world for the body, but because everybody in their dreams already knows the eternal transcendental truth which i have just tried to describe in silly words."[8]

His drug experience was intense and revelatory. He discovered that he had a fear of women, especially his mother. However, it was the final proof that he was on the "right track with spontaneous never-touch-up poetry of immediate report, and *Old Angel Midnight* most especially, opening out a new world of connection in writing with the endless space of Shakti Maya Kali Illusion."[9] His resulting text, "Mescaline," is perhaps one of his more important writings because in it he has finally confronted the complexity of his neuroses and the soundness of his writing methods. In Jungian terms, it reveals his fear of women—even his mother—but also his reverence for them because they are vehicles of creation toward death (as he bluntly states in *Some of the Dharma*, "Pretty girls make graves, fuck you all."[10]) This is apparent when he reports of "loving cunt" before it transforms into a "snapping cunt" eating everything in existence.

Kerouac's visions of Kali evoked his fear of impending death.[11] Mescaline was the key to deciphering truth and eternity. The emphasis on the "mother" ideal was recognized as one of the chief forces in Kerouac's life. His demise (physical, emotional, and spiritual) was imminent. Physicality and spirituality were interchangeable.

Gabe's appearance in Kerouac's drug vision manifested because she was not only his "mother" but she also represented the "Mother of All Things" as written in Lao Tzu's *The Tao Te Ching*. Gabe was Kali; Kali was all women. Jack writes of the many faces of God. It was not simply a "trip." It was a moment of clarity: God, Creation, Mother Earth, Suffering, Lust, Fear, and Death. The importance of "Mescaline" lies in Kerouac's journey toward understanding the truth of his existence. He had left Plato's allegorical cave with its shadows on the wall. In his hallucination, he experienced the appearance of the "Father of Light," which induced a realization that God was everywhere at last. This, then, became his last true journey. It was not the road he had been raggedly following, literally and symbolically. Nor was it in his books; it was his true understanding of Self in relation to a visible and invisible cosmos. He had tapped into the source of all things that he had formerly tried to capture from dreams, visions, endless traveling, and furious writing.

And so, we must return to the source waters of his creative journey.

CHAPTER TWO

Where the Road Begins

JACK KEROUAC WAS SEVENTEEN YEARS OLD IN THE AUTUMN OF 1939 when he left his family for the first time. It was the first of many times, a fevered habit of relocation in search of something that he could not pinpoint exactly. The drive of moving also drove his writing. It was in that year he also discovered the chief vocation that would consume him for the remainder of his short life.

His father, Leo, wanted Jack to become an All-American athlete. His mother wanted him to leave their provincial hometown and become a journalist in New York. That year, Jack had other plans. He wanted to be a writer.

To his peers, "John" was "Jack." To friends, "Zaggo." To his father and sister, he was "Jacky." To his mother, he was "Ti Jean" and "My Sweet Son." He had received a scholarship to attend college. He had his choice: Boston College or Columbia University. Gabe encouraged him: don't stay in Lowell. Lowell was the end game for many of their friends and family. They lived and died routinely punching a time clock, trekking to and fro beneath the sooty smokestacks of the textile mills. And so Jack opted to go Ivy League and chose Columbia. But first, he had to make up some classes at a prep school, and Columbia paid his way to Horace Mann School for Boys in the Bronx neighborhood of New York City.

Jack's relocation in the autumn of 1939 thrust him into a chaotic urban Babylon. He lived with his maternal step-grandmother, Amanda Dube, at 293 State Street in Brooklyn, until the spring of 1940. Every weekday he woke at 6:00 in a bedroom "lined with volumes which I rejuvenated from the doom of cellar dust." These were books he had picked up over time: Dickens, Lewis, Bacon, Stevenson, Romains, Eliot, H. G. Wells, Coleridge, Tennyson, Emerson, Bianchi, and Alexander Pope were some of them. He dressed in a required uniform and took public transportation. *Mémère* Amanda brown-bagged peanut butter sandwiches for him. The paper bag, Jack learned, was a mark of his poverty.

When Jack left the brownstone apartment, he was thrust into the restless kinetics of an ever-fueled social machinery. He avidly absorbed the myriad specimens of bustling humanity. It reminded him of Herman Melville's "Manhattoes" and the "Mannahatta" of Walt Whitman. It was the "rock" of Thomas Wolfe's *The Web and the Rock*. Saroyan's Broadway. It was what he had read about and knew in his heart. There was something liquid, refined, and almost musical in its clamor. He took a train all the way to the IRT's last stop—West 242nd Street—and got off to step into numerous bands of Horace Mann students—a new breed stinking of money—gathered with their refined demeanors and patent leather Oxfords. Jack could have blended in or set himself apart. He could have had it either way. Assimilation was a gradual process.

In class, Jack was disconsolate. Ill-at-ease. A daydreaming exile. Yet, he treasured his differentness. He felt an impulse for *otherness*. He was destined to be an outsider. He declared, "The more you study, the more you subsequently know; naturally, the more you know, the nearer you get to perfection as a journalist." But he did not want perfection but only a chance to transform his life into art. One way of getting there was to start writing a journal to document his journey.[1]

Jack pursued his truth-seeking mission as his year went by. This urge accelerated once fate intertwined with wartime. His personal writing became further removed from the amateurish juvenalia he had written since he was a boy. He found that using himself as his main subject was the most effective method to accomplish this. Autobiographical aliases like Richard Vesque, Peter Martin, and Jack Duluoz would transport him through his autobiographical terrain.

In much of Jack's early prose, we encounter a son determined to win his father's approval. In high school and in his first year at Columbia University, it was primarily sought through sports. It was also through writing, though what he showed his father was not taken seriously. Leo considered it a troubling phase that threatened to re-route Jack from his main goals: to play football and "get an education." But writing became his sole objective as Jack entered his first year at Columbia.

Kerouac favored solitude except when he wanted the comforts of a woman. But here, he failed.[2] His relationship with women remained undeveloped, perceiving them either as lovemaking partners or potential mother figures. Barely, if ever (during the early to mid-1940s) would he write about female characters with any depth because he could not understand them. His most crucial deficiency was maternal solicitude, which destroyed any intimacy he may have desired from a woman. Jack could easily pay for sex from a woman if he were without one (and he had the money). His Catholic upbringing did little to stop him from doing so. He patronized sex workers regularly from his late teens through the 1960s. All women, intimate or otherwise, fell short of his birth mother. He was afflicted with what Jung defines as "Don Juanism," when a man "unconsciously seeks his mother in every woman he meets" even if he had to pay for her services.[3]

After Jack graduated from Horace Mann, he was thoroughly educated in his urban milieu. Though he lacked any authentic life experience to populate his imaginary world fully, indeed he was catching up quickly. He became fascinated with psychology and was willing to explore the depths of his neuroses. He often subjected himself to lay self-analysis in his journal. By 1943, Kerouac knew he bore an undiagnosed schizoid condition embattled by melancholia. This in turn prompted his thirst for alcohol. Spirits either numbed him or brought out his jovial nature. Over-indulgence inflamed his temperament. As the abuse became established as a pattern, it inevitably exposed his worst inclinations.

After the spring semester of 1940, Jack returned to Lowell for the summer. He returned to his family's rented Gersham Avenue house in Pawtucketville (several of his later novels would take place there). He spent much of his free time in his bedroom. In the corner sat a green desk; chalkings scribbled beneath it bore the last remnants of older brother Gerard's long-dead hand. Nine-year-old Gerard Francois Kerouac had died of rheumatic fever when Jack was four. The somber aftermath of his wake (in the family parlor) and funeral indelibly attached itself to Jack's wounded psyche on a subconscious level. What he barely remembered of Gerard had merged with his mother's memories and relayed back to him. Thus, Gerard's sacred memory was transmuted through a maternal sensibility into Kerouac's later stories. Jack assumed the survivor's guilt and was sometimes made to believe that the wrong son had died when his mother was deep in her cups. To this, he privately puzzled a reason for his existence. Each morning he read from the Bible, not for salvation, but to attenuate his obsessive sense of guilt and failure. In his writings, he pondered an unbridgeable chasm he felt between eternity and Nothingness and wondered where he stood between them. At times he felt like crying over it. Other moments he sensed life as one vast comedy in which he was only a bit player. He bore his mirth boldly: "sometime this week I figured that the earth was a spark of light in the span of eternity in the spaceless universe and so the only thing to do is laugh at such pecunious smallness."[4]

He yearned to bind the personal with the universal, a revelation that was a "moment of new & ecstatic light." It seemed that an indifferent cosmos dwarfed his humanity. Jack's so-called modernistic[5] phase of his writing had less to do with breaking with literary tradition and collapsed social norms than it was an initiation of his future disillusionment. The immediacy of his writing became "real." He pondered the smoke of a pipe that had scoured his throat. The dissipating smoke symbolized the ephemeral nature of the world. Concepts of "civilization" are temporary. Earth is but a ray of light extinguished by darkness. To self-loathe was as impractical as a "zebra fighting its stripes." Life was a spark destroyed as suddenly as it was created. Like a swarm of ants, humankind was a mere cluster of laborers feebly cultivating a cosmic order.[6]

"I am one of the grimy coal-shovelers, supplying the fuel. I don't know now just where to analogize grime with life's grime, but your guess is as good as mine. There is grime here and grime there, so we don't have to analyze it because grime is grime no matter what you say or the philosopher says. . . . I think that our smallness is to be measured by the spark which lasts one second and dies out and all the ants have gone to waste but they supplied the coal anyhow."[7]

Jack's self-awareness entertained the certitude of a far-greater cosmic order. Later, in his Buddhist phase of the early to mid-1950s, actuality became "Nothingness." He had declared a similar ideology at age eighteen in a reflective essay titled "Nothing": "I know someday I will be nothing."[8] Ultimately, "nothing" exists. It does not exist in life or death. In an interview with news-journalist Mike Wallace in 1958, Kerouac associated the same concept he wrote of at eighteen: "What I believe is that *nothing* is happening." Confused, Wallace asks, "What do you mean?" Kerouac is forthright, and, ultimately, misinterpreted:

"Well, you're not sitting here. That's what you think. Actually, we are a great empty space. I could walk right through you . . . Do you know what I mean? We're made out of atoms, electrons. We're actually empty. We're an empty vision . . . In one mind."

In "Go Back," Kerouac analyzes the pursuit of truth through memory. Sitting on a curbstone observing a "rickety" cottage, Jack describes his childhood experience. He is assuming an early form of "sketching," a writing practice he will thoroughly utilize in the autumn of 1952, only later conducted in small breast-pocket notebooks. This method permits his thoughts to unreel a memory stream. Jack pities a passer-by's grim perseverance when he disturbs Jack's meditation. This releases a repressed memory of childhood trauma:

"Later on, I left and I went toward the house before that, where my brother had died. Here, the memories were now vague and childish. I was three and four there, three and four years old. I remembered the high snow, my sandwich, calling for my mother, weeping, all. Myself. . . . at the church. . . . unabashed, they burying my brother. Why do you cry, I ask my mother and sister. Why do you cry? Why?"[9]

He lapsed into nostalgia before brushing it off as absurd. Yet, he pledged to "hold the present now because someday it will be very precious."[10]

Through the summer, Jack sold *Lowell Sun* newspaper subscriptions and gave his parents a percentage of his earnings. He was ready for his first semester at Columbia with a $500-a-year scholarship in place to pay his way. He packed his trunk with books, notebooks, and neatly folded clothes washed and ironed by his mother. On the last day, he kissed Gabe goodbye and left. She would now have to write to her "Sweet Boy" daily to keep his spirits up and to fend off her loneliness for him.[11]

Leo went with Jack to New York so that he might find work.[12] A local job would place himself and Gabe closer to Jack.[13]

Jack was housed at decrepit Hartley Hall overlooking Amsterdam Avenue. He had a single roommate with whom he was instantly at odds. For the next several days, father and son scoured the city. On the field, Leo watched Jack train. He supported his athleticism and scrutinized Coach Little's coaching style. Jack was to be utilized, when the time came, as a "climax runner."[14] Jack was not in the starting lineup though he trained four hours daily and was prepared. His lack of varsity experience counted against him. He came to resent how the coaches treated him. Before Leo left, he advised Jack to "study, play good ball, pay attention to what the coach and the professors tell you, and see if you can't make your old man proud and maybe an All-American."[15] Not only did such advice go unheeded, but it was one catalyst for Jack's defection from Columbia.

Seemingly, with each passing day, Jack became further removed from Columbia. It was Jack's second game. He had run the opening kickoff back to the 12 yard line and was brutally tackled. He was stretchered off the field. His coaches assessed his injury as a sprain. Jack sat out the next game. He went to the Columbia Medical Center for x-rays when he didn't improve. Jack had suffered a hairline stress fracture of the tibia (*Columbia Spectator* reported it as a "split bone"). His leg was wrapped in plaster and he was placed on injured player status for the remainder of the season.

This sudden manna from heaven relieved Jack of his burden. He was, at last, alone with "my thoughts, my self-confidences." He had ample time to read lengthy tomes like Thomas Wolfe's posthumous novel, *You Can't Go Home Again* (1940). Its dust jacket promised a story about a "Lost Modern Who Found Himself." In search for his identity, young George Webber could have been a stand-in for Kerouac instead of Wolfe. The idea of America as one great poem inspired Jack. He had mostly read romanticized versions of America told through a nineteenth-century sensibility: the Concord Transcendentalists, Whitman, Melville, Twain, and Emily Dickinson. Now, Wolfe opened up an entirely new perception of their native country. Wolfe wanted to write a vast saga using American vernacular. Both Kerouac and Wolfe wanted to write the Great American Novel.

In his diary Jack noted that his writing was frivolous. Characterization was a struggle. To compensate, he read Dostoevsky's *Notes from the Underground*. The unnamed narrator who cleverly posited a moral and spiritual dilemma intrigued Jack. The book's ideology became his literary blueprint. Jack's mercurial personality wavered between determination and defeat as did the Underground Man. Both were plagued by anguish. Jack agreed that humankind and its history were irrational. Jack wrote as such in the West End Cafeteria on Broadway as he observed young people that were just like him. He concluded from watching them that "man is essentially an ANIMAL."[16] For Jack, he relished such profundities because they were vital to his artistry. For the Underground Man, animalism fed into his nihilism. The Underground narrator and Jack perceived society as false. They reveled in isolated consciousness. Kerouac's polemics mirrored the Underground Man, the vanquished dreamer. Ultimately, Jack chose to mount the mantle created for him, to rise above those people who only strove to spread further torment. The Underground Man was the opposite of what society deemed acceptable and appropriate. Jack did not desire a utopian society because, again like *Notes from the Underground*'s nihilist, such a society would remove suffering and pain, but humanity desired both things and needed them to be happy. He argued that removing pain and suffering in society took away man's freedom. He stated that the cruelty of society made human beings moan about pain only to spread their suffering to others. Idealized rationality was inherently flawed for not accounting for humanity's darker and more irrational side. Jack quoted Underground Man: "That man everywhere, and at all times, whoever he may be, has preferred to act as he chose and not in the least as his reason and advantage dictated."[17]

Kerouac's next journal began in the autumn of 1940, titled "Journal of an Egotist," which dealt with his "activities and thoughts" during his freshman year at Columbia. Jack reasoned that despite the "millions upon millions of people in the world," he remained a world unto himself. He was one among other "little worlds." Though his achievements thus far were insignificant, they were "sacred" because the very act of writing was sacred. It was a way to address himself: "It is I, speaking to you." He was certain of his direction without bravado or approval. Jack's self-image meant that he thought what others saw of him: "A young writer, unshaven" dressed rakishly like young Whitman on the frontispiece of the 1855 edition of *Leaves of Grass*. Or, maybe closer to seafaring Melville of *Typee* fame. He would pay heed to all he experienced, no matter how trite. It was all part of a legend. *His* legend. The very banality of eating meatloaf and mashed potatoes was elevated to a Homeric feast. He documented moments of indecision: Should he smoke a cigar before or after a show? Every act was significant, "every precious second, every conscious moment." The curves of a woman were an indulgence, as were food and alcohol. Yet, as a man and writer, Jack had to be part of society: "You can't be an artist unless you're a member of humanity."[18]

Jack knew his uniqueness and potential: "I had a terrific imagination. First, I imagined the most paralyzing sort of monsters, and with the years, imagined my own little world. From the age of five to twelve, I was continually absorbed in the pantomimes of my little universe whenever I could get a moment off by myself."[19] Despite this, Jack felt limited under current circumstances. He had to wait, despite an urge for otherwise though his ambitions remained noble: "I wish to be a novelist, playwright, short story writer . . . in short, a Journalist, a man of letters."[20]

The "Egotist" journal represents a record of Jack's mercurial temperament. Writing around midnight on December 9, Kerouac prepared to "let my heart out" to splatter "its delicate essences all over the page." He was hopelessly in love with sixteen-year-old Norma Blickfelt (he was eighteen). Jack quaffed six mugs of beer because he did not feel drunk. This is an alarming indicator of his addiction to come. Though he curses himself and wonders if he lacks any self-control, he continues self-medicating his despondency:

"What the hell kind of a man are you, getting drunk over a girl. You and all your high and mighty philosophy! You and your Aristotle and Plato and everybody. Temperance, wisdom, truth, etc. O hell, I'm in love and I can't stand it. Three beers," I ordered. "Three glasses of foaming, acrid beer, pungent yellow beer, ugly frothing brew, distasteful golden ale; bitter nose-contracting, stomach-formenting beer. Three beers."[21]

Alcohol elated him before it changed to self-deprecation: "John, you are a writer and a philosopher to boot, and a scholar, though a very slothful one." Self-pity transformed into despondency as the effects of the beer began to settle: "Why do I cry now. Why do I want to go home and sit in the parlor with my Ma and look at the Xmas tree? Why must a man go nowhere, and return to nowhere, and always be lost?" He continues with a run of writing that reveals a specific constancy found in his mature writings: "Of course, why do the vultures persist, you would ask—-for the vultures are the cause of it all, the Vultures of Human Sadness."

By the time the intoxicating effects of alcohol wore off, Jack had finished writing. He is depleted: "I am dead." He feels empty. Hopeless. This prompts him to write as a solution to battle an inner tumult. It is one of the myriad deaths, reflecting what he had read from William Saroyan by paraphrasing, "we would have to die many times before dying physically." At its core, the "Journal of an Egotist" is a meditation on Nothingness: "This emptiness is made out of nothing, and therefore it is endless. So let us proceed through the emptiness of time, through the void of endlessness, and let us never reach the end of nowhere, or the" ——the journal entry terminates, as if Jack fell asleep, or passed out from drinking.[22]

Despite his unhappiness, Jack was becoming a varsity star athlete. The *Columbia Spectator* reported: "One of these yearlings is Jack Kerouac. Injured in the second game of the freshman campaign last fall and unable to play out the remainder of the schedule, Kerouac nevertheless showed enough to convince frosh coach Ralph Furey that he would have to be reckoned with in the plans for next year's varsity."[23] Jack was a brightening light, but not for Columbia.

The spring semester ended in late May 1941. Jack returned to Lowell, arriving thirteen hours later after thumbing a series of rides: "I got rides from truck-drivers, philosophers, and good souls. There is nothing like hitch-hiking as a pedestal from which to study and be studied by humanity."[24] When he arrived tired and famished, it was 4:00 a.m. His arduous trip was valuable because Jack was intrigued by the "journey" as a literary device. The journey story, where the hero must venture into the world for reasons not of his/her own devising, is as old as recorded history. It is allegorical of Self and Soul. Gilgamesh's journey to the end of the earth is a search for the secret of eternal life. When Gilgamesh does not find what he is looking for, he returns home to make peace with his mortality. Homer's *Odyssey* is an epic journey; Dante's journey through hell, purgatory, and heaven pursuing divine Beatrice is a metaphysical journey. In *Don Quixote*, Quixote sets off searching for adventure after confusing reality with fantasy. Huckleberry Finn floats down the Mississippi River with slave Jim, on a journey for physical and spiritual liberation. Kerouac's physical journey was initially undertaken to save money. Later it will become a figurative journey to find the "father never found."[25] Jack shares with Gabe details of his journey by thumb. Ultimately, after a series of cross-country trips, it is to the world that he yearns to tell his story, his epic road novel.

Gabe was alone. Leo worked weekdays at a Works Progress Administration (WPA) job in Worcester, Massachusetts. He rented a room to save time and money and returned to Lowell on weekends. Though Jack loved the rigors of the road, Leo detested it. For him, it meant instability and uncertainty. Any job could be his last. He was an aging man and there was an expectation for Jack to assume the patriarchy with his education and social advantages. Leo was disillusioned with the American dream; he was at odds with its corrupt underbelly that he felt undermined his own success. However, he thought it was possible for All-American Jack. Jack, however, thought otherwise.

The "American Dream" in 1940s America meant that ideals of equality, freedom, and opportunity were available for all. For Jack, this dreamy ideology was unacceptable. Though America was once regarded as a new Garden of Eden, it was now a paradise lost and therefore should be approached with an anarchic attitude. Yet, Kerouac did not permit rampant anarchy and a challenge to authority except through his art. In his novels and in life, he latched on to others to embody this revolution (such as Neal Cassady and William Burroughs). Kerouac would document the country he passed through as a chaotically convoluted wasteland.

Jack wasted no time. On the first night, he wrote further plans for a novel. He had a stack of white paper waiting for his typewriter from New

York. Jack had been developing characters, settings, and themes. He was eager to start but had to put it aside to study for a make-up chemistry exam. He awaited a telegram beckoning him back to Columbia for a test date. The next day he received his typewriter. The words immediately clacked out in a fury. His typing mastery permitted him to keep pace with a stream of ideas. It was second nature: He just rolled a sheet into the platen, turned the knob, and began typing top to bottom, single-spaced. He'd fill the page and repeat the process in hours-long sittings.

This summer was Jack's last period of independence. His youth was flaming out. He could still be lackadaisical about responsibilities. He aligned himself with loafer-hero Whitman. Jack felt Whitman to be divinely blessed. By virtue of his reading Whitman's poetry and following his credo, he would be blessed too. He read in the library. This cost him nothing. Day after day, he scanned the pages of the Old Testament. He read plays by Sean O'Casey and George Bernard Shaw. Jack read from the "immortals" to join their ranks one day. After reading Wolfe's *The Web and the Rock* (1939), he wanted to begin his own writing process all over again. What he had written before was chaff. He wanted to break free of tradition. Throw the hawser from the capstan. Set sail. Find different shores to explore. Write as he never did before. Wolfe wrung order from chaos; now it was Jack's turn. His rapid progress manifested into a "spontaneous burst of passion." He favored observational prose, a technique utilized when he sat curbside on Moody Street[26] and documented what he saw firsthand. He was fond of this area. It had its own hospital run by the Sisters of Charity Ottawa.[27] Remnants of flimsy shelters near the textile mill had since transformed into a densely developed and self-sufficient neighborhood. There were social clubs, stores, and markets. Jack realized the impermanence of all matter, and so began recording it on paper which made him an agent of preservation. Each piece of matter took on the same importance: a landlord in bib overalls; mill girls, paying $3.50 a week for a five-room apartment, stepping out of their tenement home; clotheslines strung between porches; Judy's Candy Store. Two men smoking outside Dube's Barbershop. Matronly *mémères* at Vinnie's Shoe Store. Lovestruck teens sitting in a booth at Laura's Variety store listening to her jukebox. Mr. Giguere, the cobbler, smoking a tobacco pipe by a big boot at his front door. The rag man, Mr. Tessier, shouting, "Rags, rags!" from his horse-drawn cart. The decrepit theaters of Jack's boyhood: The Rialto, Keith, Royal, Merrimack, and the Palace were scribbled as he remembered them. Rochette's Market was baking salmon pie on Fridays, and a pot of baked beans on Saturdays. Old Man Joe Gauthier was on his front steps holding a spittoon. People were milling about. Cars passed in whooshes of white noise. Children were everywhere. The sounds of glee. A chortling fiddle. Laughter. Jack wrote, stopping not to find better words but to see the picture better. Somebody was weeping. A door slammed. The myriad sounds of humanity drifted over the Lowell rooftops like spring pollen. There were a million things he could write about:

"Every day, especially today, I see and feel a million things about which I could write thousands and thousands of words. Things come up at me and strike me—lights, colors, symphonies of sounds, dramatic movements, smells, poetic moments, Life."[28]

That weekend, Leo was at home placing bets on the horses. Jack caroused the city. He and friend George Apostolos had "tasted of Venus" despite the wooden floor making it difficult for Jack to finish.[29] He was pressured to get a job. *Stop daydreaming.* Whitman did not trouble his Spirit to be understood, why should Jack? He had a date at Canobie Lake in Salem, New Hampshire. They went to Glennies on Lowell's Pawtucket Boulevard ("Seldom Equalled Never Excelled") for ice cream floats and Belgian Butter Creams. Life was innocent. Effervescent. He had to work: $17.60 a week shoveling in a roadside ditch in Portsmouth, New Hampshire. Gabe got up at 5:30 every morning to go to work. It made Jack feel bad to see her, throwing him into "[d]ignified despair."[30] Life felt empty: "You have to keep up 'The Lie' to get along—but a manic depressive like myself does not do so steadily." All he did was sit and stare blankly at the world. He was dramatic in his journal: "death, right now, would be received very calmly." Life was a bore. He wished for war. Wouldn't that shake things up? He labored seaside watching vacationers flying down the highway on their way to the beach. He felt stupid. Futile. The men beside him cursed and sweated. Hair hung in their faces. It revealed to Jack the futility of the material world. He noted those working alongside him; they were living embodiments of Thoreau's "quiet desperation."[31] This imparted to Jack the importance of making a change to follow his own path. His life, while still quiet, no longer felt desperate.

All was empty. All was Nothingness.

And then summer ended.

Leo moved Gabe to Connecticut. Rather than renting a room and paying her rent in Lowell, it was more economical to relocate. She would be closer to him, and both would be closer to Jack in New York. They could see his games. Hit the town and make a night of it. Be a happy family once again.

It was the summer of Sibelius. Jack was fond of Sibelius's First Symphony. It was his favorite. And was not Jack embodied in its very spirit? A lone dissonant clarinet opens the first movement with a heroic and epic entrance waiting for the orchestra to follow. Low brass. High woodwinds. Strings surged like thundering waves crashing the Navy yard pilings along the Portsmouth waterfront. It reminded Jack of "stately pines in the snow." He wrote as he listened to it from his family's Victrola. Once it was the "Tarantella" he played over and over as he timed his horse-racing game to it, but now his tastes had evolved to a more complex nature. He liked Tchaikovsky's "Arabian Dance" and Wagner's *Der Ring des Nibelungen*. It elevated his mood and made him feel larger than life. He no longer thought of himself as a mere athlete or college student: "I am a poet, a singer, a writer of songs."[32]

Then the family packed their belongings. A moving truck with a pair of men loaded the furniture and left. Gabe and Jack followed with a seventeen-year-old Horace Mann classmate of Jack's[33] driving his car. Before leaving, Jack sat on his doorstep listening to the wind blowing through the trees of the dawn-lit street. He wrote, "Farewell Song, Sweet from My Trees" to remember his companions, Pine Brook, the old tenements, and its people. Saddened, he bid farewell to Lowell, which spoke to him from the treetops: "I look up at the trees, staring into their sorrowful profusion of night-green: 'So long trees. I've got to move along,' I whisper to them. 'So long. . . . . . so long . . . oh so long.'"[34] The move was unexpected, an impulsive decision on Leo's part. Lowell had no more to offer him, still, Leo, an inveterate bettor for all of his adult life, gambled a chance to start anew. He convinced Gabe that she could be closer to Jack; she still referred to herself as "your mommy" when she wrote him into adulthood. Jack was *their* bright star. However, in his journal, Jack felt the stirring of something new, an unfolding to his innermost bulb[35]: "suddenly we had to leave Lowell, and that was the beginning. . . ."[36]

* * *

President Roosevelt's reluctance to entangle America in World War II changed in June 1941. He authorized warships to join the Allies and retaliate should German U-boats fire upon them. In August, the military draft, opposed by isolationist members of Congress, was extended for another eighteen months. The clock was running out for Jack's freedom.

A gale of August rain whipped Long Island Sound's coastline as mother and son dropped their bags into the doorway of a ramshackle rental in West Haven, Connecticut. Gabe was appalled. She likened it to the dives of Moody Street and "Little Canada," Lowell's Franco-American ghetto district. Jack wrote his sister Caroline, known as Nin, complaining that the apartment Leo had picked out for them was "full of niggers, flies, and swill." Leo had not bothered to check out the place before renting it. Jack walked around the area looking for another place. The following day, Jack, Burt, and Gabe looked again without success. They stayed in a motel until they could find one. Their furniture was placed in temporary storage. On the following day, Leo consulted a French-Canadian realtor for a $40-a-month vacation cottage located at the end of a dead end on West Haven's Bradley Point. This, too, was temporary for it was not winterized. The sandy strip beachfronted Long Island Sound. There was a trolley that could take them to the center of New Haven. On a clear day, one could see across the Sound all the way to Long Island.[37]

Once they were moved in, Jack left for New York.

When he stepped on Baker Field, Jack found that he was late for practice. Coach Little snubbed him for this infraction. The team cold-shouldered him. With visions of hitchhiking, writing, and freedom dancing before him, he felt that he only had one choice. He lied to Little, showing his lack of interest in playing by telling him he had to do his laundry in Brooklyn. Then he left. It was only mid-September.

He wasn't sure where to go, and so he bought a Greyhound ticket to travel south. As the bus sped away from New York, he was invigorated yet consumed by dread. Jack despised inertia. He had to keep moving. It was like shedding old skin. He had guilt. His parents were moving partially because of him. Now he was leaving. Unwise. His scholarship would be thrown away. The draft was certain to find him. What could he gain from this experience?

Washington, DC, was no less busy than New York. The roads were congested with traffic. Everywhere, cars in the same monotonous pattern went nowhere to anywhere. Hours later he was in a cheap hotel room in a low-rent district. Bedbugs swarmed the sheets. The Capitol was silent and hot. Almost sterile. Jack saw nobody of merit and did not care. He was apolitical and chiefly enamored with artists and athletes, not nay-saying politicians with their war machines. Roaming the cold interior of the National Archives, he had no way of knowing that one day his own Navy medical records would be stored there. He returned to his squalid room. The heat felt like it was choking him. He wrote to his friend Sammy Sampas: "I don't know what I've done, afraid to go home, too proud and sick to go back to the football team, driven and weary with no place to go, I know not a soul."[38] He restlessly wept and panged with worry. The bedbugs drove him to distraction. He could not sleep. He paced his room. Yet, this experience was vital for his writing. Out of it, he typed a one-page story, "Washington in 1941."

"I am a writer, and thus it will prove valuable for me to study this place. However, before I start writing in dead seriousness, I want to add one thing. One of the remedies for American sickness is humour, there isn't enough of it to go around, and I think it ought to be fed to the people."[39]

Kerouac needed to laugh it off. He bought a used copy of Ralph Waldo Emerson's *Essays*. Emerson's philosophy of self-reliance consoled him like an understanding father: "though the wide universe is full of good, no kernel of nourishing corn can come to him but through his toil bestowed on that plot of ground which is given to him to till."[40]

And so he returned to his parents.

"Taking one last look at the shabby brick wall outside my window, there in Washington in 1941, and one last look at the skinny little tree which sprouted from between fences and barrels, I departed. As the bus pulled out of Washington, I looked at the streets and figured they were no different than any other."[41]

Wolfe was clear to him now. Jack had experienced America authentically, though the only thing of value he had seen were "three negroes standing on the corner across the street from my hotel, talking and joking."[42] The enlightenment of his trip faded once he was home. Leo was furious. Jack had an opportunity they never had. How dare he throw it away? But he had a safe harbor in Emerson and Whitman. He quoted to Sammy, "My final merit I refuse you. I refuse putting from me what I really am. Encompass worlds, but never try to encompass me."[43] Jack was trying to explain to Sammy that one must cultivate openness and awareness in order to contradict the past and present self. One must accept the unseen future. Jack had taken that chance, despite its unpleasant consequences.

To appease Leo, Jack promised that he would find a job. He applied as a laborer at a local rubber plant and worked the night shift until the following morning. Faceless, lost, he felt worthless. He tired of breathing hot rubber fumes. He detested punching a time clock, and so he did it for the last time and without collecting his pay. He resented having to wallow "in the mire of other people": "It is not right for me to give eight hours of my precious life to anyone at such a gory task every day. I should rather keep those eight hours to myself, meditating in the grass."[44]

Kerouac saw firsthand the plight of mill workers meekly accepting their tasks like beasts of burden:

"Look at him. He is middle-aged, and his face is resolute and tired in the early morning mists. He carries the lunchbox under his arm and trudges onward. He is on his way to the mill for another day of roaring heat. He is not afraid. He has been told that man's duty is work. So he is not afraid and hasn't been for fifteen years. But has he ever been uncertain? He turns around the corner and disappears from my gaze."

Leo's quarreling was incessant. Jack felt hopeless and so he did what he did best. He left. Leo had encouraged him to go out on his own and try to live as he pleased. With the help of an acquaintance, Jack moved forty-eight miles north to Hartford. He arranged a job at an Atlantic Whiteflash filling station in Manchester, Connecticut. In his knapsack were his works-in-progress, including "Farewell Song, Sweet from My Trees." He had a plan to send it to magazines. Seeing his writing in print would show them at last. Then they could get off his back. He lived at 106 Webster Street in a $4.50-a-week shambles of a furnished room. It had a grease-splattered stove, a steaming-hot radiator, some furniture, and a bed. The bathroom stank of stale piss. Despite its shortcomings, it meant freedom. He could do as he pleased without fear of retribution.

He rented an Underwood with a ream of yellow paper on October 13. He wrote dozens of pages in a matter of days. Soon he exceeded sixty prose pieces. His method of composition was to fill each sheet margin to margin, top to bottom, wrapping up his thought with the final line before closing with his initials. He whittled each to its pith using vivid impressions of Hartford and Lowell, his family, recent jobs, and his insatiable appetite for food because he was starving. He typed in a revelatory fever classifying each piece as either "SS" (short stories) or "LS" (long stories). He titled the mass of pages "Atop an Underwood." He promptly mailed the first of them to *Harper's* (who had already rejected "Farewell Song, Sweet from My Trees"). He wrote in the spirit of his heroes. Wolfe was his hub; experience spoked the wheel. On November 12, he typed the last and returned the Underwood. His days in Hartford were ending. The owner of Atlantic Whiteflash discovered that he lied about his qualifications and Jack was demoted to pumping gas. With only 4 cents in his pocket, he went into a drugstore one penny shy of a cup of coffee. An acquaintance gave Jack a cigarette and sifted through his piles of papers. He liked what he read and encouraged Jack. They made tentative plans to drive west someday.

Sammy surprised Jack with a Thanksgiving Day visit. He questioned Jack about leaving school. Jack told him, "it's allright to be an athlete if you think you're going to get something out of college. I wanna be a writer." Sammy had encouraged Jack to be a writer only two years before. Now he was mildly alarmed to see that Jack was following through with it, not as a hobby or on the weekends. The writing was to be his sole vocation.

Sammy left. Jack was alone. Two weeks later, he received a postcard from Gabe. She wanted him to return to Lowell with them. Leo was hired for a new job in Massachusetts, and so they were leaving New Haven. She was homesick and missed Jack. Caroline was still in Lowell and now living alone after her husband left her. She had space for all of them in a vacant downstairs apartment. Jack was ready to do as she wished. He had proven to himself that he had what it took to be a writer. Now he just had to prepare for the worst of what life could throw at him.

By December, the moving truck veered the peripatetic Kerouacs north to Lowell for the last time.

CHAPTER THREE

Among the Philistines

THE KEROUACS LIVED ON CRAWFORD STREET IN PAWTUCKETVILLE, less than a mile from where they had lived the previous summer. With no classes or work, Jack took to a plan for self-education. He wanted to return to school but had no scholarship to defray the cost. For now, he would educate himself with an exhaustive reading list. Wasting no time, "After hours were spent in the Library studying, where I learned more in three months than I could have learned in three years at college. I delved into everything: history, sociology, psychology, the classics, philosophy, evolution, and even psychoanalysis."[1] However, Jack also needed to work. The timing could not have been worse for he was vulnerable for the draft. Also, his parents were struggling despite Leo's promising employment. Sammy suggested a job for Jack working as a cub reporter at the *Lowell Sun*, a job he could do without much effort. This would keep him from shoveling ditches and in front of a typewriter.

Jack was uncertain about his destiny. If he did not want to stay in college and did not want to work, then he had to write. Writing a novel demanded time and dedication. Yet, he was ready for it. He was easily distracted by his vices: "Whatever I have to say will undoubtedly be of no use when a pair of stockinged limbs go clicking by on seductive heels."[2] War was a concern. Obstacles beset his path. He could be tossed into combat: "And when a guy finds himself in the path of an onrushing army of soldiers brandishing bayonets, what does all my writing or anybody else matter?"[3] Only two days earlier, a *Lowell Sun* headline screamed, "US Jap War Decision Possible Within Hours." Jack assumed a fatalistic stance by challenging God's will. He was never meant to be a writer if he did not survive the war. Jack saw himself as a "man-creature" yearning to "kick in an original manner." He had forsaken all else to write. He still felt that he could best accomplish this through novel writing. His life thus far was a "hidden legend" played out in real time. He was hyper-aware of his sense of Self. His emerging personal scope of vision was influenced by reading James Joyce. Joyce gave Kerouac the courage to move ahead with new ideas. Jack writes:

"[Joyce] has not only dragged out the truth to its ultimate veracity, but has created a new Realism in letters, (add to that a new style of writing which is not too smooth), has created a phase of Life that IS Life— Stream of Consciousness, a psychological and cerebral phenomena that everyone knows and no one realizes. James Joyce is something that no modern man can be complete without, that is, without thorough understanding of the man and his works. He has possibly begun a new age in letters, and what seems to me the ultimate age, for what can go further than complete and unbiased impeccable reality or Realism? Some people like to dream, like dreamy writers. Joyce, like Dostoevsky, dreams in his realistic works. Stream of Consciousness is one long dream, the thought of the thought, as Joyce puts it."[4]

On January 14, 1942, Jack became restlessly conflicted. He wrote "Self-Analysis of a Youth" to explain the discord between himself and those who could not understand him. It is a short exchange between a boy and a girl who senses a marked change in him:

"There is something dark and savage in your face, something sad, yet so angry! What is it?? What is there about you I cannot understand and do not like? What is that fierce wild stare? Why the savagery in the placid sea-pale eyes? Why the frown and brood? Why?"

The boy calls her a fool. To him, it is plain what it is. It is the thorny secret to life. He is highly sensitized to his environment. He feels that he alone has found the secret to life. The "boy" is Kerouac, and the girl is an anonymous girlfriend who he felt did not understand him (possibly Mary Carney).[5]

By January 1942 Jack wanted to return to New York to live. However, that required money. For now, he would have to remain in Lowell until the spring. Kerouac took the job at the *Lowell Sun*. He typed out his sports articles with a cigarette in his mouth like an old newspaper hack. His articles were bylined, though the editors misspelled his name.

Almost to spite his employers for disrespecting his surname, Jack began typing a novel on the company typewriter while he was on the clock. He titled it *The Vanity of Duluoz*.[6] "Duluoz" was the name he used for his pseudonym. The book was planned to depict the story of his life:

"During the months of January, February, and March of 1942, when I was nineteen years old and employed as a sports reporter on the *Lowell Sun*, I wrote a novel as an experiment in complete artistic freedom. Its title, 'The Vanity of Duluoz,' lends a great deal of information on the work's subject matter, mainly, The vanity of Kerouac. It was to have been a gigantic undertaking, as long and as encyclopedic as 'Ulysses,' but events, coupled with the general restlessness of youth and the particular restlessness of the young Romanticist, intervened at the sixtieth thousand-word mark."[7]

Jack marked it as a trilogy: *The Vanity of Duluoz, The Vexation of Duluoz*, and *The Joy of Duluoz*. Kerouac's namesake, "Robert Duluoz," was to be a writer for the *Galloway Star* (*Lowell Sun*) in a mid-size town in New England. He carries on a love affair with Eleanor and rebels against his father. He studies with "brooding enormity" in his bedroom by night. By day, he read at the Galloway Public Library. Jack was holding up a mirror to his life, reflecting back a "vanity" built up as legend.

At this point, Jack was only vaguely aware of his urge for emancipation through art: an "ideality in the atmosphere of fullest freedom." Though this "freedom" would emerge in his later writing, he possessed yet "the root of the idea": "I was nevertheless free in art and thus, free through art." It was art's "most satisfying definition." It represented freedom as a "source of power over nature," human and natural. He imagined three pillars, supporting themes of his trilogy: freedom, power, and beauty. Each represented the "humbler will" of the artist "by its humility."[8]

Jack worked in a manic burst to complete the novel while working in the *Sun*'s office. His Joycean influence was discouraged by Sammy, who encouraged Jack to remain true to himself knowing that he wrote best when he was stripped of his influences: "when you try (without realizing it) to be someone else, you are not great."[9]

To win his parents' confidence and admiration, Jack reworked "Farewell Song, Sweet from My Trees" to sell (it had already been rejected by *Harper's Magazine*). He mailed it to *Atlantic Monthly* and *Esquire*. He was not discouraged. However, both rejected it. Unfazed, he continued, polishing a short story, "Story of a Touchdown," a self-described psychological study of a hysterical player intended for *Esquire* with the same result.

Jack wanted no more to do with the *Lowell Sun*. At home, the fissure widened. Gabe defended Jack. There was tension between all of them.

A little after his twentieth birthday, Jack quit:

"I worked on the Sun for two months—just quit last week in order to get away from the pettiness + trivia of the job + the people who worked with me. They were a disgusting lot—except for two or three—vain, self-centered, immensely wise + satirical, (!) and above all, utterly unimportant and as sterile as dust . . . I left + decided to spend all of my time studying, which I've been doing consistently. . . . "[10]

George Apostolos left Lowell for a Civil Service stenography position in Washington, DC. Jack saw him off at the Lowell train depot. Apostolos encouraged Jack to follow him. Soon afterward, Jack obtained a letter of recommendation from a newspaper columnist that he was acquainted with. Then he packed a duffel bag and left.

In Washington, Jack spent $10 to join a local union. He worked for a month and a half as an apprentice sheet metal worker for the War Department's new Pentagon construction project. However, he became distracted and left the job site to do whatever his spirit prompted. He often slept through his shift until it was time to punch out. Writing Leo, Jack boasted of bedding women and shirking his work.

Leo wrote wayward Jack in better spirits:

"Dog my cat, so I whelped a Gigolo[11]—that's what Roosie [Roosevelt] does to everyone in America, makes 'em what they ain't meant to be.—or even dreamed they were. Ask Charlie Lindberg and others who tried to do some straight thinking. Anyway, don't let the Washington Merry-Go-Round make you permanently dizzy. Are you saving money kid? It's mighty handy sometimes. Have you sent some home—and did you remember your mom on Mother's Day, or did a blonde make you forget that? Your letter was the most welcome and it pleased me immensely—I hope you'll find time to write as often as you can. . . . You tell me you take naps on your job. Gosh, I hope, you should try to keep this job, the money you could make would probably mean a lot to you next Fall. I am rambling a lot, my mind is not on writing, and so just consider this note a little greeting and my fervent wishes for your welfare through these trying times—keep your head. Think clean, act clean, don't let your life become sordid—."[12]

Leo had much in common with Jack. They were both very literate. Leo, like Jack, was an avid reader and enjoyed theater and films. Leo had just read a brand-new novel, Upton Sinclair's *Dragon's Teeth* (1942), a "mighty clear story of what the shooting is all about. I don't know whether you'd like it—but it is a very clear picture of the rise of Adolf Schikelgruber—and shows just how the power of politics operates in the hands of scatter brains!" He also read Guy de Maupassant: "I sometimes wonder if guys like him are great writers or just plain, common double-action jerks, they sure sound like 'em in spots—but they can tell good stories, and how they love the gutters. I can imagine how they would read in French!"[13]

Discussing books was the best way to keep Jack's ear before delving into the heart of any matter.

But Jack wasn't swayed by Leo's advice, not to try and keep his job or avoid becoming "sordid." One afternoon he walked across a bridge over the Potomac River drinking gin straight from the bottle. In Virginia, he wandered through early springtime fields before returning in time to punch his time card. Eventually, the foreman caught on to him and Jack was fired. Jack worked at a lunch counter to remain solvent. An older woman there offered to take him in. Having no qualms about being a kept man, Jack spent a few nights with her before moving on. Then one day he took his last paycheck and went south. He didn't stay long before returning to Massachusetts.

When he returned home, he wanted to re-register with Columbia. He corresponded with Lou Little conveying his intentions to return to the team. He made arrangements to be there in the fall. He needed to regain his scholarship, and until then, come up with $400 for tuition.[14] Jack was torn; he was obligated to his family and needed to pay for school. But he was also drawn toward duty as the war escalated. In a romantic gesture, he desired to be with his symbolic brothers:

"I wish to take part in the war, not because I want to kill anyone, but for a reason directly opposed to killing—the Brotherhood. To be with my American brothers, for that matter, my Russian brothers; for their danger to be my danger; to speak to them quietly, perhaps at dawn, in Arctic mists; to know them, and for them to know myself . . . an elusive thing, I speak of now, but I know it is there. I want to return to college with a feeling that I am a brother of the earth, to know that I am not snug and smug in my little universe."[15]

That summer, Jack met a merchant mariner from Lowell named George Murray who was actively serving the Merchant Marine through the war. Murray shared details about its pay and benefits. When they parted, Jack handed Murray his leather-bound copy of "The Rime of the Ancient Mariner" for good luck. It was a transference of the Brotherhood of Man through verse.

Days later, at the National Maritime Union headquarters in Boston, Jack applied for—and received—an overseas passport and his seaman's papers. He joined the National Maritime Union and was classified as a general laborer. For several days, Jack hitchhiked from Lowell to Boston to wait at the Boston Seaman's Hall for ship's calls. At sunset, he prowled the docks. He wrote his girlfriend, Barnard student Norma Blickfelt:

"Drinking in the strong cod scent of the wharves; eyeing the anchored freighters and muttering: 'There are ships, and there are cities.' I repeat those words constantly. At night, in bed, I burn."[16]

In the Boston Seaman's Hall, he awaited his first assignment. The intercom piped a call. The SS *Dorchester* needed a scullion.[17] The *Dorchester* was a shipping vessel pegged for dangerous runs across the Atlantic to assist the Allied war effort. He signed on with the ship yeoman as John Keroach[18] with a scheduled departure date of July 18. He did not tell his parents.

That night he lay astir, thrilled to be one among a grand lineage of ancient mariners. He felt expiated. This opportunity brought him closer to authentic living. He planned a diary to track his day-to-day life onboard. He hoped to develop characterization by observing his shipmates. Without telling his parents where he was going, he left in mid-July to live on-board. He did not bother to explain his decision until he was away, chiefly because he could not bear to say goodbye to his mother.

At first, Leo was furious. He tried dissuading Jack.[19] After consideration, Leo considered his choice a "real job for a real man." Though his heart was heavy, he felt that harboring a grudge would not return his son should he not come back. Leo shared his feelings of willful blindness and loyalty (a "bad combination"). It was clear that Jack's "mistakes" could yield a higher purpose. Jack's mortality struck Leo hard, and so he pleaded that whatever happened in the past, that they as parents had done their best. He wished Jack to not hold it against them, and maintained that a fervent desire for life would keep him strong. Should he die, his death would be heroic instead of the "boring death" most others experienced.[20] Leo was philosophical, revealing that death was ultimately life's reward.

On July 21, the *Dorchester* cruised from Boston Harbor with a military escort of US Navy destroyers. It sailed through the Bay of Fundy past Maine's rocky coastline. Jack marveled at Nova Scotia's bleak beauty. By moonlight, they were in the mouth of the Saint Lawrence River, an area prone to torpedo strikes. While Jack contemplated death, his crew members distracted themselves by playing cards.

Dorchester was to support bases constructed in Bluey West in Greenland, a top secret mission that was hidden even from the crew. The role of merchant shipping was critical. It determined what the Allies could or could not accomplish militarily. If sinkings of Allied merchant vessels exceeded production or slow turnarounds and convoy delays severely taxed the transports, the war could be prolonged for many months. Enlistment took courage for, like their military counterparts, merchant ships suffered tremendous casualties. When Jack crossed *Dorchester*'s gangplank, he was either being brave, desperate, indifferent, or naïve.

The weather significantly cooled. *Dorchester* passed Belle Isle Strait. Pangs of loneliness pricked Jack like wasps. He peered over the shimmering waters of the open sea and thought of his mother. He wrote a July 18 entry titling it "The Great Necessity":

"If this tub gets hit tonight, you wouldn't have a chance down here in the foc'sle—here, alone, as I write, I am lost and lonely, and the room heaves slowly. I am not afraid to sleep 'down here . . .' I know of Emerson's Great Necessity. Spent my usual hour brooding on the bow, watching the weird northern sunset and the slow journey of a pale orange moon. Such beauty in this distant northern sea!"[21]

Jack was on the top deck brooding over the sea when he wasn't working. The silvery-gray ocean was hypnotic. Cold driving winds howled from the north. Ice accumulated on the deck. A pall fell over the crew. They imagined the hissing sounds of incoming torpedoes. They finally reached Greenland. The crew disembarked. They took on fuel and food for the return voyage and left.

* * *

During the voyage, Jack read of Emerson's "Great Necessity." He had avidly read his volume bought in Washington, DC. Emerson's essay, "The Scholar," was especially important for Jack: "A man's power is hooped in by a necessity, which, by many experiments, he touches on every side, until he learns its arc." Jack's desire for freedom at all costs posited a decisive stance to accept the consequences of its pursuit. For now, it was the challenges of shipboard life and the war. Later, it would be the road. Kerouac was an offshoot of New England Transcendentalism with its empiricist philosophy and Yankee shrewdness. "So far as a man thinks," Emerson wrote, "he is free." Jack sensed his fate was walled-up around him. "Dim acceptance"[22] gave him the courage to sleep in the ship's foc'sle above a powder magazine. Though he was lost in a labyrinth of circumstances beyond his control, he was determined not to be afraid. Emerson's Great Necessity was the pep talk needed to encourage his bravery. It grounded him. It gave him the fortitude to endure penurious duties and humiliating tasks. Somehow, it imparted a "necessity" toward achieving the soul of a world-wearied scholar of life. Emerson's wisdom burned profoundly in his chest:

"The scholar must be ready for bad weather, poverty, insult, weariness, repute of failure and many vexations. He must have a great patience, and ride at anchor and vanquish every enemy whom his small arms cannot reach, by the grand resistance of submission, of ceasing to do. He is to know that in the last resort he is not here to work, but to be worked upon. He is to eat insult, drink insult, be clothed and shod in insult until he has learned that this bitter bread and shameful dress is also wholesome and warm, is, in short, indifferent; is of the same chemistry as praise and fat living; that they also are disgrace and soreness to him who has them. I think much may be said to discourage and dissuade the young scholar from his career. Freely be that said. Dissuade all you can from the lists. Sift the wheat, frighten away the lighter souls. Let us keep only the heavy-armed. Let those come who cannot but come, and who see that there is no choice here, no advantage and no disadvantage compared with other careers. For the great Necessity is our patron, who distributes sun and shade after immutable laws."[23]

Nowhere else does a literary source point so perfectly to the core of the Kerouacian ethos.

* * *

Jack was discharged from shipboard duties in New York City on October 5, 1942. He returned to Lowell with Sammy, who was waiting for him at the pier. He had with him a payout of $800. He gave $300 to his mother and left the remaining $500 for her to mail to him as needed while he was in New York. Jack accepted Lou Little's invitation which was telegrammed in his absence. Fate had intervened, for without this invitation, Jack would have surely boarded *Dorchester* for another crossing. On that voyage, *Dorchester* was torpedoed by a German submarine and sunk.[24] Many of those crewmembers who befriended Jack had been killed.

Intending to salvage the remaining weeks of the first semester, Jack registered for classes two days after receiving the telegram. Little, expecting a positive outcome, had already arranged a headline in advance to be printed in the *New York World-Telegram*: "Lions May Spring Surprise in Person of Jack Kerouac."[25]

However, upon arriving, Little decided not to utilize Kerouac. He had lost weight at sea (ten pounds), and so he languished on the bench. Also, there was more than Jack's weight at issue. In 1933, Little devised a football strategy called the "KF-79." KF-79 was, according to the *Columbia Spectator*, a "complicated quarterback-halfback" used in a match against Stanford University from which the Lions achieved a Rose Bowl 7–0 victory. Jack was accused by Little of not being able to execute the play that would have returned the Lions to their former glory. Therefore, he had little use for him. During the notorious Columbia vs. Army game, Jack was put in reserves. His nemesis, Paul Governali, was favored as a wingback where Jack wanted to be. But Governali had been impressive, gaining 677 yards on the ground over three games. Thus far, the Lions had only scored fourteen touchdowns, and Governali was responsible for all of them. Kerouac was considered not ready for prime-time, and so was held in reserve as a backup, should he be needed. The *Spectator* reported: "Little has been drilling Jack in the spin back position so that he'll be able to spell Adam Spiegal at full back."

Off the field, there were difficulties when Leo appeared on campus to exact his due from Coach Little. He claimed that the coach promised him a job should he become involved with Jack's return. Little was very influential in New York, a well-known figure found most nights in renowned nightspots, exchanging sports stories with mayors, athletes, and entertainers. He was also infamous for his fantastic wardrobe, including his shoes; he had a different pair for each day of the year.[26] He was friends with General Eisenhower.[27]

With Jack benched, Little felt that he was under no obligation to honor his word. Jack reminded Little of his promise to no avail. Enraged, Leo visited Little in his office. Sitting outside the shuttered window, Jack heard them yelling back and forth. When his father stormed out, he spat that the "wops" were cheating them both.[28] Leo—unable to make gains on his own without using Jack as leverage—made things increasingly uncomfortable for his son on campus. Predictably, Jack's days at Columbia became numbered once again.

In October, Jack had met Edie Parker at the West End Bar. She was acquainted with Jack's Horace Mann friend, Henri Cru. Through the fall, she occasionally saw Jack on the street. Though she remained attracted to Cru, she was enamored with his dark husky blue-eyed friend. Jack's gradual involvement with her partially accounts for his defection from Columbia. She was open to sex, and he was willing to indulge her.

Jack asked Gabe to send money though it was slow in coming. She did mail him an abundant supply of handkerchiefs, underwear, and socks. She assured him that she was taking good care of his funds, though a gradually worsening set of circumstances made her "borrow" it over time. Gabe was not working. She broke two upper teeth; she needed $25 for warm blankets as oil rationing allotted only a limited amount with government oil stamps. Winter was setting in; she would only get colder. Leo did not send enough for her subsistence. To compensate, Jack washed dishes in the school cafeteria. Gabe inquired about Leo's appearance on campus as he did not regularly correspond with her.

Despite his parents' woes, Jack stayed focused on his classes. He enrolled in an Advanced Composition course and earned a grade of B. His papers were imaginative and insightful, writing on such subjects as "Cinema and the Stage"; a critique of T. S. Eliot's "The Love Song of J. Alfred Prufrock"; and a short story, "Joe Doakes and the Immortals." In a Humanities course, he wrote an essay on "Contrasting the Parthenon and the Sub-Treasury," which earned him a C. His dedication, after a while, became marginal. He committed himself just enough to make the grade. His personal writing was his mistress, and she demanded her due.

Leo drove around Connecticut to different job assignments. He was deeply disgruntled to have to go to such lengths when nobody seemed to give a damn. He thought Jack and Caroline did not write enough. Gabe was needy. No sooner than he cashed his check, the money was gone, and not a lot of it in the first place. He was living a miserable paycheck-to-paycheck existence. He hated Roosevelt, the First Lady, and the war. He was profoundly racist and anti-Semitic. Leo was opinionated and blunt. In no uncertain terms would he share his narrowing views with Jack. The more hurt by life he was, the harsher his invectives. In ways, Jack was in a toxic environment, though he was deeply reverential of his parents. Gabe made him feel guilty. Leo made him feel obligated to resolve his woes. Jack, in turn, resorted to desperate measures to appease them both.

He attended a college-wide assembly on October 8, 1942, to encourage recruitment efforts on behalf of the Navy via the V-12 program. They were in need of officers due to declining enrollment. Jack took an interest and kept it in his mind to fall back on should he run out of money to pay for school. He filled out an application and waited.

By the end of October, Jack's name was absent from the Columbia Lion Reserves. He no longer showed up for games. Weekends were spent with Edie.

Leo wrote Gabe, "Just read a NY paper and there's bad news again. Jack has quit again."[29] Leo blamed the coach: "the great Little is keeping up his best to make bean-bag tosser Governali a star. Wotta star!! So there's no room for a real top-notch ball carrier." Leo was unable to contact Jack, not knowing if he was going home or still somewhere on campus. He was disgusted: "all he had to do was go through the motions."[30] Gabe worriedly wrote Jack, unable to "understand the change" that had come over him. He stopped going to practice. When friends of Gabe and Leo went to the game to watch Jack play, they failed to see him on the field. They reported back to Gabe who dispatched another concerned letter:

"I know you feel restless but don't let anything interfere with school you know how you wanted to go back and now that you are in there, you seem to want to quit again, according to what you write at least that's what I detect so please honey now that you've signed up with the navy and they will let you finish school try and stick it out. I guess after the war you can all-ways wiggle yourself out."[31]

By early November, Leo was in touch with Jack, fully understanding his reasons for quitting the team. He despised Little and sided with Jack's frustrations:

"So you're out of Football at Columbia. How it bears out. My observations weren't any too far wrong. 'A fart by any other name' would stink as much. You're like your old dad—bet your boodle on the wrong nag that time—but other days, other places—it's not too late. You might try it south. . . . should you be lucky enough to get in eventually.[32] I wish the day would come when you could show Old Shit-Face that you're a better man than he is. Woops!"[33]

Jack wrote back that he was lonely. Leo reminded him that loneliness was a "sign of greatness": "If you find happiness and beauty but for a few fleeting hours, your life has not been in vain."[34]

On November 2, Jack walked into the Office of Naval Procurement in New York City and spoke with a recruiter. His decision to join the Navy Air Corps was less patriotic than it was self-serving. By enlisting as an officer aviation candidate, he could forestall the draft. He filled out the obligatory forms delving into his family history and listed four character references. Gabe ran around Lowell acquiring the necessary papers to prove his citizenship and mailed him what he needed. He underwent a physical examination and passed. On November 17, he was provisionally accepted after co-signing with his mother. On December 8, he signed shipping articles as an apprentice seaman, classified V-1, and appointed his mother as an insurance beneficiary. He was given an ultimatum: If he stopped attending classes or if he failed to qualify in any way for Navy classes (to attain a Class V-5 rating in the Navy Air Corps), he would be ordered into active duty as an unlisted seaman should his services be required. Jack didn't care, figuring he could slip his neck from the noose whenever he was ready.

Troubled and confused, he wanted to leave altogether: school and Navy. He wrote Sammy expressing his dissatisfaction:

"I am wasting my money and my health here at Columbia . . . it's been one huge debauchery. . . . I am more interested in the pith of our great times than in dissecting 'Romeo and Juliet.' . . . These are stirring, magnificent times. . . . I am not sorry for having returned to Columbia, for I have experienced one terrific month here. I had a gay, a mad, a magnificent time of it. But I believe I want to go back to sea . . . for the money, for the leisure and study, for the heart-rending romance, and for the pith of the moment."[35]

Not a week in, Jack was through with Navy regimentation. He had designs to return to the Merchant Marine, despite having taken an oath to the government. Jack spent his free time debauching in the city with Henri Cru.[36] Then there was Edie. New York was not cheap. Jack ran out of money. By skipping classes, he could not make up what he lost and to return was pointless.

Jack was home by Thanksgiving. Afterward, he went with a companion to Boston on a train filled with sailors and soldiers. They struck up a conversation with two girls. A drunken soldier clutching a bottle of Greek wine offered them a slug. By the time they arrived, they were buzzed. They decided to drink at the Imperial Cafe on Cambridge Street in notoriously seedy Scollay Square. By night's end, Jack had drunkenly abandoned his friend (who went to sleep it off in a YMCA bed) for a random woman. When Jack woke the following morning, he saw her sprawled across a bed. She was homely and snoring like an old drunk in the little room. Revolted by his actions, Jack felt nauseous. The next night, the two men met again and boarded a train back to New York.

He missed Edie.

* * *

On December 5, Kerouac wrote a one-page story of his Boston episode titled "The Wastrel." The narrative opens by employing a hybrid of what Henry James called "The Invisible Narrator." First-person narrative was difficult for Kerouac unless he was doing it from his own point of view. Otherwise, he had to work harder to disclose everything the reader could not find out for themselves. Instead, the narrative is observed through what James calls the "centre of consciousness."[37] Kerouac employed this style in other stories from this time like "The Hero" and "Life Is a Tired Thing." In "The Joy of Duluoz," Jack declared in the Introduction to Part III "your author, who prefers to remain anonymous . . . ," and he did this by structuring a fully realized form of "The Invisible Narrator." Kerouac had good reason to be pleased with his progress; these stories and others to follow paved the way for a fully realized narrative novel.

"The Wastrel" is an intriguing study because it demonstrates that these influences were rooted not only in the characters and themes of Dostoevsky, but in how he varied his narrative practices to achieve perfection in story writing. The character of Duluoz in "The Wastrel" struggles with a desire to change. His capricious nature leads him to "realize the complete dissolution and waste of his life. . . . " After a wasted night of "[b]lood-red drunkenness," he wakes in a shabby hotel to hear the wind and ships moaning in the harbor. Duluoz is horrified that he has shared his bed with a strange older woman. After inventorying his dwindling cash reserves, Duluoz despairs that he must change to reign in his uncontrollable impulses. In language echoing Jean-Paul Sartre's *Nausea* (1938), Duluoz's revulsion and regret mirror Sartre's character, Antoine Roquentin. The barest existence of things confronts Roquentin. Duluoz similarly experiences the same struggle and despair. The constant affray they wielded with their world and its never-ending state of flux left both psychologically bilious.

* * *

On December 22, Columbia's faculty military adviser, William A. Hance, wrote the lieutenant commander of the V-1 Selection Board:

"Report is made that John L. Kerouac of 125 Crawford Street, Lowell, Massachusetts, a sophomore of Columbia College, is no longer in attendance. It is understood that he will be ordered to active duty as an apprentice seaman in the near future."

Unbeknownst to Kerouac, the government was on to him. He spent most of his waking and sleeping hours with Edie and may have gotten her pregnant. She was not sure if it was his or Cru's. Neither Leo nor Gabrielle had any success in tracking Jack down.

Leo considered Jack's choices and advised him to stay out of Lowell. Leo maintained an antiwar stance and chided his home city for "celebrating because they're going to make things to kill the youth of the world." He had pride; whatever he was earning, paltry as it was, he came by it honestly: "I make a small pay, but it's all green, and is not stained red with the blood of the vast army of the world's underprivileged."[38] He advised Jack to keep a budget. He should send money home every week to help save it, "and we will find it handy later for the completion of your education." Leo had made a life for himself in Meriden, Connecticut. Once a week he went to Hartford to take in a show and a dinner. He may have been seeing another woman. All he could do was work and try to enjoy himself:

"Don't get false ideas. Don't think for instance that I've given you up. You're a strange boy, but you are still my very dear, hustling, quizzling little kid with your old fringed hat, a brown healthy tan, a craving for ice cream, and your mom's good cooking."[39]

Leo was encouraging Jack to find his own way in the world, and to conduct it with virtue:

"I don't know whether all I've said so far means anything to you, for I've given up trying to understand you some years ago. I realize the gulf between the old gang, and the new generation, there are so many things I cannot understand about you, but I have faith that time and experience will bring us around to a better understanding, and you on the verge of upheavals which will either make or break you."[40]

He closed his missive hoping to see Jack by summer.

* * *

Jack closed the year[41] with a handwritten essay, "The New Romanticism." In it, he praised poet and playwright Johann Goethe as having expressed great truths about life:

"Goethe knew that life was not our choice, that it was forced upon us each and individually; that this birth of ours was all at once a curse and a joy—the curse of clay and human agony, and the joy of living and fulfilling. And we knew that Death was inevitable as it was rewarding, and that all of life was sheer glory and beauty. He knew this paradox well, and feared not its terrible beauty."[42]

Goethe had marked entities of this world with deep reverence; he had peeked into the mysteries of human existence with the hope of decoding the imponderables entangling the lives of humankind. Goethe was, first and foremost, a spectator of life.

The New Romanticism was "life at its fullest" and "most divine." It was "chaos with meaning; bloodshed with regret"; and "victory with fulfillment."[43] Its Faustian bargain was life's paradox: death. Jack need not fear it. New Romanticism was more dogmatic than any religion. Being a "New Romantic" was to take all life had to offer and transform it into art. It paralleled the Goethean plan of humankind's salvation. Kerouac read *Faust* as a textbook of human experience.

39

Jack was also reading Oswald Spengler after he encountered him for the first time during his first year at Columbia. Spengler designated restless modern man as the "Faustian soul," the antithesis to the rooted Fellaheen of *The Decline of the West*.[44] There is, Spengler wrote, a birth, life, and death to all cultures. This belief became instrumental to Kerouac's ideology and spread throughout his writings. His Beat iconoclasts used the book as a talisman of past and current events, encouraging their assurance that there would one day be a "Second Religiousness."

Throughout his writings, Kerouac expresses the same consideration for the state of Western humanity as Spengler.[45] Many of the essential themes outlined in Spengler's analytical, historical analysis of contemporary Western society—the debilitating impact of the city on modern humans, intellectualism versus experience, the enigmatic idea of time, the role of women in contemporary society, the importance of memory, and humankind's urge for extension and motion—are played out in Kerouac's writings.[46]

Going forward, Kerouac's New Romanticism would encompass Spenglerian concepts. He would adopt a Spenglerian worldview; he had to remain up on high in order to look down.

* * *

In the winter of 1943, Jack returned to Lowell by train with Leo. He left behind Edie and her pregnancy. Cru was en route to Africa by sea. Other than Jack's absence, all Edie had left to remind herself of Jack were her memories and a love letter he mailed from Lowell. She was so enraptured with it that she committed it to memory and sold it to some G.I.s who wanted to copy it and send it to their paramours. She was alone when she suffered her painful abortion (paid for by her appalled "Grams") in a Bronx clinic. Over the next several weeks, she recovered.

In Lowell, oblivious to Edie's misery, Jack set immediately to work. Expecting a letter from the Navy, he wrote in a mad streak drafting notes for a sea novel, incorporating strands from the Brotherhood of Man tract to provide his material, which alluded to a desire for social reform that would serve a universal cause. "The Brotherhood of Man" served as the credo for The Young Prometheans, a group consisting of Jack's Lowell boyhood friends that met to discuss literature and philosophy. Their philosophy was derived from an early organ of the chapter of the Universal Brotherhood.

The idea was direct. Without the Brotherhood, humankind possesses a conscious will to secede from society. The only cure is to love all equally. Love is the great destroyer of walls, leveling each through selflessness. Love desires to unite, bonding two units into a whole. The Brotherhood of Man was believed to cure society's divisiveness. "Love, or benevolence, must seek the greatest good of the greatest number in its broadest sense," wrote Reverend Charles B. Smith in his tract, "The Brotherhood of Man." Jack's desire to bridge this gap between him and the world he perceived to be the proper path. A selfish person was the loneliest. One must live sacredly. The flesh is the enemy of the soul, and through this insatiable desire, it cheats its end goal. Through the famished lust of flesh for flesh, it destroys to endure. It becomes a struggle for sovereignty. Soul and flesh mirror Christ's divinity. Its push-and-pull is mirrored in the turbulent times we live in. Kerouac's thematic concerns endeavored to create a new spiritual movement that exists without exploitation and corruption. It was a grand idea, and so his note taking was to wrap itself around an experiential narrative.

The Navy finally caught up with him. After failing the altitude tests, he was disqualified as a candidate and was declared 1-A. Between that and his defection from Columbia, the government considered him a prime candidate for the draft. They telegrammed him a letter. Jack replied that he was sick with German measles and had to be quarantined by doctor's orders. The recruiting office in Boston gave him two weeks.

Jack began handwriting his novel for the lack of a typewriter.

Sammy left Lowell for boot camp in Camp Lee, Virginia. He was starved for companionship. Jack wrote a series of letters to placate him. The government had Sammy, why should he be treated any differently?

Jack was flooded with anxiety, torn between duty to himself, his country, and his family. He was wearied. He wrote notes for shorter, perhaps more realizable short stories like "Brother" and "Morning with the Brother." In these and others, he switched his narrative from first-person to the third-person narrator. He sketched out characters. Bulleted plot points. Wrote trial runs. He used the "Brothers" concept to explore the strands of his psyche. His main character (another Kerouac stand-in) is Wesley Martin, a pensive reserved seaman with emotional strength and compassion. He kindles a friendship with another seaman, Billy Everhart, who Wesley feels is his lost brother.

"The writing of this little novel will require exceeding craft. I believe this to be true because modern taste in this war year of 1943 demands but one thing from its novelists—the correlation of democracy and the war against Fascism, timely and pro-democratic issues dealing with change (change as symbolized by the foundation of the United Nations), and above all, the extension, improvisation, and rationalization of the modern spirit."[47]

He vowed to "write in complete sincerity" and have trust in "my own knowledge of life." He used several people he knew, including his one female character based on Edie. The more detailed his storyline, the closer he was to achieving his goal. Throughout, Jack wove in strands of his personal life:

"Main plot—Everhart decides to ship out with Martin, whom he meets in Broadway cafe in N. Y. Broke, they hitch-hike up to Boston through New Haven, Harford, Worcester, etc. Ship on S. S. Westchester a 'curious, quaint bark,' a freight-passenger oilburner, bound for Greenland. Cruise broken at Sidney, Nova Scotia, where crew goes wild in port debaucheries. (Before shipping out, they meet Wes's father in South End bar, and Edna, destitute and prostituting, a one-time socialite.) Ship reaches Greenland safely. Drama develops aboard ship depicting the folly of heated partisanship . . . Wesley's self-content wins over all. Ship is torpedoed off Greenland, sunk. Martin drowned, Everhart blinded . . . realizes then the hope of Wesley Martin, and wins vision through blindness; ends his cynicism, his futile partisanship, and resorts to weapons of the blind man. Refuses to let life stun him; will win out his remaining days, will see all in end. (Last lines of 'Morning with Brother' set to rhythm of end of Beethoven's first movement in the Fifth Symphony.)"[48]

Jack, in a sentimental mood, wrote Sammy in mid-February. He wrote that he needed to invest in what he had learned about life thus far. He refined his theme of the Brotherhood and continued developing his "Brothers" theme, insisting that what he needed most was a mastery of craft. He imbued the work with an onslaught of mixed feelings from the past year; Seaman Wesley Martin embodied America's apprehension during a time of considerable uncertainty. He was the "lost brother" Kerouac discovered in his art. The ghostly pallor of Gerard informed all that Jack felt in the pulsing mysteries of life. Wes is quiet and thin. He had black intense staring eyes. A twisted smile. He is a man that suddenly appears, having blown in from the West (a precursor to the same image of *On the Road*'s Dean Pomeroy). He and Billy Everhart go to Washington, and "there the stage is set which will reflect their colors under pressure." Through Wesley, Kerouac is able to resurrect the lost soul of America. He is the prophecy of Spengler; "becoming" has ceased. He thrums like a circadian rhythm, embodying Spengler's "cosmic beat." A "strange, ghostly spirit, yet so strong, so much in him that is best in Americans."[49]

"He rose, cigarette in mouth, and moved on across the Drive, ascending West 112th street toward Broadway. He turned uptown on Broadway and shuffled slowly along the crowded pavement, taking in the little Kosher shops, the radio repair stores, the fruit markets, the drugstores, the newstands, the dimly lit bookstores, and the shoe shine parlors with a calm and curious eye. Pausing in front of a combination cafeteria and bar, the young man took stock of his depleted funds; in his thin hand he beheld two quarters, a dime, and a nickel; then, with a flicker of a smile, which he accomplished by raising one corner of his mouth, he entered through the revolving doors and turned left into the partitioned bar. It was crowded with drinkers, some who sat ranged in front of the long bar on stools, and the rest filling in the booths across the rectangular room. Music from a nickelodeon added to the babel of voices that filled the room with a nervous, subdued din; heavy veils of smoke hung, dimming the room to a smoky gold, and serving to intensify the spirit of confined revelry that made the room almost unbearably stuffy and convulsive."

Jack was disturbed by reports of mounting war casualties. Each day there were more. There was no sign that it would ever end. Jack assured Sammy, his Whitmanic comrade and symbol of the Brotherhood of

Man, that he would visit him in Camp Lee before he shipped overseas to Africa.

He never got that chance.

CHAPTER FOUR

Shaking Off the Shadow

ONE MORNING, JACK WOKE AND HEARD A FAMILIAR VOICE. IT WAS Sammy. It sounded like he was in their living room. He hurried to find Gabe standing beside their Victrola. She was playing an acetate record recorded at a USO Club. Inscribed on the acetate disc was "The Voice of Sebastian Sampas." He was reciting a Wolfe passage. Gabe was shaken, her premonition of death foreboding.

Undaunted by prospects of mortality, Jack persisted, fleshing out what his book, now titled *Merchant Mariner / The Sea Is My Brother*,[1] would encompass, yearning to achieve a craft beyond his means. He reached eighty-three pages before stopping. Through an intense spell of writing, Jack demonstrated through fortitude a desire to rise above an imperfect culture (inklings of Spengler). A carnivore destroys flesh to satisfy flesh. Kerouac was no different. He was no stranger to the duality of flesh and spirit as symbolized by the substance of Christ's divinity. A drunken Everhart tells his comrades, "My world is imperfect, there is no perfection in it, and thus no real good. And so I measure things in the light of their imperfection, or wrong; on that basis, I can say what is not good, but I refuse to dawdle about what is supposedly good. . . . "[2]

Everhart is Kerouac's mouthpiece. He wrote what his intentions were in his "Preface to the Will":

"Into this book, 'The Sea is My Brother,' I shall weave all the passion and glory of living, its restlessness and peace, its fever and ennui, its mornings, noons, and nights of desire, frustration, fear, triumph, and death. . . . Yes, the world is cold, it reeks not my love for Wesley Martin and for the sea, it will not give me time! Time! Time to labor! Time to travail! Time to ruin the youth of my flesh in the consuming drive to wreak out my love in art . . . Ah yes! Let me lean my weary head as I write this on a cold, lonely midnight in March, let me weep my Goddamned piece, grant me that! Dare me to dare not. I shall finish this book, this work of art, despite all the odds that the world may pit me—I shall work! Work! And who is to gainsay my solitary hours, who is to cut the hand that wreaks? I dare all the Gods to try it! I shall write this book—take my body and array it in Navy Blue, hurl it over embattlements, guns thunder, war bleed to your foolish conclusion, men scorn, men laugh, men threaten, friends sneer, death come, yea, death come—I'll finish it in Hell. I'll finish it, I tell you, and I'll weave all my art into it with all the love in me, and it will tell you what I say about our life and our world, and when it is there, completed, let men marvel at it, let the world cheer; I'll hit me to my room and drop on the bed, dead . . . and only then . . . or in Hell."[3]

Jack had skirted death once by avoiding *Dorchester*'s fatal voyage. How long before his luck would run out?

He had it all figured out. The rest would have to wait until he was freed of the military. He needed to be liberated from all obligations, even his parents. He was held back. He needed to overcome any impediments, even the government if hard-pressed. The prospects were frightening, least of all combat. He feared not a ship sinking. The idea of rising before dawn, general quarters, uniform inspections, and saluting officers went against every fiber of his being.

One late-winter mid-March Sunday, he was alone. Leo was in Connecticut. Gabe was visiting her ailing stepmother in Brooklyn. Caroline had joined the Women's Army Corps. She had completed Basic Training and was sent to Kentucky at Eastern College for six weeks to attend Administrative School where she lived on campus. Riding aboard the train, she was not impressed with the ramshackle existence of "hill-billys." She found the South to be dirty ("People live in shacks.") Where she saw squalor, her brother saw the South as the backbone of the American working class. Not having much to go on in terms of a cosmopolitan experience, Nin was taken in by the simple beauty of the campus dining room. Much of it, for her, seemed like "paradise" when compared to the barracks. Where before she was engaged in endless school drilling, now she would be chiefly studying. By April 1943, Nin was largely blind to her brother's Navy troubles. Gabe and Leo chose to not bring it up and Jack had not written to her yet. Where she found freedom and opportunity, Jack felt imprisoned and anguished by the call of duty.[4]

At his pre-dawn tabletop Jack wrote Sammy. A female acquaintance, Margaret "Margie" Coffey, had just left.[5] He kissed her goodbye and shut the door. He smoked and paced before sitting down to write. Afterward, he went to church and knelt with his faithful Lowell brethren "for the sake of humanity." Haunted and drawn, Jack returned to his empty apartment and wrote Sammy:

"The ghosts of those I love haunt me in the sorrowful stillness, not leering, capricious ghosts, but loving ghosts who touch my lonely brow with tender care. I was alone. I don't know why, Sam, but tell me: Why did I begin to weep? I tell you I wept. . . . "[6]

He wept because he was alone, helpless, and scared.

* * *

Twenty-one-year-old Kerouac reported for duty at Newport, Rhode Island.[7] On his first day his tousled hair was shorn to a buzzcut. He was vaccinated after stripping his civilian attire and possessions to be shipped home.[8] He stood in line with the other recruits, most of whom were his age. Some were quite a bit older. They stood nude and shivering. The season in Rhode Island was in flux; winter lingered like a bad dream. The sun burned feebly upon denuded trees and dead grass. Supply clerks tossed Jack his uniform and gear over his extended arms with little attention paid to size. He was issued a grommeted sea bag (that he would later use on his road travels), a pillow, mattress, two blankets, pillowcases, "fart sacks" (mattress covers), and a hammock. He was given a stencil to place his surname over all of his issued gear. The sea bag and its contents were all that comprised Jack's possessions. For books, he was issued a Bible and *The Bluejacket's Manual*. He slung the pack over his thick shoulder and marched to his assigned barracks where all of his gear was laid upon a bare mattress in a specific order. He and his company were by now exhausted. It was lights out. Jack's habits were broken. He couldn't fire up his tobacco pipe, switch on his radio, and start typing. All he could do was lie there and listen to an entire company of men wheezing, crying, farting, and snoring through the dark interior of the barracks. Of all of the indignities he endured, not being permitted to be alone was the worst.

At 0430 a bugle announced reveille. It was still dark. His company commander was screaming orders. His job was to denigrate his new recruits into instant obedience like dogs. Here and across three other boot camps, the Navy was grinding out thousands of men to support the war effort. Once awake, the men began a ten-hour day over and over for eight weeks. They endured a regimen of pushups, calisthenics, and endless marching. They seemed to be *always* marching with a dummy rifle lifted over their heads. The men hand-scrubbed their laundry. Shined their boots. There were no wrinkles permitted on blankets, sheets, pillowcases, shirts, or pants. They had to respond to discipline and obey orders no matter how disagreeable. They needed to function with little sleep. Just like the ships they would one day be living in (if not a naval base), the conditions they accepted were cramped and crowded with no privacy.

Everything about this regimen was in opposition to Kerouac's spirit. He deplored taking orders. He despised uniforms. He wanted to smoke wherever and whenever he wanted. He wanted to eat and drink when the whim struck him. Possibly he was sweating out his thirst for alcohol. Though physical regimen was no stranger to him, for he had endured that and more in sports conditioning, it was the crushing discipline that bothered him. He abhorred his total lack of aloneness. There was no way out but to get out.

Eight days after arriving, Jack requested to go to sick bay. He had a headache and wanted aspirin. When he spoke to the corpsmen, he used language unbecoming of most recruits. There was a dreamy eloquence to his words. A forthright frankness and desire to tell-all, as if he were taking the sacrament of confession. From sick bay, Jack dispatched a letter to his mother to intercept any queries the Navy might make toward her. To his mother, he blamed his headaches on having written too much. His eyes hurt (though he tested 20/20 vision). He thought that maybe he was suffering the lingering effects of German measles, or perhaps a prior injury sustained from contact sports. He reminded her that his hands shook when he drank coffee (averting the fact that he was likely over-caffeinated). He was administered a nerve test on April 1.

During the examination,[9] Jack explained what he saw and how he felt. Voices resounded in an "echo effect" that repeated conversations held only days before. He explained: "My diagnosis is dementia praecox but as far as I'm concerned I am nervous; I get nervous in an emotional way but I'm not nervous enough [often] enough to get a discharge." He offered up the possibility to his mother that the Navy might "cure" him if she would only share details of his symptoms for his recovery.

The nature of his complaints warranted extended sick bay status. An officer and two corpsmen accompanied him to the National Naval Medical Center at Bethesda, Maryland. It was the largest military medical complex in the world. Within, the hallways and rooms buzzed with activity. The war was in full swing. It was understaffed, and so much of the psychological diagnoses of its patients was cursory.

Jack was initially diagnosed, as he had suspected, with "Dementia Praecox."[10] Doctors perceived hallucinations and delusions of "a bizarre or fantastic quality," marked by passivity, lack of insight, and a variant of thought disorder.[11] Jack claimed auditory hallucinations. They surmised that he was suicidal. He spoke in a "rambling, grandiose philosophical manner." His thoughts swirled in a murk of self-deprecatory worthlessness. His imagination, nurtured from reading books, watching movies, and surface philosophies made it possible for him to embellish his ailments with details uncharacteristic of the average recruit. He subjected himself to a self-analysis that became stridently accurate in the coming months. He had little sense of obligation, loyalty to nothing but family and writing.

He was reeling from reality.

In a room partitioned by curtains, Jack heard the moans of the war wounded. He was listless, apathetic, and wanted to be alone. He told examining doctors, "I can't stand it. I like to be by myself." He offered details of sexual contact with a thirty-two-year-old woman when he was fourteen. He revealed that he hadn't masturbated in a year, and that he was promiscuous. He was a "spree drinker" and could imagine "whole symphonies" like Beethoven. He was perpetually nervous like his mother. Too emotional like his father. He explained to Lieutenant J. J. O'Connell, "I don't hear voices talking to me from nowhere but I have a photographic picture before my eyes; when I go to sleep and I hear music playing." After heated talk, Jack returned to his quarters and heard the forever "talk" in his head.[12]

Then his parents were involved, each detailing Jack's personality for the medical board. On April 23, Leo, interviewed by O'Connell, stated that his son had been "boiling for some time." He described him as "seclusive, stubborn, headstrong, resentful of authority and advice, being unreliable, unstable and undependable." Then Gabe gave her input. She presumed that Jack was heterosexual and his interest in girls to be "shallow." He was stubborn and brooded when "unhappy or lonely." Then they returned to Brooklyn.

* * *

Leo felt that Jack was "bewildered," but he felt much like his son, plunged into uncertainties he could not control. He left his defense job at a printing plant in Meriden.[13] He thought that the other men alongside him were simply "cattle." He had been traveling from Brooklyn to Meriden for six weeks before he got sick. He was suffering from diarrhea. He was broke, 15 cents left in his pocket until payday. If it wasn't for a leftover $2 meal ticket, he would have starved. Traveling to Meriden and then having to stay there was demoralizing. The town was a "cess-pool." Its townspeople he could not understand. Just looking at them made him "wince."

"Thank God that I've but a few years left in which to sicken of the thought of the mess and filth this once beautiful town has become. O Canada I wonder if you too have changed as greatly now and more I feel that these United States are no place for any of us—folks like you and I we'll never see peace nor a shred of happiness again in these once hospitable shores."[14]

Mindful of Jack's conflict, Leo's letter was angrily apolitical, refusing to take sides with the government over his son:

"Don't kid yourself about [the] government, they are only as good as the people who represent them. Democrats. Nazis. Leftists. Fascists.

Communists. They all alike. If you've no stomach for politics you become what I am myself—on to them, but nothing can be done about it so I am only looking for a peaceful spot where I can live by myself beholden of no political affiliations or paid patriots."

Leo's desire to get away and be left alone mirrors Jack's affinity for solitude. Leo had thrown in the towel, as he felt reduced to a "verminous thing" because he was broke and alone. Leo was looking forward to a mid-May vacation in "lovely Brooklyn." Perhaps he could take in a day at the circus or the Jamaica racetrack. By the 13th of May, Leo had made good on his promise despite his anxious state toward Jack's circumstances. He and Gabe took in a French movie and a "poor stage show" at Radio City. The circus was old hat, they'd seen it all before. Gabe was working for a Brooklyn couple for almost no pay: "Your mother seems to be nothing more than a pennyless chambermaid. For two of the most peculiar people I had never hoped to meet." They were in it "up to our neck." Leo had had enough: "let me tell you that it won't go on, I certainly wont let your mother be a slavey for Pete or anybody like him. I'll find a way out, BUT, THIS IS THE LAST TIME. If you people don't buckle down, and stop dreaming, and go about the business of life as it should, I warn you that I will wash my hands DRY of ALL of you."[15]

* * *

On May 4, Jack informed Lieutenant Junior Grade G. H. Carr that he felt that he was improving. He felt less nervous. Their initial impressions, he informed them, were incorrect because he did not take their questions toward him "seriously." He revealed that he had "writing ambitions" which they notated in his service record: "he has written several novels, and when he was quite young, another just prior to joining the service, and he is writing now." Jack's "mental grasp and capacity" was within normal limits though he tested very high on the Weschler-Bellevue I.Q. exam: 128. His Verbal IQ was tested at 133.[16]

A recommendation was brought before the Board of Medical Survey. Their patient was deemed "unsuitable for Naval Service" reporting that his malady stemmed from "extreme preoccupation." Jack revealed that religion observation for him was conflicting: "He is trying to resolve, according to his parents, a religious philosophy that will be satisfactory to himself." He tended to brood "a great deal."

Days later, Jack transferred to another wing of the National Naval Medical Center. J. J. Head, the senior member of the Board of Medical Survey, signed off on a letter that the "Board of Medical Survey has found your present disability, Constitutional Psychopathic State, Schizoid Personality, #1543, to have existed prior to your reporting for active duty in the U.S. Naval Reserve, and was not aggravated by service conditions." Jack signed a letter concurring with their findings. Because he was enlisted for more than thirty days, he was entitled to veteran's benefits. Now, he only had to wait to be formally discharged. As he waited, Jack handwrote "My Generation, My World":

"My generation," he whispered, "is making the sacrifice. It is suffering. Only through suffering does one learn to love and fulfillment. I believe I am correct in saying so. My generation, my world is not lost."[17]

Being there, in the military hospital, he was at the front lines with the wounded. Jack expressed hope (despite his antiwar stance mirroring his father) that the future of the nation lay in his keep, despite the destruction that war had wrought upon his countrymen. The future lay in art. On June 25, he wrote:

"Living necessarily presupposes and promises hurt, degeneration, and death," and "I am young now and can look upon my body and soul with pride. But it will be mangled soon, and later it will begin to disintegrate, and then I shall die and die conclusively. How can we face such a fact, and not live in fear?"[18]

Five days later, Jack was discharged. He returned to his parents in Ozone Park, Brooklyn, with his sea bag and $200 in his pocket.

* * *

After Edie recovered from her abortion, she was hired at the Brooklyn Navy Yard in March 1943. Once she was receiving regular paychecks, she moved out of her grandmother's house and into an apartment with a married, twenty-year-old Barnard College graduate, Joan Vollmer Adams. She had met Joan at the West End Bar, where she was going in the absence of her husband, Paul Adams, a Columbia law student, who was now in the Army and overseas. Their marriage was doomed from the start; they were no longer married in spirit. She called him a "poor little soul" for him wanting to get back together with her. He consented to send her his Army allotment checks. This, as well as what she received from her father, permitted her to live in comfort. Taking on a roommate meant that Joan could live without any financial duress. Joan's apartment was located at 420 West 119th Street close to Columbia University and Riverside Park, near the West End Bar. There she would find men and bring them home with her. Paul was not her first husband, nor would he be her last. She split from both because she felt they were too basic in personality and intelligence. She would find all that she was looking for in the guise of William S. Burroughs.[19]

Joan was a voracious reader of literature and newspapers. For a while, her living arrangement with Edie suited her. Joan had her own opinions about the world. In Jack's notebook, Joan wrote: "'Freedom' is a truncated concept, an unintended caricature of human relations," and rhetorically wondered how freedom suited her husband since he was forcibly restrained into serving.[20] Joan came from an affluent suburb of Albany, New York. She left her upper-middle-class upbringing to attend college in New York City in the early 1940s and first married an unknown man, split from him, and not long after that, married Paul Adams, her second failed marriage. Joan was a Bohemian eccentric capable of unboxing Marcel Proust and James Joyce as she would of the war.[21] Her broad face and unruly hair attracted both sexes. And so Jack had established his pattern, living with Joan and Edie during weekdays and staying with his parents on weekends. Joan was libidinous and daring. According to Edie, Joan taught her how to give Jack a proper blowjob.[22]

The city Jack returned to after the Navy was not the same as when he left. New York seemed diminished, bereft of humanity as many were away serving their country. He felt disconsolate riding the El over the city on his way to West 119th Street. He did not favor his parents move to New York, wishing to separate these two worlds of his, town and city. Discharged and jobless, Jack contrasted with the rest of his family. Earlier that morning he had been sitting at the kitchen table with Leo who had asked him what he was going to do with his life now, as if the possibility of writing full-time had never occurred to him. To stave him off, Jack had an answer; he would return to sea. Leo was envious of Jack's youth and freedom and wished that he could join him. Leo's life had taken on a circuitous route. Lowell, New Haven, or New York. It didn't matter. All of it were variants of one crude monotonous cycle heading straight to the grave. For now, Leo and Gabe had weekly visits to the show and lobster dinners to boost their morale, and not much more.

"Supreme Reality" was conceptualized in March 1943. Jack described it as his "new literary form" with a "new creative structure designed to further an artistic philosophy to a point or denouement generously filled with lengthy analogisms."[23] Jack was determined to be thoroughly liberated through art alone. He would "suffer no drawbacks other than those in the essence of nature and supreme reality."[24] Not long afterwards, he was put to the test.

Unfettered from his parents, Jack lounged in Edie and Joan's apartment writing stories and mailing them to magazines, all of which were rejected. He spent more time with Edie. She intrigued him in several ways: not only sexually, but as a social companion. He latched on to her free-spirited ways despite their differences and she was content to be subservient to him. Jack introduced Edie to his parents. He had learned of her abortion and was angry, but there was nothing he could do.

Edie found her way into Jack's latest writings. In one example, he characterized her as Wesley Martin's ex-wife and sometime girlfriend. She was "Edna" and "Eddy." In a brief fictional account titled "Edna Porter Martin Tate," Wesley was drinking with Billy Everhart in the South End of Boston where Wesley's father, Charley, tended bar. Jack learned Wesley's feelings for Edna. The story's last lines evoke the tenderness he felt for her:

"Wes was silent, his head upraised in a long, blank gaze at the light; his hands trembled by his hips, long nervous fingers coiling and uncoiling shakily, taking hold convulsively of the trousers cloth . . . Still looking up at the light, Wes whispered uncertainly: 'Eddy.'"[25]

In Jim Perrizo's biography of Edie Parker,[26] he writes that "Edie was happy. Jack was sad." She was outgoing. He was introverted. He never spoke unless spoken to. He was always writing notes or reading.

She was her own woman and would not let anyone, not even Jack, pin her down. As much as Jack was her dream lover, he became, in reality, a disappointment.

* * *

That April, Sammy came home on leave for Easter before going to Rhode Island to visit Jack. He was refused admittance. It would have been the last time they saw each other. He left America for the last time and wrote Jack from North Africa on August 29, 1943. However, Jack was too involved with Edie and self-absorbed with his writing to keep up with Sammy's rabid missives. In one of his journal notations, he wonders to himself why he had not been thinking of Sampas. Sampas's last letter arrived a month later from the 8th Evacuation Hospital, where he was convalescing from a throat ailment. This time, he was self-deprecating toward his poetry, feeling it was mediocre. He signed off, "I have kept faith . . . I have remembered."[27]

* * *

After returning from the Navy, Jack began working on material he had initiated before leaving for boot camp, particularly *The Brothers*.

In *The Brothers*, Peter Martin lives in a cheap room in Hartford, Connecticut. On weekends, he goes to New York. In his room, he writes hundreds of stories. By winter, he returns home to Bennington, Vermont, where he works at a parking garage. In spring, he hitchhikes to Washington, DC, returns to New York for the summer, and falls in love with "E.P." Peter's brother, Wesley, is a mariner on a Merchant Marine ship in the North Atlantic. He docks in Boston and takes a train to New York, where he hangs around the N.M.U. Hall, attends daily meetings, and carouses the city to find his brother, "Boston Slim," in the Bowery. He eventually runs into Peter in Washington.[28]

"Big Slim" Martin lives on the Bowery's fringes. He leaves for Portland, Maine, where he gambles, drinks, and works on harbor tugboats. The FBI afterward picks him up after failing to register for the draft. He is inducted into the Navy and sent to Newport training base, where he is instantly transferred to a naval hospital after suffering from a fit of delirium tremens. He is then transferred to Bethesda Naval Hospital. After his discharge, he finds his brothers through a Marine friend Peter knew. They go to New York and ship out together. Wesley locates his former wife. Pete travels to Detroit with E.P. Later, Slim and Wesley are killed.

Kerouac's three brothers are a triad of personalities divided from one: Jack's. It is a method of characterization that he will continue using until *The Town and the City*. However, *The Brothers* flamed out after a single chapter, but it was a necessary start. "Morning with Brother" and "The Brothers" were all false starts, but he recycled the ideas for *Merchant Mariner*, the first draft of *The Sea Is My Brother*.[29] What his first version of his sea novel lacked, now is enhanced by Jack's experience from March through August 1942. His yearning to reach beyond mere storytelling was enhanced by his rudimentary understanding of his psychology.

Galloway[30] is Kerouac's rewriting of *Vanity of Duluoz* from 1942. In it, Jack wished to expand upon his Lowell subject by depicting the "deep change war brings in a country." In his "long study," he wanted to address something besides "the symbolic reality" of his hometown. He wished to utilize psychology. Formerly, his characters lacked depth; now they could be fleshed out more effectively. One way was to use his dreams to sublimate internal strife: "Dreams are the rich invention of this sub-mind, filled with the extravagance and power of its wise vision."[31] This change will become apparent in hero-protagonist, Peter Martin, from Jack's outlining of *Galloway* through *The Haunted Life* and then *The Town and the City*. His Navy hospital experience gave him some psychological depth to draw from. Also, his ensuing self-analysis that he was "mildly insane; temperamental; martyr complex; lazy beyond salvation; brilliant creative mind without direction and consistent energy" enriched his protagonist via a self-diagnosis, such as an "artist divorced from his station as a man and citizen of society." Kerouac believed he possessed schizoid traits: his "normal" half conditioned by his environment; his schizoid side questionably evident since childhood.[32] These ingredients formed the core of Peter Martin.

Jack's challenge was to write convincingly. He often failed when he pushed himself too hard to achieve sheer word count or satisfy the marketplace's needs. The result was contrived and shallow. In order to write something of any value, he had to pursue authentic experience no matter how sordid. Kerouac resorted to using multiple brothers, thereby compartmentalizing various psychological traits in each brother. He continued developing *Galloway* through September 1945. After Leo's death in April 1946, *Galloway* metamorphosed into *The Town and the City*, where all of these concepts reached full flower.

* * *

With assistance from Henri Cru, Kerouac was finally able to get a ship. He enlisted on the SS *George B. Weems* scheduled to leave New York in August 1943 and bound for Liverpool, England. A few days before shipping out, he estimated his written output. Perhaps recognizing that much of it was below his standards, he stopped submitting (approximately half a million words' worth) to magazines and increased his efforts to write quality prose that most accurately reflected his inner state. Onboard the *Weems* he wrote in peace and away from Edie and his parents and sister. He could abide by his principles as long as he had a pencil and paper. On August 18, Jack shipped out.

As the ship sailed, blackening the skies with diesel smoke pouring from its stack, Kerouac wrote further revisions for *Merchant Mariner*. His grasp of narrative suffered from a limited perspective. He struggled to achieve a broader range and dynamism. Reading parts of John Galsworthy's trilogy, *The Forsyte Saga*, Jack was inspired to interconnect his writings. He called it his "Duluoz Legend." He realized that his prose was stilted and hampered by a lack of style. In *The Sea Is My Brother*, the characters weren't fleshed out. What he was trying to express—"man's simple revolt from society"—relied on the only revolution Jack had experienced thus far, that of him being in conflict with himself. Everhart was such a man. He wanted to escape society by going to sea, like Ishmael. Instead, the sea becomes a place of "terrible loneliness." Everhart still suffers because he has no place in his world to find his peace.

"He loses his eyesight but has won vision. In the dark moor of his blindness, he will conceive a life of love, service, devotion, beauty, and perfection. He sits in his window and listens to the streets sounds while a comrade reads him poetry, and he realizes he is free at last, shorn of all vanities, follies, and idle desires. His will be a life of fulfillment through freedom, but for a moment the awful knowledge of his blindness assails him, life's brutality stuns him, and he denies jeering Fate with a closing denial: 'I won't let it! I won't! I won't! I won't!'"[33]

Kerouac's maritime prose, through all of its variants, resonates with his dispossessed spirit. The themes are linked to a quest for the Brotherhood, yet yearning for something more satisfying. He continued to go to sea, not only because he needed money, but because he felt that with each trip, he would arrive closer to what he was trying to achieve. Shortly after midnight, four hours before sailing, he wrote his "Outline of Position":

"My only ambition is to be free in art. This ambition is a moral synthesis. To be free in art is like the refueled, repaired, reconditioned, and 'fit' ship that I have signed on, and which is ready to sail in 4 hours from now. From there on, the ship is on its own, but it suffers from no drawbacks other than those in the essence of nature and supreme reality. I am, as yet, not free in art."[34]

He was faced with obstacles no different than five years before: a responsibility to his family to satisfy their economic conditions. However, Jack also knew that he had a duty to his generation: "I must take part in the sacrifice of my generation, otherwise I should not seek their love in the future. It is an ethical matter of great importance and spiritual and social significance. THUS: I sail this ammunition ship."[35]

On August 23, the *Weems* docked in Liverpool for several weeks. Jack hitched to London and attended a Tchaikovsky concert at the Royal Albert Hall. He went AWOL and was caught. The misdeed was entered in the ship's log: "On this day, August 24, 1943, JOHN L. KEROACH, O.S. was absent from vessel without permission. For this offense, he is fined the sum of one day's pay amounting to $2.75."

Answering his charge on the 30th, Jack stated: "it was all right." He prowled wartime Liverpool observing its sights and sounds, most of which he found depressing. Women were huddled in shawls for lack of clothing, standing in line for sickly looking meat and wilted lettuce for their allotted portion. He saw droves of ill-fed children, unkempt and dirty. In general, the city's poverty made him miss America. While in port, he wrote "The Romanticist." He went on shore leave, got drunk, lost his money and return ticket, and was left stranded. Drunk and reflective, he hand-wrote his "Liverpool Testament" on September 24. Looking back:

"During the months of January, February and March of 1942, when I was nineteen years old and employed as a sports reporter on the Lowell Sun, I wrote a novel as an experiment in complete artistic freedom. Its title, 'The Vanity of Duluoz,' lends a great deal of information on the work's subject matter, mainly The vanity of Kerouac. It was to have been a gigantic undertaking, as long and as comprehensive as 'Ulysses.' Still, events, coupled with youth's general restlessness and the young Romanticist's particular restlessness, intervened at the sixteen-thousand mark."[36]

Over six pages, he wrote of an art form that expresses "degrees of freedom" and revels in the function of the artist for the world and for one's self: "I do not know of what use the artist is to the world, but as to his to himself, I can understand that his art contains him and is greater than he, and its power gives life to his spirit as nothing else can."[37]

On that same day, the master of the SS *George B. Weems* wrote an inter-office memo to the captain that Kerouac, on ship leave, found himself stranded without funds over two hundred miles away in London. The London office gave Jack the necessary money to return to the ship and deducted it from his wages. Upon his return, Jack collected his pay and went to New York City in mid-October. He found a job as a switchboard operator to scrape together his part of the rent for Joan. Not long after Jack paid her, he quit.

Jack was more interested in celebrating his return. He accompanied Edie to 52nd Street, where they met such influential musical luminaries as Lester Young and Billie Holiday. They also met Burl Ives and Ernest Hemingway at a party. Jack had also promised Edie that he would marry her. Her parents were bothered by her cohabitation with a man.

In November, Joan Adams realized that she was pregnant, but did not know who helped conceive it. To remedy this, she schemed for Paul's return so that she could have sex with him and create the ruse that he was the father for the child's financial security. To accomplish this, Joan pretended to be mentally unbalanced, walking in the rain half on and off a sidewalk, one foot in the gutter. Edie and two other female companions watched from across the street as accomplices to her charade. Finally, some witnesses summoned the authorities. Joan was admitted for examination. Paul Adams was notified and immediately went on furlough to be with her. The trap was sprung and he stepped into it.

In December, Kerouac was delivering telephone directories to buy Christmas presents for his family. Joan had a job typing for an agency. Edie signed up for an art course at Columbia.

And then the year was over. Jack had come far. His problem was that he was either grounded by his morals or unspooled by their lack. His recent experience with Navy psychologists likely sparked his curiosity. He read psychologist Alfred Adler's *The Case of Miss R.* (1929) and *The Neurotic Constitution* (1917) and drew parallels between those studies and himself:

"I was reading Adler in the bath, reclined lazily in a maze of hot water, steam, and hot towels, as a result of my fiancee's suggestion. 'I am so nervous today.' I had told her, 'that my feelings toward mankind are nil. I would as soon knock the man out of my path as walk around him. If he were dying there, I would not pause to help him. I don't care about anything and I don't give a damn who knows it!'"[38]

To paraphrase questions from Adler: What was the real meaning of what he was saying? What was Kerouac's attitude toward life? What did his words mean in light of his deeds? How did he meet life's demands? How did he behave toward his fellow human beings? How did he perform his duties (or fail to perform them)? Did he tend to reality or illusion? These questions among others fed into Kerouac's self-absorption, preparing the way for his confessional novels. By examining himself not as someone abhorrent in personality, only unique, he was able to lock down solely on his key subject: himself. Extreme preoccupation had its benefits, besides mere egoism. Through Jack, it turned into an art form.

Adler theorized that the development of a human being was largely determined within the span of the first four to five years. What had impacted Kerouac's development within that time frame? The death of nine-year-old Gerard when Jack was four for certain. If Jack was too young to truly comprehend the phenomenon of death, he surely felt the impact on his family. The fallout of grief and its impact is most profoundly detailed in Kerouac's confessional letters to Neal Cassady during the winter of 1950–51.[39] In these letters we read of flashing lights upon a ceiling, falling plaster, souls shaking in their graves below the Kerouac house, a rainy funeral, Gerard's coffin, Gabrielle's ensuing grief, and other paranormal events occurring in their home. We read of Jack's resentment from his crib as Gabrielle tended to sick Gerard. His sense of a "conspiracy" between Gabe and Gerard against himself and Leo, with Caroline left out. The family dynamic ruptured; little Ti Jean was left to fend for himself. Then, Gabe's breakdown after Gerard's death. Her teeth had fallen out.[40] Then there was the sudden dislocation after the Kerouacs moved away to a nearby home, separating themselves from the house that bore the dead body of Gerard in its parlor. Jack's resentment at moving from the residence of his final memories of Gerard marked him indelibly. Adler writes:

"And so when an adult tells us of an early remembrance (it matters little whether it is the first or not) which is particularly clear to him, we are able to interpret from it the speaker's personal attitude toward life."[41]

What does it say about Kerouac, who hallucinated sounds and sights to be resurrected later in the novel *Doctor Sax*? Of a maternal co-dependency that endured through adulthood? Navy psychologists had diagnosed a "psychopathic state" in Kerouac replete with auditory and visual hallucinations. Four-year-old Jack began to form cognitively when his brother suddenly died, and so it only took his vivid imagination to tap this trauma as a resource. Through late 1944, Jack would be forever unfolding in an attempt to solve the "problem of myself." As he wrote elsewhere, it was a "symbol of becoming":[42]

"We are all too sensitive to go on: it is too cold, and our bodies are too exhausted. There is too much life around. The multitude is feverish and ill. There is war where men sleep on the snow, and we do not desire to go on when we wake from sleep. I hiccup very violently, twice. This is an age that has created sick men, all weaklings like me. What we need is a journey to new lands. I shall embark soon on one of these. I shall sleep on the grass and eat fruit for breakfast. Perhaps when I return, I shall be well again."[43]

Kerouac's guilt did not recoil from his callous use of women. As he lay in a bath reading Adler, Edie cooked him a meal that made him feel like a "king." He was proud that he possessed the "talent" to use Edie "for my own ends." His self-analysis revealed a capacity for selfishness and cruelty. He had a contempt for humanity. Thoughts of "reality" grated his senses with a "nervous protest." He isolated himself emotionally from Edie. She only fulfilled him sexually and domestically. She was not an artist and Jack craved intellectual stimulation. He preferred male companionship. He wrote in his journal that he used Edie as he did any other woman. He played mental games without her suspecting. Her waiting on him made Jack feel superior: "The very fact that she tended me indicated her inferiority to me."[44] She told him that if they married, she would work and he would stay home and write. By mid-January 1944, she continued asking. There was a fight over their "marriage business": "Won't do it for the sake of her folk's feelings over our 'impropriety.'"[45] Though he professed his love for her, he was determined not to marry until *he* was ready.[46]

Then, on January 14, Edie knocked on their shared bedroom door (he had been writing a letter). He had just woken up at noon. Edie showed him a letter from her mother, Charlotte Maire, who had denounced Edie for "wasting her life with a bum." Edie could have had more wealth, happiness, and a higher social status without him. She was languishing in mediocrity. Charlotte wished for Edie to return home to Grosse Pointe. Charlotte was a Ground Gripper shoe company proprietor and was labeled bitterly by Jack as a "working woman." He called Charlotte's letter "smug" and "righteous":

"My mother sits at a dirty shoe table in a shoe company shop eight hours a day, toiling like a slave for 1/10th Mrs. P's income. I'm infuriated at her allusions to me. This is the goddamnest business!"[47]

To Jack, Charlotte Parker and her ilk were "too class-condescending for this era." They were "hypocrites and fools": "I may be a tramp, and a no-good, but I'm not a hypocrite and a fool." He was flummoxed for an answer on what to do. He loved Edie, but he could not marry. He felt obligated to help pay his parents' rent. Mrs. Parker knew nothing of economic struggle: "What does she know of unsheltered youth?" Jack stayed in Ozone Park. Seymour Wyse visited. Jack went to a show with his father and they had literary discussions. Four days later, Edie and Jack made up and resumed relations.

Through the winter, Jack stayed his course. *Galloway* was approaching thirty thousand words. Since Edie was on his case, he saw her less often. Most of his writing was done at Ozone Park. He finished writing "The Problem of Myself," which he felt was hardly a "seriously constructed attempt" though it reveals a carefully worded single-draft of interlinked essays. He asked himself, how does the artist function in society? Must he obey his neuroses?

"The pattern is simple. It needs only more understanding and kindness on my part, redoubled energies in my 'works' and toward helping others as humbly and awkwardly as I can (I know my limitations in that direction), and a mutual acceptance of the fact that weakness in one part may allow for double power in another. If I am weak and ineffectual 'morally,' I may be strong and competent 'artistically.' If some have been strong in both respects (as Dostoevsky doubtlessly was), it can only mean that all kinds make a world. Compassion was Dostoevsky's greatest gift; it is not mine, though I should like to believe so—or develop compassion, as I am attempting today."[48]

He did not feel obligated to marry or to honor any firm commitments other than to his mother and father; he was in service to art and nothing else. He wrote a four-part poem titled "Supreme Reality" along with a note addressed to himself:

"Jack:—Oh Reality, thou hast reigned supreme! Supreme Reality, lift thyself before my eyes in any form you choose! Improvise the theme of yourself. Be endless and all-changing, confuse me with your whimsy."[49]

Of late, he was suffering with ennui: "I am bored at the thought of Sebastian and the others. I am bored with the whole picture of it. I can bring to it no enthusiasm." He was ready for a vastly more laborious mature undertaking. Working on *Galloway* was a "force of habit": "I feel that the novel as planned falls far short of those powers I now command: it is merely an introductory piece to more mature work, it is a prelude, an overture to a symphony."[50]

His newest relations then were seminal, almost as compensation for who he did lose: Sebastian "Sammy" Sampas.

On March 2, Sammy, who felt fated to die young, succumbed to injuries in a North African hospital. In a mid-March letter, Jack was grief-stricken. He had lost a vital comrade and had fallen into despair. As with Gerard, the memory of Sampas was cached in Jack's imagination to rise again in his books.

* * *

In February 1944, Jack was hired by Columbia Pictures to do "script work." He read unproduced screenplays and summarized them into a pithy synopsis complete with a brief summary of the completed screenplay's core concept, major plot points, and main character arcs. Studio executives saved time by only reading the synopses and not having to pour through entire scripts.

He only saw Edie occasionally. His time was chiefly devoted to *Galloway*, reaching the thirty-thousand-word mark by mid-February. In the novel, Jack sought to "shape the substance in a form correlative to the substance. Supreme Reality as a cosmogony I should like also to see as a form, or at least, fitted into a form related to Supreme Reality."

He felt that he was on the verge of a "flowering"[51] and made plans to record himself reciting the poem "Supreme Reality" on Seymour Wyse's recording machine where he worked at the Chelsea Record Shop in the Village with Jerry Newman. Of vital importance to Kerouac's artistry was his exposure to Wyse and Newman and their respective contacts with the jazz scene of New York. Through them, Jack picked up on jazz rhythms and breath phrasings, learning to utilize this musical technique in his writing. "Supreme Reality" was Jack's acceptance of "two forces": "the individual and that of his world under all circumstances."[52] His recording of it initiated a process he would continue to improve upon by reading works like "Old Angel Midnight," *Visions of Cody*, and "Brakeman on the Railroad."

"Oh Reality, Thou hast reigned supreme!
Supreme Reality, lift thyself before

My eyes in any form you choose!
Improvise the theme of yourself,
Be endless and all-changing confuse
    me with your whimsy"

Jack's "supreme reality" was, in his estimate, the "restrictions imposed upon an individual will by the general will" and vice versa. Through the general will imposed upon him, Jack planned to forge it into art. This would be expressed in *Galloway*. The novel was to capture America's "deep change" during wartime. The point he wanted to make was that one had to accept change and realize that such manifestations led to a "new life." People, Jack felt, accepted a change to their lives as a vital process of disintegration. Using the character of Peter Martin, Kerouac sought to depict his challenging odyssey. After returning to Galloway, Martin is surprised by throngs of happy children, jubilantly greeting him despite the war across the waters: "this strikes a sad but truthful note. And the change, though saddening him, has awarded a chance to make his own world."

In order to best capture the spirit of the "olden days," as Kerouac referred to it, he listened to baseball games on the radio, remembered Lowell's summer trees, Pine Brook, fresh lemonade, and his Lowell gang. Through past, present, and future, there was a strangeness and a mystery to life weaving through the supreme reality of it all. Jack must take all of it, even the most commonplace, and honor Whitman's ode to the ordinary ("The nearest, cheapest is me"). He had to record them again "exactly like the wash of waves." He had to imbue the commonplace with holy reverence.

Only days before his birthday, on March 4, 1944, Jack wanted to reconfigure *Galloway*. His Wolfe-like ambition yearned to weave peace, restlessness, and a fevered frenzy to defeat his ennui. He intended to accomplish this task and dared God to cut his life short. If he should die, "I'll finish it in Hell." On Easter Sunday, as he listened to Handel's *Messiah*, he handwrote a new passage for *Galloway*.

* * *

In April 1944, Kerouac met Lucien Carr and his companion, Dave Kammerer. These new associations opened a new phase for Kerouac. Lucien was a living incarnation of Rimbaud, minus the poetry. He almost looked like him. In that vein, Kerouac's choice of reading via Carr began to include French Symbolist poets. His current writing reflected these readings.

For no clear reason other than he may have been trying to find sea work, Jack formally disenrolled from Columbia on April 30 and left for New Orleans. There is no extant source detailing Kerouac's sudden departure to New Orleans. It is barely mentioned in existing journals, chiefly because Kerouac failed to keep any for the spring and summer of 1944.

Jack was in flux, having lost Sammy Sampas before meeting Carr through Edie. Lucien was a constant habitué of the West End Bar, where he drank copious amounts of beer. Jack was in the process of redefining his literary voice via his new associations. He was not tempted to write about his latest life events, including the Navy stint, Merchant Marines, or his Columbia cohorts of New York. Having achieved an effective physical distance from Lowell, he was able to objectify it as new writing material. In *The Haunted Life*, he would resurrect Sebastian Sampas along with a re-rendering of himself, capturing the summer of 1941 when his mother and father were in their fighting prime, ready to aggressively challenge life to fulfill their respective destinies. The same for Jack; the latent talent he possessed during the months before the war opened up a proper avenue for his *A Portrait of the Artist* approach to the legend of his life.

* * *

Seventeen-year-old Irwin Allen Ginsberg, born on June 3, 1926, in Newark, New Jersey, was a Columbia University student attending via a Congress of Industrial Organizations scholarship. He had already won the recognition of the prestigious trio of Columbia literary scholars: Mark Van Doren, Lionel Trilling, and Raymond Weaver. Although Allen had initially aspired to be a labor lawyer, the influence of these professors convinced him to switch his major to English.

Allen frequented the campus outskirts among a select few who straddled Village bohemia and respectable academia. He, too, spent time at Edie and Joan's apartment conversing with two other men: nineteen-year-old Lucien Carr and thirty-three-year-old David Kammerer. It was rumored that Carr had stuck his head into an oven as a suicide attempt. When cops asked why, he professed it as an art experiment. He was placed under examination at Chicago's Cook County Hospital. From this incident, Lucien had dodged the draft.

Also, there was eighteen-year-old Celine Young, a Pelham girl from the Class of '45 at Barnard. She fit right into the group with her "disarmingly frank" personality (as the Barnard yearbook described her[53]), and her knowledge of literature (she was an English literature major). She was also fond of tapping the Columbia music library and tea time with Barnard. Celine was an ardent admirer of Lucien's who competed for his affection with rival Kammerer. Allen, like Jack, kept a journal. Unlike Jack, he was already documenting dreams, noting such episodes as staring creatures, flying, and a dead father. Thus far, his journal was mostly dream content, finding in them a possible key to his psyche that otherwise eluded him. By June 1944, he was dreaming of Jack.

Joan Vollmer's apartment was now a refuge for many, including Lucien and his new girlfriend, Celine Young. Lucien was young and troubled. He was also intelligent and handsome, possessing a sinister charm equally alluring to young Allen and eager Jack. Lucien was central to those gathering in Joan's apartment. Though he was literate, he did not write and, according to Allen, would not do so until he learned how to attain perfection.[54]

Jack was keyed into Lucien's speech-pattern, sensing with his musical ear a repartee that he analogized to Shakespeare. It was high drunken talk imbued with an entirely new vocabulary so fresh and unique to Allen that he listed some of the more scatological words in his journal.[55] In hindsight, Allen was initially more taken by Carr than Kerouac and had undertaken an extensive "character analysis" of Lucien in his journal.[56]

Lucien drove David Kammerer to an obsession, having followed Carr from St. Louis to New York as a relentless grooming paramour.[57] Lucien knew how to straddle the line between intriguing Kammerer and repelling him. If he wanted his college papers written, Kammerer was willing to do it. Likely what he did do, he did it for a price on Lucien's ass. Otherwise, Carr cruelly deployed a variant of sadism to demean and diminish lovelorn Kammerer. Though Carr may have created an impression that he was successfully deflecting Kammerer, it is plausible that David would not have followed him so aggressively if he was not getting what he wanted, at least occasionally.

Jack and Lucien were avid conversationalists; Lucien's intellect impressed him because it was centered mostly upon art and morality. Lucien feigned boredom much of the time, as he was incapable of pedestrian talk or commonplace ideas. He was a walking enigma, mostly because he did not write. There was no rendering of his ideas into art of any kind. It was all talk with him. Because of this, nobody, not Jack or Allen or his girlfriend Celine, knew where he stood. Unbeknownst to all of them, Lucien was haunted by a homicidal impulse toward David Kammerer that lay dormant in ideation until falling into its deadly nadir in late-August 1944.

Though the others could do something with their intelligence besides speaking about it, Lucien could not commit his high thoughts to paper. He claimed he had neither the patience, time, or opportunity to do so. Lucien had a girlfriend, as did Jack. Allen was the odd man out. He was lonely and closeted. Frustrated and death-conscious. There was madness in his family. Insanity burned a hot streak through his private journal jottings.

Lucien and Jack formulated a "New Vision" in their fevered discussions, though it was Carr that encouraged this philosophical dialogue between himself, Jack, and Allen. For Jack, the New Vision was an extension of "Supreme Reality" and "New Romanticism." In happenstance the ideology of the New Vision was rooted in Oswald Spengler's meta-historical study, *The Decline of the West*. It took umbrage with Western values by addressing the values which contributed to the decline of civilization and culture. Carr's approach to curtail this was to seize upon texts that had either fallen off the canon, or were never there in the first place. It was preparing for the exfoliation of High Culture then merging into Civilization. The "New Vision" anticipates Spengler's "Second

Religiousness" (the final phase of a civilization's spiritual development). This stage comes "after history," when all interior growth is exhausted. The only possible transformation is accidental or through the attempted reconciliation or union of different or opposing principles, practices, or parties in philosophy or religion. It also refers to a period when a primordial religion returns: holy individuals, decrees, and sites outweigh the theological systems initiated by civilization earlier in its record, as well as the doubt that briefly supersedes religion among the educated. With the coming of the Second Religiousness, there is no longer any significant divide between popular and select opinions on these issues. Now it had gestated into something else. The New Vision asserted self-expression as a path and summit of artistic endeavor. It sought to discard traditional writing in favor of expressing personal experience uninhibited by technique or structure. Allen defined it in his journal: "Since art is merely and ultimately self-expressive, we conclude that the fullest art, the most individual, uninfluenced, unrepressed, uninhibited expression of art is true expression and the true art."

* * *

In May 1944, Kerouac took a solo bus trip from New York City to New Orleans to be accepted for work with the Merchant Marines. The result did not pan out, but he did write the first part of *The Haunted Life*.

Jack sketched the idea back in 1943.[58] Back then, he wished to focus on the effects of World War II on an "average American youth in an average and beautiful American town."[59] He moved its setting to presage the war. The ideas of loss and loneliness serve as thematic constants for much of Jack's writing of the mid-1940s. He also wanted to write about a pair of characters pursuing "something" across the American continent. At times it was a woman, a lost inheritance, or the "father we never found." In *On the Road*, the "something" pursued would be called "IT."

The Haunted Life suggests a necrological meditation on Sampas and another Lowell friend, Billy Chandler. It focuses on their philosophical/sociological mindset before the war. However, since only Part I has been published, the fate of these characters cannot be read. The remaining sections of the book are not extant. Jack had lost part of the manuscript in a taxi. Readers would not learn the outcome of Tourian and Sheffield, but it may have been incorporated into *The Town and the City*. In that novel, Garabed Tourian's name is changed to "Alexander Panos." Dick Sheffield becomes "Tommy Campbell." Panos mourns his imminent fate and his Galloway brethren in the war:

"After a few months, we'll probably never see each other again for the duration of eternity. Many of us here in Galloway, your brothers and my brothers, and the kids we know, will get killed in this war, many of us. Tommy Campbell is only the first to go, don't you see? 'So we'll go no more a-roving,' Pierre."[60]

The Haunted Life and *Galloway* made possible the writing of *The Town and the City*.

* * *

Jack returned to New York in June. By August, his circle grew. Beneath this circle (they called themselves the "Libertine Circle") was a simmering undercurrent of dread. Lucien's manifesto, "The New Vision," encouraged Jack to follow by example. The New Vision was a call to arms to challenge authority. To slay conformity in art and themselves.

Jack met Lucien through Edie (she and Lucien were in a life drawing class), and his first impression was that he was a "mischievous little prick." Between Lucien and Jack, there was also the remainder of the Libertine Circle: Burroughs, Ginsberg, Joan Vollmer Adams, David Kammerer, Celine Young, and Edie:

"Lucien, brilliant companion, most amazing figure in this neighbourhood of amazing figures. Yet, he is cold, not warm. We rout out together the curiosities of Greenwich Village and allied cultures. To Lucien, archetypal circumstances are cliché. Still and all, he would make a wonderful anthropologist, another Aldous Huxley."[61]

Lucien was nicknamed "Claude De Maubri," an epithet Kerouac would utilize in his future fiction. Carr was troubled by Kammerer's menacing behavior. For Jack and Edie, it was like Verlaine in hot pursuit of Rimbaud. Lucien's relationship with Jack grounded him into a new dynamic of male bonding. "It was Jack," Caleb Carr wrote journalist Mark Judge in 2014, "with whom he shared heterosexual laughs and pursuits (and sometimes women), and it was the friendship with Jack that made him begin to see not only the inappropriateness but the psychologically devastating and indeed criminal nature of his relationship with Kammerer."[62]

That summer, Carr's world opened. He was a man among men, respected and revered for his intelligence and not the boyish good looks that enamored Kammerer and Ginsberg. Carr and Kerouac pursued women, though their mainstays were Edie (for Kerouac) and Celine Young (for Carr). This angered Kammerer to the point of insanity. Carr was beginning to assume a masculine identity for himself. Whenever Lucien kissed or nuzzled Celine, it bristled Kammerer. Sometimes, Lucien did it intentionally.

There was drinking at Minetta's Tavern where eccentric Village Bohemian Joe Gould held court, squawking like a seagull to tourists, and poet and novelist Maxwell Bodenheim, a Jazz Age relic, sold typed copies of his poems in exchange for gin (Allen had bought one). There were discussions of Rimbaud, drinking Pernod, and smoking marijuana. T. S. Eliot, Faulkner's *Sanctuary*, and Robert Briffault's *Europa* were some of what passed through the hands of Jack, Lucien, Allen, and Bill during this time. Lucien was also unstable and capable of abrupt randomness. One time he stepped into a crowded subway and peered disdainfully over the commuters yelling loudly, "When cattle are put in trains, they copulate."[63]

Wanting to go to France together to follow Rimbaud's path, Jack helped Lucien obtain the necessary papers from the Union Hall so that they could ship out together. They signed on board a vessel, but an irate boatswain's mate began harassing them. They bounced out of this opportunity to reach Paris *gratis* and drifted, jobless, through the remainder of July into August 1944.

Their conversations about the New Vision comprised three tenets:

1. Naked self-expressionism is the seed of creativity.

2. The derangement of the senses expands the artists' consciousness.

3. Art eludes conventional morality.[64]

The first tenet, the "seed of creativity," expresses the pursuit of truth in art. Art, of any kind, necessitates honesty. One must not become self-conscious in this enterprise. To do so would nullify the meaning of art. This doctrine, coined by Carr, makes him the progenitor of "first thought—best thought," not Kerouac.

The second, the expansion of an artist's consciousness, necessitates not necessarily the ingestion of alcohol or drugs but being open to new experiences. It is openness to experience. It is the freeing of the soul from convention. An expansion of the senses can liberate art.

Lastly, art transcends contemporary standards. It is linked to the spiritual. It tears morals and social mores asunder. For Lucien, there was no fear of breaking moral codes. His alleged "bad" behavior, according to Nietzsche,[65] was not bad at all. At his level, "being bad" had no guilt connected to intention. Lucien's ultimate act of criminality, the slaying of David Kammerer, possibly left him feeling indifferent to the gruesome task while he was in the grip of the New Vision.

Jack, for his part, was still under pressure to work. Edie wanted to marry. He consented to blood tests to receive their marriage license and, hopefully soon, marry. He was still living with her and Joan. According to a list kept by Kerouac, he somehow found the time to bed Joan almost two-dozen times.

On Monday, August 14, Lucien was drinking with Jack and Allen at the West End Bar. After leaving Lucien, Jack saw David Kammerer on the Columbia campus. David queried Lucien's whereabouts. Jack pointed to the West End Café and went on his way. The next time he saw Lucien, he was standing at his door, pale and distressed.

Lucien and David had been walking to Riverside Park. It was dark and hot. Kammerer made threatening comments toward Celine Young. Whether this was to harm or woo her is unknown. Lucien, perhaps using this reason to dispense with David once and for all, stabbed him several times and let him fall and succumb to the deep tears into his heart and lung. He weighted the body and floated it into the slow-moving Hudson. He watched Kammerer sink into the inky depths and left.[66]

Edie was sleeping when Carr unfolded the sordid events of the past few hours to Jack. There was no going to France to follow Rimbaud's wayward path now.

Jack and Lucien walked the pre-dawn streets searching for a place to dispose of Kammerer's eyeglasses and a blood-encrusted knife. In Morningside Park, Jack pretended to piss in a bush to keep watch. Lucien buried the eyeglasses. On 125th Street, Lucien dropped the knife down a sewer grate. Lucien confessed to his psychiatrist later that day as Jack sat in the waiting room. Afterwards, they went to a movie and wandered around the Museum of Modern Art. Lucien left, at last, to ask his mother to call an attorney.

That evening, Jack was with Edie (she was still oblivious to the killing). Two plainclothes detectives knocked. Edie answered and led them to Jack. They inquired about his knowledge of the slaying, and he was arrested as a material witness. He was jailed and held (along with Lucien) on bail. "All of our lives had changed," Edie later wrote in her memoir, "drastically, all because of Dave, who Lucien had tried to avoid, just as we all did."

* * *

"If any man's work shall be burned," Kerouac later quoted from Corinthians 3:15 into Ginsberg's journal, "he shall suffer loss; but he shall be saved, yet so as by fire."

In his cell, Jack was desperate to be sprung by Edie or his parents. He had sheets of paper to write on with a pencil and wrote what he titled "Jail Notes." All of the notes are testimony to Kerouac's convictions about the role of an artist in society. Over the preceding several years, he had written numerous essays about art and artists and how society perceived them. He explained in the "Definition of Art for the Layman":

"Art should be regarded as we respectively regard the individual. We seek no value in the individual: he may be of value to one, in that he may assist in livelihood, but to the rest of the world he has no value: he exists, is a human being, and is regarded, with no considerations of value, simply as a man or a woman. He stands on the dignity of his being. Art, too, should not be regarded as a thing of value. Art exists, in Spinozean terms, through the necessity of its nature, like man. It is not to be used to satisfy the appetites of readers, like a courtesan. It is not to promote political ideas and social ideas in the spirit of propaganda. It exists and lives, like man, and is regarded as a thing of beauty and truth to be understood and loved for itself."[67]

Jack vowed to "unlock the mystery of the world": "Then give me the key to every mind, every soul in the world, and give me extraordinary powers of deduction and movement, and I shall unlock for you the mystery of existence itself."[68]

But first, he had to get out of jail.

Jack's arrest had disturbed Leo and Gabe. They could not bail him out, so Jack resorted to desperate measures and finally married Edie. By arrangement with her mother, Edie was able to make bail.

After staying with Jack's parents for several days, he promised Edie they would go to her home in Grosse Pointe. On September 1, at Edie's urging, Jack wrote a letter to Charlotte Parker stressing his willingness to settle his debt with her. He clarified that they had not cohabited before their marriage and that he was sleeping on a merchant ship in dry dock. This would ensure that their arrival in Michigan was a little less awkward.

Jack then had to clarify matters with first the shipping commissioner of the US Coast Guard and then the Seaman's Union. He thought that maybe Edie could find a job there because she had Red Cross and longshoreman contacts and could draw upon them. Harry R. Durning signed a letter requesting permission for Jack to articles for one voyage only. The only offer for Jack was a ship transporting live ammunition across the Pacific. He passed. In a photo taken by Edie from this year, Jack is wearing his Merchant Marine cap. Scrawled on the back of the picture that Edie kept in her possession was "*Apparition de l'enfer* . . . John Kerouac 1944 C.U., NYC."

Jack worked through September at a factory to make weekly payments to Mrs. Parker. They were anxious to see Jack succeed as a competent husband. But he was peculiar at best. Though he was mannered and kind, there was a darkness that they could not reconcile. They were alarmed that most of his free time was alone in the bathroom keeping company with the Bible and Shakespeare.

At night, Jack restlessly slept. He dreamed of bloodied faces. Murdered men taunting him. When he could not sleep, he was studying Edie's silhouetted form as she slept. He wrung his hands, frightened of his delicate existence. He concocted stories, trying to pair his violent thoughts with creative material. When he finally fell asleep, he again dreamt of violent death "and of myself shielding my body against this violence with the body of a friend." When he woke, he felt his gut curdling. Guilt had weighed heavily upon him and he was unable to sleep. On paper, he tried to justify his tendency for compulsion (marrying hastily) that steered him from his life's purpose to be a writer. He made amends with his parents, content to believe that his incarceration resulted from bad associations: "They looked on me as an errant but innocent son victimized by decadent friendships in the evil city."

Grosse Pointe bored Jack; their marriage continued for two months. He wrote Allen of his new goal: to work vigorously to earn his riches and buy a flat in Montparnasse. He encouraged Allen to abandon his studies at Columbia and join where the "New Vision would blossom." In Lucien's absence, Jack was latching on to Allen more exclusively. With Allen, Jack felt more at ease. Lucien was too self-loathing. Unpredictable:

"Lucien is different, or at least, his egocentricity is different, he hates himself intensely, whereas we do not. Hating himself as he does, hating his 'human-kindness,' he seeks new vision, a post-human post-intelligence. He wishes more than Nietzsche prescribed. He wants more than the next mutation—he wants a post-soul Lord only knows what he wants!"[69]

Jack opposed the idea of going to sea. He wanted to be exclusively writing, even if it meant starving. However, Edie was relentless, insistent that he should work to build their future "nest egg." Her promise to work as he wrote was a ruse.

Edie's father arranged a free truck ride for Jack to go to New York in October. As he waited for his ship to depart, Jack stayed with Allen, hiding from his mother, who was writing letters to him every day, waiting for word from him. Like Edie, she assumed he was already at sea. Without a typewriter, Jack unleashed a flood of writings throughout the month. He wrote in his notebook some short notes, titling part of it "A Dissertation on Style":

"In reporting on experience, one is confronted with problems at once difficult and dubious—the problems, in this case, of style. For it is perhaps wholly true that the master is too pregnant with message to experiment with forms."[70]

He explained that the *Galloway* project sought to shape its "substance in a form correlative to the substance" In that regard, Jack was seeking a cosmogony where "Supreme Reality is the true form itself; that of the individual and the 'world under all circumstances.'"

He joined Allen and Celine Young in a West End Bar booth. Allen described the setting in "The Bloodsong," an attempt at retelling the lurid events of the Carr/Kammerer murder:

"We were spread out in a dim red booth in the Radical Café. We liked the bar mostly because it served pernod and it had always attracted the campus bohemian, the whores, the fags, the sterile drunkard, and all the intellectual maniacs that clustered around the college. Jack Kerouac had just come back from a visit to his wife in Cleveland [*sic*: Detroit]--Edie Parker, a rich, bird-brained intelligent female who had been his mistress for two years before he married her. Tonight was his last night and we were all a bit melancholy."[71]

As they drank, they talked. Jack got drunk and banged his glass on the table. He blamed Edie for him having to ship out just for the money. Allen asked why he married her in the first place. Jack's response was glib, that she was an "animal." He was with her only for the sex. However, his guilt made him want to run back to her whenever he was away from her. Celine defended Edie. Ginsberg condescendingly patted her on the head. She resented that. Jack was frustrated for Celine, seeing in her a potential conquest.

Jack vowed to write a novel while he was hiding from Edie and his parents. He would salvage his loss. Jack criticized Allen for not using New York as his sole tableau vivant, as he did with Lowell: "All you can write about is Rimbaud and Lautréamont. Look at you—a Jew from Jersey City and you don't have a feeling for your country."

Jack intended to put all he remembered of Lowell into *Galloway*, to utilize, like Faulkner, his intimate knowledge of his hometown, engaging its rhythms as only a native could. Jack felt that Allen showed more signs as an academician than a poet.

As they spoke, Celine flirted with an eavesdropping sailor. He called to a shipmate: "Hey Joe, come 'ere and listen to these two talk over here. Looks like the real stuff."

Outside the West End, drunken Jack took on both sailors with mild intervention by Allen. Jack ended up on his back with one sailor beating his head against the sidewalk. Bruised and bloodied, he returned to Allen's room at 627 West 115th Street, where Celine was sleeping for the night. In bed, Jack lay his head on her lap, crying. Allen recited Shelley at his desk before turning off the light. He slept on the floor. When he heard the bedsprings creaking, he left and walked along Riverside Drive alone.

The following day, Allen accompanied Jack to board a brand-new liberty ship, the SS *Robert Treat Paine*, designed to boost the supply line of the war effort in the North Atlantic. Jack signed articles on October 18 after showing his letter from the shipping commissioner. Jack and Allen parted dockside. Jack hoisted his sea bag and a Modern Library volume of *The Philosophy of Nietzsche* borrowed from Allen and waved him off.

"I won't see you for a year," Jack said, "please tell Celine that I love her. I mean it."

* * *

The *Paine* sailed south to Norfolk, Virginia, for replenishments before turning to Italy. Jack, despite his misgivings, was relieved. He had instant clarity. He was away from alcohol, Edie, family, and his lovelorn feelings for Celine. In his free time, he read *The Birth of Tragedy*. He was particularly taken by a line from "Preface to Richard Wagner": "Those earnest ones may be informed of my conviction that art is the highest task and the proper metaphysical activity of this life. . . ."[72] It struck to the core of Kerouac's convictions, justifying his belief that writing was central to his existence. Everything else was secondary. He was seduced by Nietzsche's maxim. Freed from distraction, he could sink into self-absorption, entertaining ideas that were otherwise irretrievable: "I can find no time to compromise—I am the revolutionary." Each person to his own work or their hedonism. Jack felt that thus far, he did not have any opportunity to "realize my relative intellectual immaturity." The task at hand, he realized, was to "lose society and find one's self." This meant discarding society's traditions and mores. This influence upon Kerouac was not purely Nietzschean but also Carr-inspired.

The influence was so strong that Jack was swayed to episodes of self-destruction. Carr possessed those characteristics Kerouac craved, a thorough disregard for laws or convention. However, Lucien could not write. "He had the vision," observed Kerouac, "but not the method." Now, Lucien was in jail. It was up to Jack to carry his torch. Here on a war-bound merchant vessel, there were no dreams or drunkenness. The voyage to Virginia was cut short, so he barely had time to settle into his old habits. According to Kerouac, a crew member became enamored with him and was aggressive in his pursuits.[73] He told Allen that he had gotten into a fight. Allen called Jack the "Neurotic Personality of Our Time."[74] After the ship docked, Jack left for New York. This dereliction of duties disbarred him from the Merchant Marine for a year. On the US Customs letter Jack carried with him, he crossed out his name and identification and wrote in pencil, "Merde alors!"[75]

Another reason for his sudden departure was to return to Celine. He thought he was in love with her. Though she flirted with him and permitted him to join her in Allen's bed, the feelings were not mutual. This did not stop Kerouac from throwing away the one job that he did not really mind turning to when times got tough.

When Jack arrived in New York, he checked into a cheap room for three days. While in hiding, he wrote at least two compositions: "Dialogs in Introspection" and "The Dark Corridor," using a pencil and red crayon he had at hand. In "Dialogs in Introspection," Kerouac proposes two life views by positing his "Creative" half against his "Moral" obligations, thereby exchanging warring perspectives. He begins with "Creative" (in lead pencil): "Creative pregnancy justifies anything I do short of criminality. Why should I live a moral life and inconvenience pre-disinterested emotions towards it?" "Moral" (in red crayon) counters: "If you don't, your creation will not be sound. Sound creation is moral in temper. Goethe proved that."[76] The Creative force summons writers that Kerouac had read to support its argument making references to Goethe and Dosto-evsky's Raskolnikov from *Crime and Punishment* among others, each in support of an argument that favors creativity over moral obligation. This is the same truth Emerson perceived when he spoke of "the ravishment of the intellect by coming nearer to the fact," even as he perceived the further truth that, since the poet is a man among men, so his concrete-ness becomes universality, when he said: "The young man reveres men of genius because, to speak truly, they are more himself than he is."[77] This then, is the essence of art as understood by Kerouac. Genius strives to ful-fill its hunger for immortality beyond natural begetting—its knowledge of soul and flesh, both of meaning and importance, and by the necessity of prediction and transmission, declares its oneness with and its love of its type.

This, then, according to "Dialogs in Introspection," is with or with-out morality. It asks, "can each remain separate?" Righteousness is found within, not without. If it is true that one could cause pain in friends and family, then this pain, Jack reasoned, is "the law of the artist's life." The artist is the "final distillery of emotions."

Kerouac's moral dialogue explains that it is still possible for people to lead good lives. But are they really "good"? Or just merely decent? Decent people with dignified lives are dedicated solely to their comfort and secu-rity. However, this comes at a cost. Genuine emotions are repressed to the degree that they become materialistically evaluated. This, according to Kerouac's creative dialogue, is the actual indecency. Kerouac's role as an artist will come with a price, as it would and should. A dispassionate atti-tude toward life is the only artistic attitude. It cannot be a philosophy for humanity because it is, at its best, anarchic. The artist's superior morality must be *immorality*. Art needs no moral justification. "Dialogs in Intro-spection" signals conflicted Kerouac in exile from Edie and his parents.[78]

Jack called Allen from a Village bar (Kerouac's Greenwich Village was a "spiritual Bowery") asking for him to meet him there. "I had it all figured out," Kerouac explained, "when I got back, I decided I'd stay in the Village—get a job as a counterman, find a room and write. I wasn't even going to tell anybody I was back. Remember, don't say a word of it, or Edie will hear and come storming into town to know why I haven't been out earning money. Well, I'm going to hide myself in the Village and work on *Galloway*. I wrote a lot last week on the boat."[79]

Jack roomed with Allen at Warren Hall. He asked about Celine. Allen advised him to forget her. Jack wrote her a note in French (she could read and speak French), translated thus:

"About my dog heart . . . I love you like crazy; like a young girl without pride, don't ask why! Unreasonable loves! I want to look at your eyes—again! Don't leave me / My heart aches, as always. I'm miserable again—Jean."[80]

When she arrived, Jack embraced her. She cold-shouldered him and they got into an argument. She shied from any suggestion of sexual contact. Despite this, Jack was desperately lovelorn. She told him to go back to Edie. He was conflicted. She was, after all, Lucien's girlfriend. She was Edie's maid of honor. Jack thought Celine was a "tease" because he thought she was flirting with him. On October 26, he went to Flynn's Bar on Broadway where Celine was supposed to meet him clandestinely. He sat at a table and wrote on the reverse side of his letter permitting his voyage on the *Paine* the depths of his anguish:

"She has not come yet. Probably, she lunches casually this moment weighing whether or not she should come. Here I burn in hell. This paper is the mirror with which I reflect myself burning in hell. Sing the happy solipsist!"[81]

Over a beer, he brooded dark thoughts. He did not want to work and would avoid it at all costs. Yet, he was faced with the problem of how to "make a living." He felt himself "a weakling like Rimbaud" and wanted to be "well-versed in true nihilism." He was unable to meet the demands of such a life-path. As he continued waiting for Celine, he drank until he was despondent. Besides the fact that he was married to her friend, Jack's stance on working could not have made an attractive candidate to win Celine's affections. She was determined to steer herself upon her own path.[82] For Jack, Celine personified true beauty; "her presence matters more than this loss of pride, this abject cravenness." He lay bare his emotions amid the noontime drinkers: "I have no more money; I do not want to give myself up to the family. I do not want to be lonely or to work, I cannot be practical and I cannot die and I am an apprentice nihilist . . . This, then, is hell. Oh Celene, come, come!"[83] He wondered if Lucien really loved her. If he did, it did not matter to Jack. He loved her more. In this moment of crisis, Jack was through being loyal to Lucien, a "pasty-faced punk kid from St. Louis." Did Allen convey his message? Or did he choose to betray Jack?

Either way, she never showed.

* * *

Jack received a letter from Lucien. He was planning a novel (never to be written):

"The novel of Claude de Maubri [a moniker for Lucien Carr] if you will. But Claude has changed somewhat since you last saw him due to various vicissitudes which he has undergone. Still introspective, he will never cease to see, like Thoreau, all of life in a drop of water. He is still convinced that the secret of morality lies within and not without the self, though he has learned that the self is far fuller (pardon the solecism) entity than he ever thought it before. He is not disillusioned with the intellect and its power but has relegated it to a position of less importance. He has begun to wonder about the meaning of the 'spirit.' But *notre garcon* still worships fervently, more fervently than ever before, at the shrine of parturience. And he has begun to see a little more clearly, along the ascendant path of self-consummation. Once when de Maubri read the 'Symposium,' he said, 'Ah Aristophanes! How true was thy half jest,' and then he wondered what that little rhetorical outburst meant. Now he has begun to find out."[84]

Kerouac called the period between October and November 1944 his phase of "Self Ultimacy." He, too, sought the "secret of morality" if only he could discard it. Self-Ultimacy was his New Vision. Kerouac's source for his ideas was taken from Nietzsche's *Thus Spoke Zarathustra*. He quoted Nietzsche: "Now I bid you lose me and find yourselves; and only when ye have all denied me, will I return onto you."[85] This credo became the core of an attempted novel (it got as far as sixty-three manuscript pages) titled *I Bid You Lose Me*, written between November 4 and November 15, 1944.[86] It was a rewrite of *Galloway*. Jack adopted Nietzsche's maxim ("Of all that is written, I love only what a man has written with his own blood") to its extreme by cutting his finger and smearing the word *BLOOD* in blood on its title page. He then wrote (in pencil): "He flees from reality to mysteries and himself—a mere naturalist. Symbols conceal the real causes of his despair. His symbols color him; his hue is vivid: he postures."[87] In black ink, he added a Nietzsche quote from *Ecce Homo*, "How much truth can a mind endure? How much truth will I dare?" Jack sought to enact Nietzsche's dictum to recognize that he was no longer an integral part of society. Though he was a tax-paying citizen (though his income was too low to pay taxes in 1944), he turned his back to it. After leaving his wife and hiding from his mother, all that was required of him now was to sleep, eat, and write. He tallied his accomplishments thus far:

"I wrote close to half a million words since 1939, when I first began to write. Poems, stories, essays, aphorisms, journals and nine unfinished novels. . . . Art so far has rationalized my errantry, my essential Prodigal Son behavior. It has also been the victim of an ego craving fame and superiority. I have been using art as a societal step-ladder, proving that my renunciation of society is incomplete. Self-Ultimacy I saw as the new vision—but I cravenly turned it to a use in a novel designed to gain me, the man of the world, respect, idolatry, sexual success, and every other thing that goes with it. Au revoir à l'art, then."[88]

Jack set himself apart from his friends when they argued over art, religion, and politics one evening. He referred to Nietzsche's maxim: "The man of knowledge must be able not only to love his enemies but also to hate his friends." It was an excellent "transvaluation," and he remembered weeping over the conversational brawl between his companions. They were, in his estimate, "idiots," and he was one even more for taking the time to understand them. He hated his friends for hating his enemies. He realized this was why he related so closely to Nietzsche, recalling how he did not adhere to his writings the first time he read them. Jack felt that Nietzsche, more than any other philosopher, was the most "timely" in wartime America.

* * *

"The Dark Corridor" of autumn 1944 is a dialogue conducted by Kerouac in a dream state. He wonders about his guilt and transcribes from a recent dream: "Is this the way I'm supposed to feel?" Jack explores this guilt through a maze of words supported by symbols, allusions, and occasional French phrases. It is a journey into subconsciousness, memory, and myth. Buried phrasings from books and places that he has read and experienced (southern Greenland, London) flesh out the core of this ten-page essay. Within "The Dark Corridor," Kerouac challenges those who doubt his convictions as an artist:

> Now, these dreadful guilts come out to
> Shame me and unman me:
> They challenge the soundness of my
>   Cosmology:
> In the corridor I pause awhile and in
> So nervous a state, I must
> Knead the flesh of my face, incessantly
> Scratch my hair, my arms:
> *She repeated her plight to me tonight!*
> I want to become mad—I am ill
>   with sanity:
> Who can gainsay my best while
>   I lasted?[89]

Kerouac was twenty-two years old. Within the past four years, he had evolved from a naive romanticist to an "apprentice nihilist." He yearned to embrace his madness, to lose his sanity if only to bring himself closer to genuine emotions stripped bare of falsehoods and pride. He imagined disease as a posse chasing him, that with the disease there lies wholeness. "Disease is my salvation," he wrote as if daring himself to embrace hostile forces that threatened to topple him. He addressed an imaginary audience, much as he did with "Dialogs in Introspection." Both texts reveal a conflicted artist plunging deeper into his disturbed neuroses. He converses with his opposition: "You do mad things!"; "No mind, he is gone." Kerouac retorts, "This is the way I'm supposed to feel!"

> It is cold here, and lonely: at one time

or another my heart is warm,
My mind in place.
And then my heart congeals, the cosmology
    falls to the icy ground
And shatters:
I must kneel and regain the pieces in
    cold, shaky hands:
I kneel there and gave mutely at the
    hands, I tremble:
There is no one to report the truth,
    Little Jean is working,
His work exists! The cold wind blows.[90]

His recent reading of Nietzsche encouraged a new social awareness: "What is the first and last thing a philosopher demands of himself? To overcome his times and become 'timeless inwardly.'"[91] Jack has made the same demands for himself; he, too, must become timeless through art. He must not be swayed by any impediment discouraging him from his path. This entire process was Lucien's gift to Jack. The "New Vision" was put into play.

* * *

By November 1944, Jack stood at a crossroads. Without external distractions, his conclusions were his own. The despair he endured, he had to learn to bear. He might use that despair, for it expressed an authentic experience. He needed to arise from darkness to light. Rimbaud proposed a "derangement of the senses" which advised Jack that his first mission was to explore his burgeoning awareness entirely. He had to pursue his soul, not hide from it. He had to learn to scrutinize it. He had to learn to test it. To become a visionary, he had to make himself a visionary and embrace its suffering essence, and reach out to madness and love and devour all that lay within.

Jack once saw a sign over a door: "Better to live in heaven than die in hell." Jack quipped, "Better to live in hell than die in heaven." But it was an "aesthetic hell" in which he'd happily perish. Reason had cast its spell over him. He was a wandering poet searching for a symbol. He was adrift on an ocean of madness. He had strayed from Whitman, yet something else lay frustratingly beyond his grasp: "Is this the way I'm supposed to feel? I am ill with sanity."

After reading *The Sea Is My Brother*, Columbia professor Raymond Weaver suggested a reading list to Jack: Eastern texts, the New England Transcendentalists, *The Egyptian Book of the Dead*, Plotinus, *Pierre*, and Gnostic scripture. It was his first exposure to theological and Eastern spiritual writings. Jack borrowed Allen's library card and checked out Nietzsche, the Comte de Lautréamont's *Maldoror*, Aldous Huxley, Yeats, and Rimbaud. He embarked upon a series of readings from several sources: sexual neo-Platonism, political liberalism, the decline of religion in the Western church, Freud, and H. G. Wells.

On November 16, 1944, Kerouac estimated his written output: "I wrote close to half a million words since 1939 when I first began to write—Poems, stories, essays, aphorisms, journals, and nine unfinished novels. That is the record—600,000 words, all in the service of art—in five years . . . Tonight I stored away my writings of the past month, plus an unfinished novel, a total of 75,000 words, in my drawer."[92]

Throughout late autumn into winter, Jack was reduced to sharing potato peel soup from the same bowl as Allen. In the Village, a bum told him, "Life is a bowl of cherries, my son, but try and get one." They slept in separate beds in Ginsberg's room: "Ginsberg is my eagle—*Ach! j'ai fini*[93]—."

Their living arrangement led to problems when a local bartender reported to a Columbia dean that Allen was drinking every night at the West End until well after 3:00 a.m. They returned to 360 Riverside Drive, near the scene of Kammerer's murder, and slept in Burroughs's apartment. He had just returned from St. Louis after his implication in Carr's crime. Bill found Jack's Self-Ultimacy quest absurd, seeing no use for asceticism to achieve high art. Instead, he recommended a "bang of morphine" and assisted in administering Jack's first bang, approximately ½ grain. The high lasted nearly six hours. Under its influence, he wrote poems: "Straighten your limbs, or you will not become an arrow for a flight along a parallel."

He finally broke his silence with his parents by late December. Gabe's letters flew to Grosse Pointe like a wounded arrow aimed straight for Jack's heart. She was not used to his absences, and not hearing from him via correspondence sent her into a frenzied panic. Jack, unwittingly did not realize her distress. He had ignored her letters. On Christmas Eve, he finally showed up on their doorstep.

He had a new altar for worship. Jack sat at the feet of the High Priest of Morningside Heights, Bill Burroughs. Jack listened to him unwind long unsettling narratives. He thought Burroughs the "authentic devil" who could have his way with you through silky seduction. Bill gave Jack another dose of morphine on January 19, 1945, and from this experience, Jack wrote some exploratory poetry titled "Notes Gleaned from a Voyage to Morphina":

Contemplate the universe—close your
    eyes—and sense,
Without word or image, sound or
    shape, the
Impulse of God.[94]

In his drugged haze, Jack felt that the worst of humanity had annihilated his joy. Yet, he realized its benefits: "God enters me."[95]

Drinking alcohol sedated him into dim acceptance. Morphine cracked his thoughts with sacred insight.

Around Christmas 1944, Edie returned to Jack. Afterward, they moved in with Joan Adams in her spacious five-bedroom flat at 419 West 115th Street. Parker reveals in her memoir that she had "spoken with Celine [Young], and she told me he tried to seduce her, but she wasn't having any of it." Jack could not be deterred. He appealed to Allen to once again help seduce her. Celine stayed cold. Allen called her a "simpering school girl" willing to "vomit to drink the blood of a poet."[96] His true motives exposed, Jack turned to his writing for his customary self-absorbed venting. "Society bleeds geniuses," he poured out in Ginsberg's journal. Both attempted to honor Nietzsche's mantra that Art is the complement and consummation of existence. In self-absorption, Jack watched the busy street from the window. It seemed like an enormous flowing river of humanity passing beneath a bridge. Who was he in the eyes of others? Jack asked Allen: "You must think, just by spending an evening with me, by the perpetual gloominess on my face, that I am the most unhappy bastard of the weight-of-the-world type you ever saw." Ginsberg responded, "No! As long as you wear that expression, you are most happy."

A batch of books swept through Jack's and Allen's hands courtesy of Burroughs: Kafka's *The Castle*, *Moby Dick*, Jean Cocteau's *Opium*, and *Crime and the Human Mind* by David Abrahamsen, who stated that the capacity for "criminalistic tendencies" existed in all humans. On his own, Jack read Andre Gide, Joseph Conrad, D. H. Lawrence, Denton Welch (inspiring the book he would soon be writing with Burroughs), and Blaise Pascal ("Our nature consists in motion; complete rest is death."[97]). Jack's Libertine Circle had morphed into the Beats. They were his *other* family, a group of like-minded compatriots actively discussing art, literature, life, and barely outside the law.

With Edie, Jack wished for a new start despite the fact that he was open for infidelity with Celine. He invited Edie to visit his family for the holidays. Though Edie had first attempted to bond with her in-laws, she found them too provincial. Leo's fawning attempts to ingratiate himself into her privileged world (from which she was so eager to escape) seemed pathetic. However, there was ample reason for compassion.

Leo was diagnosed with Banti's disease, characterized by congestion and spleen enlargement. It would later be cancer. He was coughing blood. Life's constant disappointments had come full circle. Resigned and defeated, he sat at home playing the radio at total volume. Jack lamented his father's misfortunes in *Vanity of Duluoz*: "My poor father had to see me, while dying of cancer, come down to all of this from that beginning on the sandlot football field of Dracut Tigers Lowell when the ambition was to make good in football and school, go to college, and become a 'success.'"[98]

Leo longed to return to Lowell. His sickly pallor and detached manner witnessed his wayward son coming and going between Manhattan and Ozone Park. Sometimes Jack brought Allen or Bill with him. Leo distrusted both. Gabe did not like them either; she thought Allen was the "devil himself." She did not like Jews. Leo was a bigot. Sometimes Leo reluctantly discussed politics and religion with Allen, whose radical opinions earned Leo's disdain. Leo refused to accept Jack's ambitions, dismissing him as an oddball like his new friends.

Bill conducted lay psychoanalysis on Jack. He revealed to Jack that he did not want to be successful. There was something destructive willing him to failure. Bill felt that maybe Jack harbored disdain for Gerard. That he secretly wished him dead and that ever since he was damaged beyond repair. It warped his being. The circle of failure began once Jack left Lowell for New York.

Jack's writing continued despite his father's disapproval. It was an apt introduction to 1945, a year Jack described as "LOW, EVIL DECADENCE."

CHAPTER FIVE

The Impulse of All Creation

KEROUAC HAD CONSIDERED WHAT THE PREVIOUS YEAR HAD STOOD FOR in the trajectory of his life thus far. His world shined in a new light. His self-assurance was growing. He could better articulate his life through art. The Rimbaudian fever dream of the past six months was falling behind him in favor of a more Spenglerian worldview that would transfigure his thinking and writing, finding its most lasting impression in his first major opus, *The Town and the City*. Though Lucien Carr's influence was profoundly felt, some of it was usurped by Burroughs who saw nothing of value in Carr's willfully destructive nature. The New Vision philosophy was transforming into the ethos of what would become the Beat Generation. If Burroughs felt destructive, he was self-destructive, shooting drugs through a needle.

With ailing Leo's failing health a constant concern, Jack was obligated to maintain stronger home ties to care for him. Gabe was always working. Without school, the urgency of paying for it was gone. Edie no longer expected Jack to become a breadwinner for their nest egg. She had vanished from his life. With his Navy discharge in hand and the threat of the war now over, these distractions were gone from his life. Jack had gotten what he wanted. He could write without obligations.

A flood of writing signaled the arrival of the new year. He had newly written notes documenting the events of the past four years. He titled one such effort *An American Marriage*. Kerouac understood the futility of marriage, because his had ended. To most observers, not much seemed to have gone badly between the two except for the domestic disputes once the honeymoon period had finished. Kerouac felt that all of this was undetected by friends and family, a point analogized in his journal where he seemed to be having a ghost conversation with German philosopher and poet Friedrich Schiller: "On the other hand, it was contrary to my nature to talk over my poetic plans with anybody—even with Schiller. I carried everything with me in silence, and usually, nothing was known to anyone until the whole was completed."[1]

The new ten-chapter chronological novel was compared to a necklace of different gems. Each gem was a self-contained chapter telling its own story. It was a scaled-down version of his Duluoz Legend. Scenes were to swirl in an impressionistic dance of settings. The central chapters contained episodes like his Bronx jailing, city hall wedding, a stay in Detroit, a trip to Ontario, Canada, his attempted seduction of Celine Young, and the resulting breakdown in Flynn's Saloon. It was a meticulous restructuring of events inversely and outwardly expressing a simultaneous heaven-bound/earthbound synthesis of love and time. To achieve this, he would have to stand apart from the world while staying within its folds. Through reading Goethe, Kerouac found assurance in the German master's belief that "he who does not keep aloof from all this, and isolate himself by main force, is lost."

An American Marriage dissolved. Part of the writing was repurposed for *An American Passed Here* at the end of June 1945. This proposed novel was to begin in 1936 and unreel through time, using the family history of the Kerouacs. *An American Marriage* had been transplanted from Jack and Edie to Gabe and Leo (possibly to avoid libel suits). *An American Passed Here* was a panoramic exposition of America, illustrating a primary ideal crushed by the Great Depression and Kerouac's self-realization as an artist amidst an ensuing turmoil. World War II would be pitted against the personal conflict to a final revolt between good and evil in late 1944. He was searching for a higher communion between nature and the mind, much like Emerson's spiritual discourse in the essay "Nature." The pathway from one to the other, he felt, expressed what it meant to be human. He was seduced by Siren voices—family, religious, moral, sexual, literary, philosophical, and political—ultimately conceding to the ventriloquial version of his voice committed to his soul. It was further propulsion of the growth spirit as it evolved in stages. Only five years before, he had staked a claim to his identity and stood by it: "I am my mother's son. All other identities are artificial and recent. Naked, basic, actually, I am my mother's son. I emerged from her womb and set out into the earth."[2]

Back then, his conviction was to plant a stake into the world, to be a writer of substance and a writer of merit. It seemed, in retrospect, all so clear back then. By 1945, he had survived the raging "self-fighting" that had plagued him since 1943. He was led wrong, slightly caught up in war hysteria and other life impediments. He was baffled by commitments he was not prepared to honor.

Others were concerned about the influence of Burroughs on Allen and Jack. Jerry Newman expressed concern about Bill giving Allen drugs. Jack wrote out a transcription of one conversation between Joan and Bill:

Joan: Did you hear how Jerry was so upset about your giving Allen drugs?

Bill: In what way?

Joan: Oh, just generally, as though she felt you spend your life just doing things like that.

Bill: Corrupter, hey?

Joan: And of course, there was an element of racial solidarity in— she thinks of Allen as her brother, as her fine indomitable kinsman fighting against the Philistines. It upset her terribly—she wanted really for us to get together and do something about it.

Bill: Does she feel that I'm undermining the Jewish race? . . . But hell, how can I or Allen or anyone else become drug addicts if we can't get drugs? We're handicapped from the very start.

Joan: Oh, a fine indomitable young man like Allen ought to be able to overcome that. . . . [3]

1945 was a turning point. Jack felt a "crucial sense of an 'end' and 'beginning.'" Because of this, his written output increased: a collaboration with Burroughs on a novel; a novella, *Orpheus Emerged*; essays on Blake,

Nietzsche, and Yeats; and a plethora of short prose writings trying to find its way into a more extensive work. By February, Kerouac finished his sections of *And the Hippos Were Boiled in Their Tanks*. Bill and Jack wrote alternate chapters (except at the end of the book, where Burroughs wrote three in a row). Their subject was the events leading to David Kammerer's murder without explicitly focusing on the killing. Notwithstanding the gossip that spread from the Columbia campus through the entire city, the offense in the novel is muted, not occurring until the book's closing chapters. Burroughs, writing as "Will Dennison" and Kerouac as "Mike Ryko," offer not very different perspectives on their motley group cavorting from couch to floor to various locations like the Minetta Tavern where the phantom relics of the past Village lingered long after the tourists dissipated.

Kerouac and Burroughs were constant companions through March. Kerouac let Burroughs perform psychoanalysis. On the 16th, Burroughs resolved that Kerouac was too reliant on his mother and ultimately she would emotionally strangle him as he got older. Burroughs was aware of Gabe and Leo's hatred of him and so his study was likely biased toward them. Kerouac wrote: "the psychoanalytical probing has upset me prodigiously." In his journal, he warned himself that psychoanalysis could help achieve a "grasp of living" but could do little to gain the "grasp of life." For that, only art or religion could work."

Bill introduced Jack to New York's colorful underworld of drugs, thieves, pimps, and whores. Kerouac recalls in *Vanity of Duluoz*:

"One of our 'friends' who came in to stash a gun one day turned out, after he hanged himself in the Tombs some months later, to have been the 'Mad Killer of Times Square,' tho I didn't know about that: he'd walk right into a liquor store and shoot the proprietor dead: it was afterward confessed to me by another thief who couldn't hold the secret he said because he hurt from holding it."[4]

Bill was eager to share his underworld paradise. It wasn't long before Jack was sampling a variety of narcotics. He smoked pot (introduced to him by Lester Young in a cab, according to Edie Parker), ingested the blotted paper from Benzedrine inhalers, and took morphine (Burroughs's drug of choice). The excessive perspiration and loss of appetite from the speed caused Jack's weight to plummet thirty pounds. Benzedrine caused hallucinations that exacerbated his depression. He applied makeup to his face to give it color. It didn't help. Jack's physical and mental regression gave Leo new reasons to indict Bill and Allen as criminal delinquents. Jack composed a list of "horrors." He feared obligations of what he had to do the next day, such as jobs, errors, and appointments; of being alone in the dark; of leaving his room for the streets; "of your intently seen self-rising to the surface"; and coming down from Bennies, when everything became dull, unpleasant, unamusing, "perfectly hideous," and horrible. Looking back at his writings of the previous year, all of it stuffed two inches thick in a manila envelope, he conceded that there were so many ways of saying the same stupid things.

Disturbed, Jack approached Ginsberg at Livingstone Hall. Kerouac was *persona non grata* on the Columbia campus after the murder. There were multiple operatives in effect: Allen wasn't permitted to host over-night guests, especially Jack. Jack slept in Allen's room until the campus authorities were notified of his presence. They knocked on Allen's door. Jack ran to a bed and buried himself under the blankets, leaving Allen to fend for himself. The assistant dean followed on a report of Ginsberg scrawling obscenities on his window. Consequently, Allen was suspended. Without a place to stay, he moved into Joan Adams's apartment.

Joan's husband, Paul, returned home to find her and her strung-out roommates high on drugs. Disgusted, he left her the sole guardian of the baby daughter after realizing the baby was not his. He also ceased his allotment checks to her. Joan's $80-a-month five-room apartment became costly. Because she wanted to finish her Columbia degree, she continued taking in boarders. One was Herbert Huncke, a junkie and thief who frequented Times Square. Huncke, seven years Jack's senior, was the apotheosis of "beat," the Times Square junkie slang of being reduced to one's essentials. Huncke's high, guttered, ecstatic, bleak exis-tence impressed Kerouac. Haldon "Hal" Chase, a Columbia student of anthropology and a prolific wooer of women, received Jack's respect for his natural ease and sexual prowess. The culmination of this chance gath-ering was the "Night of the Wolfeans," a literary discussion split between "non-Wolfeans" (Ginsberg and Burroughs) and "Wolfeans" (Kerouac and

Chase). The non-Wolfeans associated themselves with French Symbol-
ists, while the Wolfeans were fundamentally traditionalists. In a broader
sense, the schism also reflected their sexual identities, with the former
as homosexual and the latter mostly heterosexual. Such literary conversations became vital to Kerouac's developing artistry. It opened him to
new ideas. The gatherings were reminiscent of those held in 1944 when
Lucien was on the scene instead of behind bars. Now it was all mostly
under Burroughs's influence. Jack found a new place to resort to when he
wanted a break from his parents.

Missing Caroline, Leo was an active correspondent. He was the
forebear of Jack, sitting at a typewriter with a sheet of paper rolled in,
thinking of what to say before blasting out the words that crowded his
mind. Most of what he had to say to her was his personal diatribes about
his son's doings. That March of 1945, Leo rightly sensed New York City's
seedy corruption and had much to say about it. He would have to "write
a book," he wrote Caroline, who was now remarried and pregnant. He
scorned the city's depravity, politics, and people and was thankful, at least,
that he and Gabe were living in a small apartment far enough away from
the locus of everything he saw wrong with the country. Leo brought up
Jack, sharing that he had written a novel (the Burroughs collaboration)
that he hoped to publish, without any success: "It tells the story of some
European whacky who comes here at a tender age, and finally lands in
the jug after a murder he commits because he is being pursued by another
man??? Just imagine that!!!!" Leo would have preferred the entire Carr/
Kammerer business that put his surname into the pages of every local
newspaper he could put his hands on to just go away. He apprised Nin
of Jack's comings and goings: "He went away last Friday night and now,
Sunday afternoon, he hasn't shown up." Of his jobs, or lack thereof: "He
had a few dollars he earned with small jobs and went on one of his intellectual binges, I suppose." For himself, Leo struggled to make ends meet,
earning, when he was at full throttle, $71.25 for a week's pay and was
finally able to save money, possibly, for a vacation. But it was "subbing"
for a newspaper, so he could not depend on that income reliably. He felt
the sting of his poverty. He needed new clothes and suffered from broken

teeth: "I feel like a bum as usual." Now, Leo was bedbound, and could not work at all.[5]

Of Gabe, she complained of fatigue, so who was more tired, Leo, Gabe, or Jack? Bitterly he added, "Jack sleeps all day anyway, so that makes it even." Gabe's postscript was less accusatory, "I have to feed him when he always comes home rather hungry." And so she did, cooking beef stew and strawberry shortcake for her boys "just like old times hey."

In the coming months, Leo championed Caroline as the sole family member who held the Kerouac banner high. It was as if he had given up, cutting loose Jack's moorings and letting the ship drift. Jack, possibly in an attempt at damage control lest he lose his sister's favor, typed a letter dated March 14. It served the initial purpose of thanking her for her birthday card and present (he had just turned twenty-three years old) but also apprised her of the book he wrote with Burroughs. Kerouac wrote that he had sent the manuscript to Simon & Schuster, describing it as an effort to describe the "lost generation." If they passed on it, they'd keep trying to sell it through a literary agent (Kerouac would keep trying to sell it until 1952, even after Lucien Carr wanted the book to go away), who insisted that Columbia Pictures had an interest (they didn't). Should the book succeed, he and Burroughs would follow it up with a second novel. Then there was the novel Kerouac had been writing, he reminded Nin, since he was nineteen. He had to complete it someday, and if he couldn't publish it, or anything else, he'd be up against a "stone wall." The letter was less confident than he intended, accomplishing little to dismiss Nin's apprehensions about Jack's intentions and how it would ultimately impact Gabe and Leo's welfare.

Family responsibilities hampered Jack. He had tentative plans to hitchhike to California on October 20. He spent most of his time with Gabe. They watched despairingly as bedridden Leo writhed with pain when they performed abdominal taps. They cut into his body, drained it, and sutured it closed. On August 21, Jack wrote of Leo having a tumor extracted from his abdomen: "we are all rotten inside, that's what we are. Life is, by nature rotten. All of nature is rotten." From that experience, much of his later prose would be steeped in the mortification of people. Slow relentless decay was the underbelly of living. Leo's mortification would influence Jack's writings exponentially as he got older. He frequently alluded to aging and decay. He noticed his father's balding head, his graying skin, and his once robust frame now thinning. He was different. He had changed; his racial slurs went away. It was as if he were humbled into meek acceptance of the world: "he sees all men now how they are, one by one . . . and all women, of course."

Before leaving the hospital room with Gabe, Jack wanted to grasp his father's hand. He wished to practice "constraint in the face of death" and realized that his father was going to someday die.

That night Jack tried to write, but the words failed him. In his diary, he exposed his vulnerability: "MY FATHER IS DYING AND I CANNOT FIND THE LANGUAGE." Looking at his father's empty bed, he wrote: "My father is a great man. That is borne by facts which I shall later bring out." The next day Leo's prognosis was better, "there were discrepancies in my mother's gloomy prognostications." Jack went to the hospital with Nin and spoke to the doctor, who suspected that Leo only had an "oversized spleen." The family was relieved.[6]

Rejuvenated on Labor Day, Jack's ambitions swept him up into a whole new perspective of his work: "I felt a resurgence of the old feeling, the Faustian urge to understand the whole in one sweep, and to express it in one magnificent work—mainly, America and American life." Kerouac no longer required a "New Vision": "it's the method I want."[7] The "Faustian urge" originated from his heightened understanding of *The Decline of the West*, the "urge" of Western civilization to confound spiritual distress and grasp at existential meaning. Spengler applied the word "Faustian" to Western culture by suggesting a similarity between Faust's tragic figure and the Western world. Just as Faust sold his soul to Mephistopheles to attain greater dominion, so then has Western man sold his soul to technology. This is the Faustian soul Kerouac references so frequently throughout his writings. The Faustian soul relies so much on his technological miracles that he has forgotten to live without them. The fate of the Faustian soul suggests that there is no possibility of spiritual deliverance. Different characters in Kerouac's books (Ray Smith, Sal Paradise, Jackie Duluoz) strike out in their Faustian urge to control their respective destinies.

The yearning for spiritual deliverance reveals another important aspect of Kerouac's appreciation for Spengler: the Second Religiousness. A civilization must become fully formed before there is a decline of the West. It anticipates a religious awakening before the endpoint of a civilization, suggesting not an utter extinction of religion, but that which is on the wane. The Second Religiousness is not a religiosity of high culture. Those people unaffected by this, the "fellaheen," will increasingly populate Kerouac's writings as he moves from the late 1940s through the 1950s into his mature writings.[8]

* * *

Having little opportunity to use Jack as his sounding board, Leo reached out to Nin, writing her on September 27 that he had been recovering for two weeks after his last drainage: "Old Mississippi flows on, and it's discouraging." His cut had not healed; he was prone to infections. The savings he had acquired, over $1,000, were now being spent on x-ray treatments. He felt "jinxed." Gabe, by autumn 1945, was earning between $70 and $75 per week. There would be no help from Jack. Leo wanted him to "straighten out" to ease his worries: "he is going further and further away from me, and nothing I can do or say does any good."

But Jack was writing a new book.

Orpheus Emerged, or The Half Jest, began as a series of notes from January 1944 with an outline of thirteen characters, the last being Marcel Orpheus, who is "never seen." He divided the story into ten parts and developed it over two complete drafts. Jack used journal entries to flesh out "Leo" and "Paul":

"Here's the way it goes," Leo says, beginning to read. "Contemplate the universe—close your eyes—and, like God, begin to sense, without words or image, sound or shape, the impulse of all creation. This is the pure moment of God's imagination before the epileptic fit of fault and history begins."[9]

Orpheus Emerged is allegorical with all of its literary and musical allusions; it also portrays Kerouac as both twenty-two-year-old Paul, the "genius of life and love," and twenty-two-year-old Michael, "the genius of imagination and art." The story is about Paul's return and his ultimate rejoining of the group. According to Kerouac's notes, Michael "suffered the wound of his calling" and had deliberately sold out to Paul. The underlying symbolism is Kerouac's attempt to portray Michael as transcending "human emotions to those of God—emotions of creation, or Eternity, etc." To do so, Michael had to discard his "human self" and strike off for the "High Regions," as Orpheus did when he went into the underworld to lead his wife, Eurydice, back from the dead. Michael becomes "lost, lonely, and out of his element" in the High Regions. His humanity retains him, and he "finds that his life exists unquestionably on human terms." His "wholeness" is only achieved in being the "Lyre of God." In essence, Michael embodies the "new vision" of Kerouac. There are references to *Faust*, Lucretius's *On the Nature of Things*, *Also Sprach Zarathustra*, Kenneth Patchen's *Journal of Albion Moonlight*, T. S. Eliot, Brahms, and Stravinsky, among others. At the head of the typescript, he typed "John Kerouac." Upon completion, he crossed out his first name in pencil and replaced it with "Jack."

In a journal entry, Kerouac assessed his written output into stages. He did not live by a "calendar of personal events" but by the "almanac of artistic directions." These stages begin with "Sunset at Six," a short story written in Hartford in October 1941 ("Saroyan" period); *Galloway* (Joycean period); *The Haunted Life* (Wolfean period); "I Bid You Lose Me" (Nietzschean period); *Orpheus Emerged* (Yeats period); the 40,000-word *Philip Tourian* (Spenglerian period); *The Sea Is My Brother* (the American period); and "Supreme Reality" (Self-Ultimacy period).[10] In truth, all of these efforts with their attending influences bleed into each other with no clear cut delineations.

Jack wondered that his writing was beginning to reflect not his ideas, but those of his mother. Burroughs's influence upon Jack was powerful and convincing. Through his objectivity and experience, Bill could sense the lay of the land of the Kerouac family dynamic as clearly as he saw his own. Trips to Ozone Park were infrequent, but it would take only one visit to see where Jack stood with his mother. He found Gabe domineering and opinionated. Clearly, she had Jack under her sway.

Kerouac's circle of friends was drifting apart for the time being. Edie was back with her grandmother in Asbury Park. She refused to reply to

Jack's letters. Joan was with her parents in Loudonville, New York; Burroughs was with his parents in Clayton, Missouri. Ginsberg had joined the US Maritime Service (he needed to come up with funds to pay for school since his expulsion). There were others, but for the time being, Jack stayed in Ozone Park trying to figure out his next move.

There was no going to sea. The US Coast Guard had suspended his seaman's papers after he neglected (and abandoned) his duties in Norfolk in October 1944. For other jobs, he felt unsuited. He planned to attend UCLA but that went nowhere.[11]

He was driven to fulfill his goal of completing a novel before his father died. He had several in mind. He wanted to rewrite *And the Hippos Were Boiled in Their Tanks* and would commence upon it in August 1945, titling it *I Wish I Were You*.[12] Without Leo, Jack would be the figurative "man of the house" and expected to help support his aging mother. As with the probability of the draft, Jack felt the pressure caving in on him, and so he immersed himself thoroughly in his projects.

In mid-August 1945, Jack wrote that he was waiting for the "only authentic revolution on this earth: The inward revolution." But there was no time to wait for *that* revolution. There was nowhere to go but return to his instincts as an artist. He was an outcast, even where he thought that he was accepted. Ginsberg wrote in July 1945: "Jean, you are an American more completely than I, more fully a child of nature and all that is of the grace of the earth."[13] But Kerouac did not feel it. Instead, he felt that he was always suffering in so many ways: spiritually, emotionally, physically (his legs):

"The nature of life, it struck me, is suffering; a doctrine, I realized, which reduced happiness to a by-product of that suffering, just as love is a by-product of the anarchic nature of man. Everything in life suffers, and where it is poetical to say that suffering is the price things must pay in order to live, to know life, it is more just to say that living things, being vouchsafed the light of life out of an eternity of darkness, are subject to the nature of life whether or not the light be as compensation for the penalties involved in being alive. No, justice is not the intention of God, wherein lies man's ignorance of the nature of life. The intention of God is light, after and before eternal darkness; and at the root of that light lies the dark uncertain pit of our souls, the pit that Pascal saw, as a natural condition and remnant of our true circumstance, which can be a reminder if we will so understand of the true nature of all life. A hint, so be it, of where we come from and where we shall return."[14]

It was only through writing that Jack could avert suffering, or take advantage of it constructively. He felt that the "artistic personality" was the basis of all outstanding achievements: "I recommend it for all human beings."[15]

Out drinking one night with Bill, Jack got drunk and lost his "psychic balance." He stole a copy of Louis-Ferdinand Celine's novel, *Voyage au bout de la nuit* (1932). This book exacerbated Kerouac's narrowing views of the world. He saw no end to darkness and human malice. He read it in its entirety. It consumed him with envy. How he wished he could write such a book! He became intoxicated with its thoughts. He was "mad to find out more about Louis Ferdinand Céline, but no one seems to bother about him." Céline drove Kerouac "into a new mad flight of thought . . . perhaps he has changed my life." No other writer, he wrote, had moved him as much "from top to bottom as it were."

* * *

Written in New York beginning in January 1944 through early 1945, the second draft of *Galloway* and its preparatory notes (referred to by Kerouac as "The Plan For The Novel Galloway") sheds light into his working method. The notes contain twenty-two sections that break down scenes for the novel. Within are revelations of different characters (himself, his family, friends, etc.) and how each could be developed through their respective arcs. Although eventually, he would not choose to include most of this content in *The Town and the City*, he later incorporated it into *Maggie Cassidy* and *Vanity of Duluoz*. The second draft was based on the "Duluoz" trilogy of 1942 (which Kerouac regarded as the first draft of *Galloway*).

"Morning gray in Galloway. Dalouas stretched his legs toward the foot of the bed and rubbed his chest with voluptuous afterthought. Why do I feel so marvelously awake? For once in my life I shall get out of bed in the moment of awakening. Allons!"[16]

The character of "Dalouas" (a variant of "Duluoz") is once again based upon Kerouac. "Pater" is Leo, who from the outset despises Galloway. He is at odds with "Callahan Brothers," a stand-in for Leo's real-life employer Sullivan Brothers who bought out Leo's printing company after the flood of 1936 had destroyed his press. In the opening paragraphs of *Galloway*, Pater is jobless. He is bitter and resentful of the foreman, O'Boyle (Pater labels O'Boyle an "asskisser" and a "faker"). Galloway itself is far from the Promised Land for Pater. Instead, it is "the city of a thousand defeats of the soul and as many minor commercial triumphs."[17] The *Galloway* second draft character of Allan MacKenzie, also based on Jack, broods alone in his Galloway room listening to records and reading books like *Crime and Punishment*.

Galloway suggests a Joycean influence on Kerouac:

"Blue Bagdad sky in Galloway. The air is vibrant with coming night. The sky, deep dark blue back there in the East, pastel directly above, faint luminous grayblue over there West. Lovely world. I am the Caliphate. Blue Bagdad sky in Galloway."[18]

Jack was driving toward something uniquely his own. In section 19 of the *Galloway* notes, he wrote:

"Whereas, in most novels, the climax of the narrative is dramatic, this, not being so much a narrative as a fugue of moods, must be a musical climax—the climax in 'Galloway' must be referred to as such:—it is not the dramatic outbreak of a narrative's laborious building up, but sheer triumph erupting like a mood without cause over the mass of life—moods strung and woven thereunto. The same method I applied in 'Orpheus Emerged,' where realism was established to vent full and glowing truth of a mystico-spiritual experience . . . although that work was of the poorest quality, really."[19]

Galloway was Kerouac's "supreme objective." Besides evoking a picture-perfect rendering of Lowell, Jack felt that he was now in a position to pour into it all that he had learned thus far.

Nothing could stand in the way of his completing it.

* * *

Kerouac felt that art can help form personality. The artist can strip "human" from "being." They seek to Be. The artist must become a synthesis of martyr, prophet, and devil. The artist must be able to adapt to either end of the spectrum (martyr to devil) and transform it through artistic awareness. The modern artist must not be deterred from evil because they are the face of the future. He was not alone, nor should he ever expect to elevate above his compatriots: "Art can be a cure—to organize and carry out and complete an artwork is to heal the breaches in a sickly will, and set the precedent on how to live, and future art."[20] The path was clear, and he would take to it with no reservation about the sacrifices he would have to make.

Despite the doctor's prognosis, Leo's health continued to fail. Because of their financial difficulties, Gabe remained at the Manhattan shoe factory, leaving Jack to care for his dying father. Jack watched as doctors and nurses attended Leo every other week, futilely lancing his stomach. As Kerouac put it, his father "withered" before him. While keeping an eye on Leo collapsed in his favorite chair, Jack sketched an outline for his subsequent work, a considerably longer novel in which he would explain "everything to everybody." When he needed to get away, if only for a few hours, he left, usually on the weekends when Gabe was home.

The city seemed dead as he rode a bus from Queens into Manhattan. He wrote of one such ride on November 25[21] after noticing its mostly empty seats: "who would be sitting in them had the war not happened? What manner of men would be here returning home from an evening with their girlfriends?" Caught in self-awareness, he reminded himself, "we are the only ones left." There were "thugs" at the rear of the bus; the "formidable killers" of the next war: "They were ready for anything that history had to offer, any time, and the bigger and bloodier the better; for history, to them, represented only some kind of authority from above to which they were prepared to pay enthusiastic allegiance." He reflected on his generation, that of being not a "lost" generation, but the "last" with a "devil-may-care" attitude toward life. His New York City companions exemplified it: Bill, Allen, Hal, Lucien, Joan, and Edie: "somehow this generation of mine seemed the finest, the most interesting, of any previous generation, & would walk into the maw of the West's decline with a beautiful air, effecting a grand and marvellous exit as no Lord Byron ever dreamed. Suave and gallant, we are the last—And we are full of strange joy! I gave us three years at the most, cheerfully."[22]

Jack heard it best from Herbert Huncke; the "last" generation was a "beat" generation.

* * *

Jack's addiction to Benzedrine had taken its toll upon his health. It had been his drug of choice, and it had helped him stay up for many hours at a time. It gave him hyper-focus on his writing. He talked nonstop. He was gregarious without drinking alcohol. He disliked morphine. It made him sick. Amphetamines gave him an edge that alcohol lacked. However, his health became compromised. While crossing Brooklyn Bridge one day with Allen, he collapsed to the ground. He was immediately hospitalized in a Queens VA hospital. Deep within his leg, blood clots had developed. He was diagnosed with thrombophlebitis.[23]

By April 20, Jack was continuing his notes on writing with "Michael Martin's Christmas Joy," evoking in first-person the child Martin, like the "little son of God," lying among a group of elders. Here his prose becomes deeply reverential, not only of God and the Lamb but of the mother and her duty to her child. Kerouac was newly charged through the remainder of April into May, finding hope and redemption in his work. An "experiment" conducted on May 12 was made up in his mind that every day would be a "dream of greatness interrupted only by a painful sifting of doubts through the mind into their proper repository: I throw nothing away." There would be nothing that could dissuade him from his goal.

At midnight on Easter Eve, Kerouac titled a new passage, "Notes by a Young American Faustus," and explored the idea that he no longer had to fear man, as Dostoevsky did when he was imprisoned in Omsk, but only that of his mind. This was the Faustian enigma of space, the idea that one can go as fast and far as one wants with nothing to stop them. It was the discovery of space and finding in it an infinite emptiness. He had gone for a hike at sundown through the city and asked himself if he was the first to disregard original sin in favor of "original virtue"? He wondered of the dual natures of Dostoevsky, Nietzsche, Rimbaud, and Stendhal. Why did he always feel so mixed up?

Kerouac sensed that damnation and disease were the only flaws in the breathtaking flow of the world swirling past him. There was beauty everywhere but so little within himself: "as it corrupts me and destroys me from within, the beauty and order in the worlds crumble before my small blind eye of weariness and I am prepared to give it all up. Is there anything left for the sick and weary? The great hand one had to yield power is the same that can be stricken, palsied into paralysis. What was cancer then, but life overbrimming with growth?"[24]

On a Friday afternoon (May 17, 1946), Jack was arguing with Leo over how to brew coffee when his father begged, "take care of your mother whatever you do. Promise me." Without another word, and before Jack could respond, Leo slumped forward in his chair. Jack assumed he was asleep. With "awful understanding," Jack reached for Leo's wrist and placed his hand on his forehead, and was surprised that it was still warm. Leo had died in his sleep at the same age as his father, Jean-Baptiste, at fifty-six. For all of his struggles, all Leo had to show for it was his ink-stained fingertips.

Leo Kerouac's body was driven to Nashua, New Hampshire, in an undertaker's hearse. His wake was held on May 19; the funeral was held the next day at the same church where Leo and Gabe were married. Among the pallbearers were Jack, thin and out of place, and his new brother-in-law, Paul Blake, who had recently returned from Okinawa, where he was stationed. They mournfully carried the casket with Leo's brothers to the Saint Louis de Gonzague Cemetery to be buried in the unmarked grave side-by-side with Gerard. The sight of his father lying in a coffin profoundly affected Jack. He would carry this tragic pathos into his books. On June 23, he finalized his notes for Emil Martin's funeral in *The Town and the City*:

"It seemed to Peter as he saw his father laying there in the coffin, surrounded by the beloved sisters, brothers, and friends of his life in Galloway and Lacoshua, in the fine old New Hampshire house that had been made into a funeral home, while the hill night brooded softly upon that beautiful little town where his father had known boyhood and youth decades ago, it seemed to Peter that a great and gentle demonstration of life's one supreme meaning was being made, before his very eyes, as right there and then his father reposed at last after the bitter years of Brooklyn's clangorous air, of illness, of bitter anger, and of longing to be back in old New England with the kin, friends, and lovers of a younger time, in the green, wooded, white-steepled, fume-of-smoke stillness of its soul and land, and as now it was all being returned to him fully at the moment after his death!"[25]

After he returned, Jack's trips into the city became less frequent. He focused his energy on his novel: *Galloway* had morphed into the first stages of *The Town and the City*. When he did go out, he stayed, despite his *persona non grata* status at Columbia, with Hal Chase at Livingstone Hall. Chase had, for a time, lived in Joan's apartment but moved out once Joan was away in Loudonville. Another student Jack met was a friend of Hal's, Ed White, who was taking classes under the G.I. Bill. White's habit of carrying pocket notebooks with him also encouraged Jack to do so. Before, his journals were mostly sheets of lined paper that he stapled together. This simple act was not for the mere taking of notes, but would eventually assume a compositional strategy over many of his published writings.

Hal Chase regaled Kerouac with tales of a young man he knew named Neal Cassady. Hal considered Neal to be a mad genius. Cassady, according to Chase, had a propensity for stealing cars and womanizing. He was the son of a Larimer Street flophouse alcoholic. Chase had a collection of Cassady's letters from reform school, which he let Allen and Jack read. Almost five years younger than Jack, Neal was brought up in a $4-a-month cubicle that he and his father shared with a double amputee. Cassady lost his virginity at age nine. His libido knew no bounds after that, having sex with everybody he could, from prepubescent girls to the elderly. Jack would later dub him a "cocksman of the West."

Before long, Neal's sexual identity became a blur; he would move with schizoid ease from male to female purely on the moment's caprice. His car thefts matched his sexual conquests: He stole an estimated five hundred cars (by Cassady's count) between the ages of fourteen and twenty-one. Intrigued, Jack and Allen were eager to meet him. However,

Jack was hot on his book and determined to finish it before the year's end. His determination caused Allen to call him the "Wizard of Ozone Park." Jack's chronicling of a large mill-town family was filled with insightful, vibrant characterizations. In his journal, Kerouac prayed for divine inspiration to help him finish. He prayed. He read from the Holy Bible that lay on his desk. This gave him balance and solace. It put him in a better mindset than a year ago. A more practical solution to composition crowded out thoughts of the New Vision and Self-Ultimacy. To succeed, he only had to work.

* * *

On September 18, 1946, in Michigan, Edie filed a decree demanding an annulment. She asked that her maiden name be restored and a restitution of $1. Though Jack missed her, he was relieved. For the rest of the fall, Jack remained in Ozone Park. He had spent through ink ribbons, clacking at the keys of his father's Underwood through the night. Time flew in his absorbed state.

In December 1946, Jack met Neal.

In late 1946, twenty-year-old Neal and his young wife, Luanne, arrived in New York. Their first objective was to find Hal Chase. They needed a place to live. With $35 between them (leftover from their stolen $300), they moved into a Spanish Harlem cold-water flat. At a Village bar, Hal introduced Neal to Allen, who was seated with a companion. Because Allen was with someone with whom Hal was not familiar, they sat in separate booths. By his estimation, Neal did not see Allen again until January 1947.

Ed White and Hal Chase brought Jack with them to meet Neal.

Cassady's speaking voice sometimes bordered on gibberish. Every so often he said something that made him seem that he was well-read. He was a hybrid of a street-wise hustler and an intellectual bookworm. Jack took to him, seeing in him something he was already vaguely familiar with through his imagined characters. These were the road-weary philosophers from his various drafts: Peter Martin; Big Slim Hubbard; Wesley Martin. Neal's blue eyes and savage gaunt features lent him an air of some strange mystic cowboy. Neal was not afraid to ask for what he wanted;

when he couldn't have it, he'd take it. There was a world-weariness to his eyes. He was at once radiant and distant.

A synthesis of madness and sobriety, Neal liked to share his life stories. When he spilled them out, they were spoken in a river of scatological cross-thoughts. His life revealed to Jack the archetypal myth embedded in the Western hero that he had been seeking. This was the understory of all he was trying to capture in his stories. It was clear to Jack that here was a man worth writing of. In Neal lurked various and partially formed personalities: the intellectual powerhouse, the sexual dynamo, the charismatic showman. These aspects of Neal embodied the rush that Kerouac felt was lacking in his prose. One night, Neal asked Jack to teach him to write as he was doing. He had stories of his own that he wanted to put on paper. For those few days they were together, Jack was wedded to Neal as comrades. He was what was lacking in Allen. He was a vague relic of Sammy, but somehow more sordid and real.

Jack wanted marijuana to smoke. He took Neal with him to meet his dealer on West 89th Street, a red-headed woman named Priscilla Arminger (also known as Vicki Russell). She was a tall beauty whom Jack had sex with at least five times. Neal, who had left his wife behind, had eyes for her. In her company was Allen. Immediately, the two paired off, Neal and Allen, leaving Jack behind. Allen was on his way to years of heartbreak from Neal. Jack had before him the answer to his dreams. Although Neal had turned off many people in Jack's circle, Jack saw something in him that the others did not.

However, Neal managed to turn off his wife. Luanne had had enough of his neglect. There came a tremendous snowstorm, but this did not stop her from boarding a bus and returning to Denver to her mother (who was not pleased that her sixteen-year-old daughter had married Neal). Neal left his rented room and alternated between Jack and Gabe's house and Allen's dorm room.

In Luanne's absence, Neal manipulated Allen's affections. It was a con job all the way. By toying with his affections, Neal could get through his predicament. He had no money and nowhere of his own to stay. Allen, left vulnerable by Neal's unconditional acceptance of him as a gay man, was lovestruck.

And then Neal was gone.

Jack made tentative plans to go west. Neal had sold Jack on the Western myth. He ate it up with relish. Jack took a Texaco road map and drew a long red line along wavering Route 6. If he followed it, the road would take him clear to Long Beach, California, if he wanted. However, he only had to go as far as Colorado, where Neal lived. Jack told Neal that maybe he could leave in July.

He still had a book to finish.

* * *

July 1946 came. It was hot and humid. Jack despised these conditions. It slowed him down. His writing faltered as the humidity sapped his physical stamina.

In mid-July, he gathered his things and began his first journey across America.

Frugality and proper planning were the rules of his journey, which would set a precedent for the rest of his travels during his lifetime. Planning on arriving in Denver in one week, he boarded the Seventh Avenue subway and then boarded a trolley to Yonkers. He successfully hitched a series of rides north along the Hudson River. However, he stopped under a bridge in the pouring rain. He was under the hollows of vast Bear Mountain. It was dark; the land boomed with strange new sounds.

Jack was fifty miles north of New York City at the junction of Route 6 where it had been unwinding all the way from Provincetown, Massachusetts, through Connecticut into New York. The sky thundered. He was on the Appalachian Trail, a backbone of mountains reaching as far north as Maine and unspooling twenty-two hundred miles south to Springer Trail, Georgia. Jack was behind schedule. He had to think fast. He did not want to exhaust his limited funds. In desperation, he took a ride from the first set of headlights that flashed out of the night. The travelers were heading north, ten miles in the opposite direction, to Newburgh, New York. He bought a ticket at a bus depot that returned him to Penn Station. Peeling dollar bills from his precious bankroll (he only had $50), he bought a bus ticket to Chicago to save time.

Jack's uneventful journey dropped him off at Chicago's bustling Loop. A truck driver in Joliet drove Jack out of Chicago. An older woman needed her car driven to Davenport, Iowa. On this leg of his journey, Jack got his first glimpse of the Old Man, the Mississippi River. Apple pies and ice cream. He ate his skimpy meals with relish. He was almost there, and his elation filled him with anticipation. Jack stopped in Cheyenne, Wyoming, and then on July 28 reached Denver.

He needed a rest. A temporary layover before moving to San Francisco where he had hoped Henri Cru would have arranged a ship for him to sail on with the Merchant Marines. Only then could he replenish his money. He barely had money to leave Denver, so he sent Gabe a postcard to wire him $25 via Western Union. Hopefully, through his ten days in Denver, the money would come and he could leave.

Allen was already in Denver, and Jack feared that he would not be able to spend any time with Neal. Neal was caught in a triangle between his wife Luanne, Allen, and Carolyn Robinson, another woman he had been seeing on the side. Allen alerted Jack to Neal's three-way fiasco. Carolyn in one hotel, Luanne in another, and Allen miserably holed up in a dive of an apartment. Somehow, Neal held on to his job amid his nightly debauches.

Neal made plans to go to Texas with Allen to visit Bill Burroughs. Luanne was vexed by Neal's lack of attention toward her. She despised Allen. Neal told her that just because he was going to Texas with Allen it did not mean he felt any less for her. They returned to Neal's room in the Hotel Colburn. At four o'clock in the morning, Allen appeared. They all went to bed together until Carolyn showed up and caught them in a threesome.[26]

Jack's introduction to Carolyn came one day when Allen accompanied him to Neal's room. Allen knocked on Neal's door and ducked out of sight after realizing that Carolyn was with him. He had gotten on her bad side as well. He was forever the outcast. He was Neal's third wheel on every occasion.

Neal opened the door in a towel. Neal introduced Carolyn to Jack and then dressed and left. He assured Carolyn that he would be right back.

Neal had arranged for both of them the company of a pair of nurses who were also sisters, Rita and Helen Gullion. They invited a Denver acquaintance, Bob Burford, over as well. Ultimately, a party ensued. Cassady ducked out for an hour when things were well underway to keep his promise to Carolyn. And then he was gone. Before he left, Neal was pleased to see Jack.

* * *

By the end of July, Jack was eager to continue his journey. He wrote Gabe to remind her that he would be needing more money to continue his travels. During his last days in Denver, he spent most of his time on Larimer Street. He began nurturing an idea for a book about "the father we never found." The theme had ties to the Prodigal Son searching for the lost father, which he explored in various notebook drafts. It had spiritual connotations steeped in mysticism. He could write of sorrow and human things. He felt them truly in his heart and became an expression of his humility. When cars sped by under the Nebraska sun, he knew that the passengers were pointing at him. He was a thin struggling figure of the American Badlands. He traversed the unbroken expanse of the wild, dark night. Jack was urgently desperate to reach California to board a ship. He would then return home to take up his pencil and start writing out this new concept with concentrated fervor.

When Jack received his wired funds, he bought a bus ticket. Hitchhiking through the Rockies, the Hot Basin, and the Sierra Nevadas was madness. He could just as well experience the Western lands through a bus window. He was two weeks late in meeting Henri Cru. Getting off the Greyhound at Market Street, he was surrounded by thick soupy fog. He was tired and hungry. He walked the San Francisco streets. He was badgered by vagrants begging for dimes. He crossed the Golden Gate Bridge into Marin County. Shortly after arriving on August 10, he became restless. There were no vessels ready to ship out. All was not lost. His visit to San Francisco and the road experience had given him the ending he needed for *The Town and the City*. After the death of the Martin patriarch, Peter Martin would go on the road.

Upon arriving in New York, Jack felt the differences between the West and the East. It was the lonesome rolling open spaces that he favored. No more would he be the young man of Horace Mann awed by shiny skyscrapers and teeming crowds. No sooner than he was home he had thoughts of going back.

Gabe remarked on Jack's gauntness. She was not aware of the sacrifices he had made for his art. Outwardly, he was making the trip to work on a merchant ship. But that was to justify the trip. In reality, Jack wanted the experience. He wanted to write about it with conviction and actuality. In his rucksack rested the journal that contained the heart of his next novel, *On the Road*.

The first week home, he wrote nonstop after some useless efforts to get back into the swing of it. Then, all at once, the words spilled out in an inspired surge. It was liberating to indulge in his vast family saga. He was blinded no longer. His vision was sharp, delivering the sweep of his saga with an effortless passion. He had the foresight not to bog himself down with vivid descriptive detail, but instead to knife the edge of his prose with a narrative swing.

On the Road was to be different than the deliberate labors of *The Town and the City*. *On the Road* required him to capture the peripatetic trekking across the continent. It was animalistic. He loved the feeling of being a vagabond. It was raw and real. The smells of the land. The earth under his feet. He itched to begin. The road meant exhaustion, physical defeat, and self-neglect. The heat of the tarmac baked through his boots. The sun burned his neck. All of it was worth it.

The road permitted him to mark his endurance. Putting himself out there meant testing himself. His enthusiasm to put it all down on paper before he forgot it all threatened to derail the two years of effort already put into *The Town and the City*.

Jack's feelings for the road made his New York associations unsavory. He was weary of the pessimism of Allen and Bill. He thought that they were still wrapped up in the same ideas as when he first met them. He wanted to go on the road to get away. He felt different from them. Bill had no use for traveling unless he needed to get from one place to another. Allen did it so that he could follow Cassady (though he became a world traveler in the years to come). Jack settled his sights on Neal.

* * *

In December 1947, turbulent and unhappy, Neal wrote Jack that he felt something within that needed to come out. Ideas for writing. He wanted to dispense with rules and literary convention. He thought that one should write as if one were the first person on earth. Maybe he would be the one to do it. Jack had completed almost all of *The Town and the City*, a staggering 280,000 words. It was, in Jack's estimate, only a month and a half from completion. Despite feeling that the world was against him, Kerouac was in high spirits. The novel was a "monstrous edifice" he felt manacled to. Looking over the fat manuscript, he saw it as an unwieldy mess chiseled by a young man blinded by zeal and optimism: "Somewhere I took the wrong road, and I did it earnestly and with furious energy, in great irretrievable labours."

Jack retyped a page of the manuscript and mailed it to Neal. He responded but made only a scant reference to his writing. Allen visited and listened as Jack read from the manuscript. Allen thought Jack might have surpassed Melville. Maybe it was even the Great American Novel!

Jack was hesitant to accept Allen's grandiose assessment. His disregard for Allen meant that Allen knew he was like everyone else, and that was what drove him crazy. Jack thought that Allen was beyond help because he could be a god in one moment and a monster in the next. He was annoyed by Allen's sexual obsession with Neal. Jack was attracted to Neal's brain. Allen, his body. However, Allen had his purposes. He was a great sounding board for sharing his ideas. He had no one else he trusted in New York. Allen's emotional encouragement boosted him tremendously. Despite Allen's concern, Kerouac debated the worthiness of such associations:

"These Ginsbergs assume that no one else has seen their visions of cataclysmic emotion, and try to foist them on others. I have been a liar and a shifty weakling by pretending that I was a friend of these people—Ginsberg, Joan, Carr, Burroughs, Kammerer even—when all the time I must have known that we disliked each other and were just grimacing incessantly in a comedy of malice. A man must recognize his limits or never be true."[27]

One visit by Allen interrupted a furious stream of twenty-five hundred words that he had completed at 4:00 in the morning. He wanted to tell Jack that he felt like he was going mad.[28] This bothered Jack. He sensed Allen's melodrama and had wished he would push his madness into verse instead of theatrics.

Throughout the spring, Jack continued polishing *The Town and the City*. In early May, he finished the first draft and immediately began working on an initial draft of *On the Road*. This version, Jack felt, was too imitative of Theodore Dreiser. Jack was determined that his work would compel people to recognize him. However, even more work and self-sacrifice were required before this happened.

At *The Town and the City*'s first anniversary on January 17, exactly one year since his beginning, it was now a staggering 225,000 words. He had fifty thousand left to go. When he looked back, the brunt of the early work was completed in March 1946. This was spurred by a desire to impress Neal. Jack's goal was to complete the novel before his twenty-sixth birthday. However, there were complications. It was not the novel he saw in his head, but it was the best that he could do. For now, Jack would have to be satisfied. This was no "psychotic sloppiness" like Joyce's *Finnegans Wake*. This was the work of a comparably sane writer. Joyce had given up trying to "communicate to humans." Jack only felt that way when he was miserable or drunk.[29]

Neal's writing sought to express the inexpressible. He wanted to reach into his individual will. He felt that he had something that he needed to tell, but could not find a way to do it. Possibly, writing just wasn't his chosen task. Perhaps it could only spring out of necessity. Perhaps his will to write could only be manifested under extreme duress.

Jack needed a different way to break out of his torpor. He walked two miles a day after finishing writing, and before he went to sleep, as well as numerous sets of pull-ups. Drinking only soured his mood. He woke up with hangovers. His sleep was plagued by nightmares. When he woke, he did not know who he was.

Then his birthday came and went. He was getting older. He could feel it. He wasn't yet out of his twenties and still brooded the day of his death. Time made him weary. He was haunted by the graves of his father and brother. He neared the end of writing. It seemed an eternity. On March 22, he finished the "city" half of the novel:

"I want to be a significant writer and I also want to live in a vast and significant way, like Twain almost. That's my present feeling, no Faustian torments that swirl futile and self-destructive around oneself, but a life that reaches out to others like two arms."[30]

He revised sections concerning Francis Martin, the funeral of the father, and the concluding chapters that would see Peter shoulder his rucksack and take to the road. Jack was elated. He felt rugged. Strong. His will lie yet within his grasp. He was the only one that could control what he was doing. What he was writing. No more was he the dazed broken man of October 1944, swooning over Celine. Crying in her arms. It seemed like a thousand years ago. The end was in sight. He had broken through, reached beyond a river of botched efforts and broken drafts. This was a novel, sure and true. It bore the mark of his passion.

Then, more drama. Allen begged Jack to hit him in the face. Jack did not, but he secretly wrote that this was the end as far as he was concerned.[31] He wished he could strike Allen to wake him from his maladjustment. Jack diminished Allen and his kind to "unimportant neurotics." "I go to see them in a happy, fond frame of mind and always come away baffled and disgusted. This does not happen among my other friends . . . therefore I should heed my feelings in these matters and stick to birds of my own feather."[32]

Kerouac realized that his pride was undermined by his doubt. His idea of "universal sympathy" had no real place but in writing: "Such things are for idiots, hypocrites, and mad charlatans of the soul":

"I will recognize that I'm human and must limit my sympathies, my active sympathies, to the life I have and will have, and that any other course is not true."[33]

In Denver, Neal's romantic triangle was so vexatious that it began to take its toll physically. He broke out in hives. His throat swelled. His hand was in pain. He owned a used car, a Chevy bought for $225 which he did not keep for long. Despite his car, Neal was grounded in Denver by his domestic foibles. He wanted a divorce from Luanne to marry Carolyn. Carolyn was playing hard to get. She was impatient. Allen was writing to him, as sick and weary as ever. With his cumulative troubles, Neal did not write to Jack for six months.

Jack took to his own proclivities. He drank beer at Ozone Park and the harder stuff in the city. He preferred pernod in French restaurants, which he used to drink with Edie, red port when he had little money. When he wrote, he stuck with Benzedrine. When he wanted to get higher, he smoked weed. His addiction to alcohol was alarming to his family and friends. Despite the great accomplishment that he had wrested from himself, he had found himself unworthy. He sought to annihilate his self-loathing with liquid fire. There was a world-weariness he was incapable of expressing other than through frustrated jottings in his journal. The era of the Brotherhood had slipped far into his past. Writing Allen, Jack expressed that "men cannot know what it is to be together without otherwise knowing what it is to be apart."[34]

CHAPTER SIX

The Forest of Arden

THE END OF 1948 YIELDED REMARKABLE PROGRESS FOR JACK. He rarely left Ozone Park to go into the city, either wary of its perils or content from his travels. He wanted to stay put. No more did he find himself in the Dark Corridor of his mind. He was on the open road.

Writing one page at a time, he saw the words accumulate in rapid-fire. No sooner had he rolled in a sheet of paper, then he was pulling it out and repeating the process. Jack was satisfied the higher his manuscript pile rose. He worked on the "Greenland" section by referring to his sea diary of 1942. He felt that it would bring authenticity to the text. Then he became distracted by the holidays. Pack the bags. Board the train. Sit with Gabe watching the countryside rush by in their one-day trek to Rocky Mount.

Jack was vexed. He felt that Allen and Neal had left him behind. Jack thought that they were making themselves obnoxious. They were condescending. His paranoia surged to the point that he would call Allen and scream at him over the phone. He thought Neal was being indifferent.

To Allen, Jack wrote, "It seems to me that both you and Neal are making yourselves obnoxious with your condescending attitudes toward the rest of us."[1] He was humiliated by Neal's indifference. It cost money to mail his long letters and manuscript pages. He was taking a risk; some were original drafts.

However, at last, Neal was writing.

Though Neal contrived to obtain an annulment from Luanne, he still sought her covertly. To Jack: "Aside from the emotional difficulty there is another and, I feel, more interesting problem—i.e., keeping Lu and Carolyn separated. This game has been going on for a month and is exciting in many ways. I am with both of them at different hours of the same day, daily, I must be on my toes to keep Carolyn from knowing."

Neal exemplified everything Jack lacked, not only in himself but in his book's characters. Neal's brazen confidence was missing in his characters. They seemed sedate by comparison. Where they always wanted something, Neal just took it. No questions asked. Though Hal Chase resembled Neal in some ways, he was too self-destructive (according to Jack), self-absorbed, and vain to benefit as a protagonist. Neal was authentic. Raw. True, he was a con man, but Jack did not care. He would con him right back. He would yield from Neal his raw essence to flesh out his next book. Cassady may have been the inspiration, but his soul would occupy the spirit of Dean Moriarty.

Through the summer of 1948, Jack revised sections of *The Town and the City*. He accompanied his mother to Rocky Mount. Caroline's problematic delivery (a Cesarean section) and her extended hospital stay strained their finances. It seemed that way always with the Kerouacs; money, or the lack of it, haunted them like a ghoulish specter. Now they were in debt. Jack piped up that there were worse things that could happen. He knew nothing about it, having had few obligations in his life so far and no family.

While in North Carolina, Kerouac developed a relationship with a nurse named Ann. But she was a far cry from Manhattan girls, who seemed more licentious. Not much happened between them. After a short stay, he returned to Ozone Park without Gabe. Selling *The Town and the City* took precedence over all things—domestic, romantic, or otherwise. He had a contact, through his friend Ed Stringham, with the chief editor of Random House, and they arranged a meeting. He also renewed his Columbia contacts despite his *persona non grata* status with officials. He gave the manuscript to Alfred Kazin who could negotiate a book deal. Kerouac would accept as little as a $2,000 advance, enough to allow him to move to California. However, his plan stalled. His editor recoiled at the manuscript's unwieldy length. Dense Wolfe-sized novels were no longer in favor. Americans found more satisfactory ways to pass their time. Televisions assumed the place of radios. Most families had a car. They, too, could traverse the states in search of something they would never find. The publisher advised Jack to cut the book down to commodify it better. He was an unknown author. A risk. Disgusted, Jack rifled through the ragged pages looking for ways to shorten the manuscript without disturbing the meticulous scaffolding he had assembled to make the work stand on its own.

Neal wrote Jack that they were expecting their first child. Neal supported Jack's idea of buying a ranch to live on. Since they perceived similarities between Carolyn and Gabe, they reasoned that they would get along like mother and daughter. This conclusion was wishful thinking. There was absolutely nothing they had in common other than their gender.

Jack felt Neal's approval of the ranch plan had grounded their friendship. Jack needed this approval. He always thought that finding someone else to keep his mother company while he wrote and traveled would relieve him of his burden. Once they were back on their feet financially, he would invite Caroline and Paul to move to Denver to be closer to Gabe.

Jack did not like to be alone. He was contradictory; he craved solitude but also loved to be in the company of others that could make his life easier. The empty Ozone Park apartment depressed him. He wrote to Neal: "Alone in the house . . . cooking, sweeping floors, washing dishes, working, sweating, sleeping, terrified dreaming, and the most yearning lonesomeness."[2] Expressing his need for companionship obliquely, Jack strove to orchestrate the ranch idea to suit his life. By living together, he would fulfill Leo's wish to provide for Gabe, have Neal by his side for inspiration, and be free to write. His mother would cook and clean. He had Carolyn nearby to serve his romantic delusions. Maybe, eventually, he could find a wife.

For now, there was California. His prospects ranged from high-paying Hollywood jobs to working as a railroad brakeman. Maybe he could ship out to sea with Henri Cru. He never decided, but he did not swerve from his intent to move with his mother. He desired to obtain the necessary funds by selling his novel, which would be sufficient to support them.

He feared Neal would back out. Or, worse, he would fail to commit. He fantasized that they could write books together and revolutionize American letters.

Neal did not share Jack's enthusiasm. His writing, he told Allen in a letter in May 1948, was "terrible, awful, stupid, stupid trash. . . . I see no greatness in myself."³ Despite their praise, Neal felt insufficient for the task. When Allen attempted to encourage him, Neal blasted that it was all bullshit. He mocked Allen's poetics. Venting his frustration at writing not even a single coherent sentence after a month of steady effort convinced Neal that he was sub-par at best. He could not keep up with Allen's intellect. His love for Cezanne and Shakespeare was over Neal's head. He had no knack for merging poetry with mysticism. He preferred to root his narrative voice somewhere between the bed and the street. Jack's writing was beyond him as well. Neal's frustrations suggest that he was depressed, allocating his former interests as futile obsessions. He wrote Allen that he was wasting time by loving him. Even Carolyn and the baby were diminished to a secondary plane. Women were all whores. The only constant that kept his interest was listening to bop. His final warning to Allen was clear: "Let us stop corresponding."⁴ Allen felt that Neal's letter was a blow that he could not comprehend; however, Allen was accustomed to Neal's mood swings, as he was with Jack, and resolved to endure them.

Neal did, however, have enthusiasm for a communal farmstead (or, as he phrased it, their "Shakespearean house"). Though Carolyn was concerned, Jack assured her not to worry. Their relative lack of privacy mattered little to him, nor did the likelihood that Carolyn and Gabe were incompatible. Very few of Jack's female partners emerged unscathed from Gabe's biting commentary.

Allen had taken Jack's finished novel to read, returned it, and expressed that he found the ending profound. Jack, he felt, would finally attain his much-deserved triumph. Despite Jack's earlier suspicions of Allen's enthusiasm, his perspective shifted when Allen was optimistic: "The madness has left Allen now, and I like him as much as ever."

Jack's retyping was formidable labor. He stuck to it with fierce determination. By July 22, he retyped nine hundred pages with two hundred pages left; he entirely rewrote ten pages of conversation between Francis and Peter Martin. He bought a five-inch-high packing box to stow the manuscript. It wasn't deep enough.

By the end of the month, Jack read Joseph Conrad, Dostoevsky, and Mark Twain. The sparseness of Conrad's writing style inspired Jack to rethink his work. He revised the last chapter with a more casual approach to gauge its readability. It was too lengthy. Though there was a slight risk of wordiness, the implicit truth of it nullified its risk. Should he de-emphasize his novel's meaning? If he did, he risked sullying the rousing expansiveness of his prose. The white heat of his typing was a step in the right direction. It was a goalpost to the final destination.

Babe Ruth's death marked the genesis of his renewed ideas for his road novel. In an August 17 journal entry, Jack wondered who Babe Ruth's father was. Who spawned this giant of an American? Ruth exemplified the American spirit just as much as Neal did. The genesis for both was the American enigma. There was a burning torch shining through the hinterlands of the groaning continent. Emerging from the shadows was a wandering phantom the "Father" never knew: IT.

The prospects intrigued Jack. He had ideas of merging *Doctor Sax* with *On the Road*. In each, there was an American mystery, the anxieties of childhood in one and the complexity of adulthood in the other.

The rain-swept night and America's endless spaces intrigued him. For his next work, he had in mind a story about two men hitchhiking to California in search of "something they don't really find." Instead, they return to their respective hometowns desiring to find "something else." Jack was vague on what that "something" was. In late summer, he expanded his ideas into a storyline. Perplexed by a working title, he called this book *On the Road*. It would be one of many proto-versions of the final draft.

In the first week of September 1948, Jack reworked chapters (at one point retitling the book *The Soul of a Family*) and extracted a lengthy excerpt from his eleven-hundred-page book for publishers to read.

Although Jack realized that books of Wolfean grandeur were no longer prevalent, he still wanted *The Town and the City* to be published as it was written. He began the arduous job of mailing it to publishers. He intended to send it to the larger New York publishing firms like Scribners (his first choice because they published Wolfe's novels); Random House; Houghton Mifflin; Knopf; Little, Brown; and Macmillan (the first to reject it). He needed to step out into the light after working so many months without seeing daylight. It was now time to prove himself.

With no word from Neal, Jack felt distanced. He wondered if he offended him. Or did Neal exclude him from his life?

Gabe left New York to visit Nin, Paul, and their new baby, Paul Jr. Her absence allowed Allen to stay with Jack in Ozone Park, where Gabe forbade him. Rarely tolerant of her son's visitors, she singled out Allen because he was a Jew and, possibly, his sexuality. Jack told Allen that he felt lost in his apartment, as he had in July when she had gone to Rocky Mount. Once again, the room struck Kerouac as stark and lonely, as he felt back in the late winter of 1943 when he was alone in the parlor of Crawford Street. Attempting to fill this core, this centerless center, Jack persisted in his dream of building a ranch with Neal. Without money, it was impractical. Jack's utopia depended upon the financial success of *The Town and the City*. Jack wrote Neal that he was entitled to $5,000 from the G.I. loan program if he could prove that he was bringing in a profit. They could grow cotton or some other crop. Conspiring with Neal to parlay this possible opportunity was a guaranteed con job. Jack realized that he lacked the audacity to do it.

Reluctant to leave the city in case a publisher should accept his novel, Jack gave himself until the new year for it to happen. By October, he was impatient and too broke to fulfill his wishes. He needed money to pay rent. Jack wrote his brother-in-law, Paul Blake, to tell him that he would be coming to Rocky Mount sooner than expected. Blake offered Jack a job helping to run a parking lot adjacent to the annual county fair—an excellent opportunity to earn fast, easy money. He could write in the Blakes' shack while not assisting Paul. However, Jack's moneymaking opportunity was a washout; a downpour turned the parking lot into a quagmire. He had no money, and now he was stuck in North Carolina. Rocky Mount offered little to do in contrast to New York City. There were the old-timers in the country store to chat with, but little else.

Once he returned home, Jack enrolled in classes at the New School for Social Research. He was utilizing his G.I. Bill benefits. Attending classes entitled him to a monthly allotment of $75 to $90 per month. The first class he signed up for was Elbert Lenrow's "20th Century Novel of America."

Lenrow had once encountered Kerouac on a street corner and knew that the young man was reputed to have already written over a half-million words. Now he was one of a hundred students enrolled in his course for credit. Lenrow asked Jack what he was writing lately. Jack told him. Later that fall, he brought in his manuscripts. Lenrow read avidly. He was impressed by Jack's knack for observation and his imaginative scope of language.

Jack also enrolled in Alfred Kazin's course (beginning in November 1948), whom he remembered when he wrote Kazin after seeing him on television, "You were as great as you ever were at the New School." He taught "Five American Writers": Poe, Whitman, Hawthorne, Emerson, and Melville. Jack was especially entranced by Kazin's Melville and Whitman lectures. He learned to read *Leaves of Grass* "like a novel," that "the observer, the events, the vision of one man playing all the parts. Whitman is the 20th century in that he is split," he has more than one mind, but several. It would be Kazin who would ultimately recommend *The Town and the City* to Harcourt, Brace.

Writing to Neal on October 18, Jack implored him to write letters more often, even though he knew that Neal's "sufferings" were rooted in "pure unreasonable demand arising from loneliness." Though they were physically separated, Jack felt closer than ever. He praised Neal's writing style and called him the "great Walt Whitman of this century."

"I'll tell you who you really are Neal, and in telling you this, you will see that we are not far apart from not seeing each other for years, but that we are as close as before. You're not Shakespeare, at least not in tone, I don't want to discuss Shakespeare anyway. I think that there's a possibility that you might become the great Walt Whitman of this century. (Remember that I say this in the same spirit with which Hal once told me I was the Dostoevsky of America: that is, a spirit of friendly speculation, egoism, etc., perhaps groundless because we are blinded by our own sense of our own circle's importance, yet in a way true.) Laugh at Walt Whitman do you?"[5]

That afternoon Jack read "Calamus" and "Children of Adam" in Union Square. He had revisited Whitman through a college course with Kazin. These two sections inspired Jack, particularly because they represented a departure from a transcendentalist celebration of the unity of all things through a recognition of the "self" in a world fraught with ruthless unfulfilled change. Unwittingly, this "world" would be the one that gave rise of the Beats. Whitman's intonations, coupled with his new perspective on his life, art, and America, allowed him to discover the poet's work anew. By bringing this poet to Neal's attention, Jack insinuated that he was Whitman's Adamic man, the sexual revolutionary who would become *On the Road*'s star attraction. Passages from Kerouac's 1948–1949 *On the Road* journals reveal the erratic path of the novel's development, strongly implying that Jack was awash in romantic ideas about art and artists and that he owed his vision to no one philosophy, person, or event in particular, but rather to a broad confluence of ideas and events, though certainly the Whitman-Cassady idealism and enthusiasm stimulated Jack's new shift in characterization. When Jack tells Neal, "we are as close as before," it is because he feels the spirit of Neal as much as if he were with him in the flesh. Cassady's narrative voice leaps out from the page as effectively as it should in any novel.

Whitman was, to Jack, a literary figure "greater than Melville." He was Shakespeare's equal as a "bard of the humans," a poet of the intellect. Jack quoted with evident relish to Neal: "Oh furious! O confine me not!" Jack did his best to justify his ideation to Neal:

"Why. Because Whitman is not only a poet who writes in waves of verse like sea-waves of the holiness of the body and of sex and love and brotherhood of man etc. but also a mighty thinker. Think how long that man has been laughed at. . . . Whitman the prophet, with a vision of athletes and great women and Democracy and friendliness and real hipness. No hipper poet than he."[6]

The lineage was clear to Jack: "Is this not Neal Cassady?" Though Neal did not follow Jack's logic, it didn't matter. Jack had transcended Neal the man into Neal the symbol. This symbolic lineage came to mark a turning point in how he viewed *On the Road*. Later, in 1959 during an appearance on *The Steve Allen Show*, Allen would describe *On the Road*'s narrative as "poetic." He asks Jack "who else writes poetic-type" novels? Kerouac mentions Whitman. Allen laughs, thinking that Jack is putting him on (as Whitman is known as a free-verse poet) until Jack clarifies, *Specimen Days*, an autobiography written by Whitman. However, *Specimen Days* is less a traditional autobiography as it is a collection of fragmented prose written poetically. Whitman described it as a "*mélange* of loafing, looking, hobbling, sitting, traveling—a little thinking thrown in for salt, but very little— . . . wild and free and somewhat acrid—indeed more like cedar-plums than you might guess at first glance."[7] The sentences can be cadenced, a technique Kerouac will consciously use in his mature works (even in some sections of *The Town and the City*). Whitman writes, "Dilapidated, fenceless, and trodden with war."[8] Compare with Kerouac, who takes this writing to another level in *On the Road*: "I was far away from home, haunted and tired with travel, in a cheap hotel room I'd never seen, hearing the hiss of steam outside, and the creak of the old wood of the hotel, and footsteps upstairs, and all the sad sounds, and I looked at the cracked high ceiling and really didn't know who I was for about fifteen strange seconds."[9] His cadence is hypnotic, leaving the reader spellbound as it does Sal Paradise who does not know who or what he is for several seconds. The invisible tongue utters long multi-syllabic passages cadence-like like the road under the wheels of a car. Cassady utilizes hyphens to tie together his stream of thoughts as they hurl out onto the page in "waves of verse" without constraint or obedience to sentence mechanics:

"This madness has been unlike any I've ever known, entirely different-I feel as if I've never had any life before-I do childish things-I think in new, distorted, over-balanced levels. I burn with agony-I sense a loss of most all wisdom I've ever had. When I see a girl tremble-I spit-I'm lost."[10]

Though Cassady would ultimately dispense with the hyphens, Kerouac would utilize them to indicate breath pauses. For all of Jack's conviction that Cassady was a reincarnated Whitman, Neal could not see it.

How he wrote came naturally to him. It was the only way he knew how to keep up with Allen and Jack if he wanted to impress them.

* * *

Jack was relieved to return to the city where he was never at a loss for socializing. As usual, there was a never-ending circuit of parties hosted by friends. Feeling forlorn and lost, Jack spent most of his time searching for Hal Chase. Hal had concealed his new address from Jack, but Jack was determined to find him.

In October and November 1948, Kerouac sketched out three novel-length works. One, *The Imbecile's Christmas*, concerns an "Imbecile" that was based loosely upon himself. The Imbecile has faith in "everybody" and "everything" much like Prince Myshkin. The Imbecile has no judgment on his fellow humans. He has no car which means that he relied on others for transportation. He did not finish it.

In October, he outlined elements of *Doctor Sax* with an alternate title, *Myth of the Rainy Night*. *Doctor Sax* explores the "American myth" and its relationship to children. He included recurring rains falling upon the earth and rising as fog and vapor. There are baptismal associations of the river flowing from a tributary of waters. There is darkness and hints of long-dead Gerard. Based on Kerouac's Lowell adolescence, the nonlinear plot focused on his childhood and concentrated on the nature of evil, glee, townspeople, and supernatural occurrences. *Doctor Sax's* plot would climax with the 1936 flooding of the Merrimack River. After a short start, Jack shelved it to focus on *On the Road*.

In November 1948, he further outlined the road novel. It became an "American-scene picaresque" detailing the arduous realities of road travel: hitchhiking, loneliness, and hunger. Its theme was the search for identity.

At Bickford's Cafeteria, at 4:30 in the morning, he was having the "most horrendous thoughts"[11] in a long while. Outside, it was cold. It had just turned to December; October (his favorite month) had gone by so fast that he hardly knew it was there at all. He was in a Benzedrine haze. He hated the stuff, but it helped him type. It kept him razor-focused on his text, typing so fast he could have fallen off the page. But this morning, he was thinking murderous thoughts. The drugs had taken their grip, and his perspective narrowed. Though he saw the joy of humanity on the road, here in the ugly city people became expressionless and gray-faced. He could have killed every one of them. He would slay them by the hundreds. Benzedrine is a highly addictive amphetamine. He lost weight on it to the degree that Gabe thought he was sick. His pallor made him appear as if he were blanched. Though Allen deplored it, making him have tangled thoughts that never helped his poems, Jack liked it. The high was mild and calmed his mind. It kept him on task. However, it sped his heart rate. He could not take it for longer than two days at a time. After that, Jack was agitated. He suffered nightmarish visions and occasionally, as he did this morning, a violent psychosis. Then came the crash.

During the autumn of 1948, Jack again wrestled with *On the Road* and *Doctor Sax*'s prose experimentation. He commenced on *Sax* three times before settling upon a beginning that he liked. He found that what he had written was forced. It was not sincere enough. He may have been distracted by his classes. He felt like he was fucking around. Despite his distractions, he gave himself two months to make any progress on *Sax*. Per its subject matter, it was worlds apart from the road book. Though Kerouac sensed a mystical connection in his mind, he was unable to put it on paper. He dug into his older material. It was too juvenile. It read like he was searching with no answers. Just blind plodding in every direction. Now that he had a better sense of what he wanted to say, he found it even harder to do it. He may have been too addled by Benzedrine to sort the wheat from the chaff. He also felt there was no authenticity. Though he was very capable of remembering Lowell in his childhood, he had little feel for how to merge it with *On the Road*. For the sake of it, Jack typed six thousand words before giving it up. Term papers and exams had distracted him. Then he had writer's block. With regret, he put aside his work and began thinking of new ways to rid himself of his writer's block. A feeling of "falseness" hindered the unbridled freedom he felt only a week before.

Jack was also distracted by his anxiety as he was waiting for any word from the publishers he had contacted in regard to *The Town and the City*. To cope with his frustrations, he swallowed Benzedrine and wrote long letters to Neal and Allen, his typewriter clacking into the deep midnight hours. He regularly walked, taking long excursions around Brooklyn in an amphetamine haze. He lost himself in his thoughts. As he walked, his mind raced. Without writing, the Bennies were a waste of time. They brought out Jack's worst tendencies. He conjured "daydreams of destruction." He imagined drawing a gun from a holster and shooting at moving cars. He felt the mental urge to wrap his hands around the necks of passing people to choke them. He was Colonel Kurtz, he thought, dark and brooding in the hot malarial jungle, wishing to "exterminate the brutes" with "complete honesty."[12]

It all cleared days later. It always did. His mood changes were fast and sudden, and his mercurial nature either remained pent up or lashed out, often hurting or confusing even his closest friends.

In the ensuing days, he burst with "mad new ideas." Time shifts, new characters, and adventurous elements all transmuted to a fresher, more honest artistic sensibility. He wrote 32,500 words in November. However, in order to be able to write at this pace, something had to give. Jack was skipping classes, continuing a trend he began in high school through Columbia. This time, it hurt him monetarily. He lost his $75 a month stipend. Since he had no money coming, his efforts for school diminished. He began making plans for the road, the only true university he wanted to attend. The road of life. He was counting on Caroline and Paul to move to Ozone Park to be with Gabe. This would diminish the guilt he had whenever he left her behind alone in their apartment. With no money, all of this was not possible. He needed to sell *The Town and the City*.

Neal also needed money. He lost his railroad job. He had a month-old baby. He wrote Jack: "We failed at fusion because we were both old enough to have our own—& separate—portraits of knowing." Their "private knowledge" had "gone too far for us to share. . . . & fuse into welded counterparts." Key to Kerouac was something else Neal wrote: he was merely "thinking along as I write." He was "writing without thought." He was "just [stringing] together abstractions that aren't even understandable as gibberish."[13] To Neal, it was gibberish, but for Jack, it came closer to the truth. Neal felt that he was too busy to write. By his assessment, he was spending two-thirds of his day on the road and slept the rest. Then, he continued this cycle. And, he had a baby and a wife. He did not have much time for writing. Jack, who in comparison was free as a bird, could not understand this.

It was imperative that Jack became physically closer to Neal. He wanted to capture lightning in a bottle even if he had to hitchhike. He was anxious to kick-start his stalled road novel. Jack wrote that they could ship out on a Standard Oil freight liner. They could possibly earn themselves $200 a month. Jack was willing to leave shortly after the new year. He would not wait to hear from any publishers. The one response he received in the interim was grim. Little, Brown rejected the manuscript, not on the grounds of quality but because of its hefty page count. Disgusted by the massive pile of manuscript pages to which he had devoted nearly four years of his life, he felt that the idea of being a published writer amounted to nothing more than a fantasy.

Bill wrote from New Orleans. He had bought a farm and had some success growing cotton, peas, and lettuce. His property bordered swampland. He could shoot his guns. He had enough firearms to hold off a siege. He, too, was fighting his heroin addiction. Sometimes he hunted small game. Most times he brooded on his porch. Jack mapped out his itinerary to include the Southeast so that he could visit Bill and Joan.

On November 20, Jack drafted an essay for Kazin. In "Whitman: A Prophet of the Sexual Revolution," he listed several "revolutions" that a person can experience—religious, political, economic, and social—asserting that each can cause one to stray from the "point of real unspeakable human desire."[14] The ultimate breakthrough, the "Forest of Arden," was Kerouac's term for a purified state. Kerouac's view was that the only revolution worth fighting for was the sexual revolution: "a world where it is finally admitted that we want to mate and love, eat and sleep, and bask in the days and nights of our true, fundamental life."[15] Kerouac tapped unknowingly into the future ideology of the Hippies: the pursuit of primal urges no longer inundated by consumerism, a social revolution no longer tied to conservative society but to the grand vessel of life itself.

In mid-December, Neal placed a long-distance call to the pharmacy below Kerouac's Ozone Park apartment. He told Jack that he had a new car. He thought that he could save Jack a hitchhiking trip and pick him up. He had to break the new car in.

Neal borrowed money from his friend Al Hinkle. He also confiscated Carolyn's savings. With combined funds, he managed to finance a 1949 Hudson Hornet straight off the assembly line. Jack suspected that Neal either stole the car or that he was running from creditors. Carolyn thought Neal was simply reckless. They had no savings. They had no reliable source of income. There was the newborn to care for. They were living in a "cardboard dump" furnished with orange crates. Despite his inhibitions, Jack agreed to join Neal if he picked him up in Rocky Mount. His one stipulation was that they had to move Gabe and her belongings from New York to North Carolina.

After classes, Jack left Brooklyn for Rocky Mount to spend Christmas with his mother. There he wrote, clicking on his typewriter keys at all hours of the day. His brother-in-law got angry, and so Jack had worn out his welcome in a matter of days. He took long walks through the woods to be alone. Sometimes, he walked the roads where locals viewed him as some strange alien creature. Caroline was griping, feeling that her brother wasn't doing enough to help their mother. Paul thought Jack was lazy. Gabe defended him, assuring those that would listen that Jack would one day be famous.

* * *

On Christmas Day, the dirt-splattered Hudson drove up the Blakes' driveway. Jack had been playing Dexter Gordon's "The Hunt" on the Blakes' Victrola. To Jack, the trio looked beat. Tired. Worn-down from the long cross-country caper they agreed to. Neal turned the record player up. He clapped his hands and jived to the music. The Blakes and other relatives stared aghast at this creature that washed up on their shore. They stayed at the Blakes for several days before the car made a quick one-day drive up the eastern seaboard to New York. The Hornet stormed through the night, passing through Washington, DC, Baltimore, Philadelphia, and Camden before safely arriving in Ozone Park.

There were risks in being around Neal. He was stealing. At the Clique Club, Neal stole two dollars from Lucien's wallet. At Elbert Lenrow's apartment, after inviting Jack, Allen, and Neal into his home. Afterward, Jack and Allen left and Neal stayed behind and slept on Lenrow's couch. The following morning, Allen dropped by to retrieve Neal. Days later, Lenrow returned home to find his door busted in and the contents of a dresser drawer pillaged of jewels (though his cash was overlooked). The police told Lenrow it had to be an "inside job." A "hit and run" robbery. Lenrow concealed this theft from Jack and Allen until eighteen years later when he wrote Allen about the crime. Allen initially doubted it was Neal but he could not shake off his involvement. Jack dismissed Neal's theft, feeling mildly intrigued by his savagery.

Allen had been quietly waiting to mark the New Year together with his old paramour. Their New Year's Eve was festive, frantic, and high. Jack was attracted to Luanne. They felt that they were tagalongs to Neal's misadventures. That ultimately, he would ditch them both. When he did, Luanne would be with Jack. Alone. They made plans to bond once that happened.

On February 2, Neal's escalating arguments with Luanne prompted him to strike her across the head. His hand deflected. He suffered an incomplete fracture of four bones around the base of his thumb. This set a precedent for the trip. In pain and seething with anger, Neal was a markedly different man than he was the first time they went on the road.

Kerouac was also having problems with a married model he had been seeing named Pauline. "That whore," Jack spat into his journal. He was unhappy at how their relationship ended, even though he was the cause of its dissolution. In a letter to Jack, she described how she had revealed her indiscretion with him to her husband, that she had had sex with another man. Her husband tried to put her head in a gas stove. He turned on the burner without a flame so she had to inhale the fumes. Their baby was crying. He went into the next room to cry as well and demanded Jack's address. Pauline had no idea where it was, except that Jack was living above a drugstore. He was to make her pay "dearly" by seeing a Jewish woman he knew. Pauline's letter took a decisive turn by indicting Jack by comparing him to her husband. She attacked his work ethic, writing, and lack of spirituality. She accused Jack of being a pale pretender of Neal, who also was a "crock of shit." Angrily, she informed Jack that he would end up in hell at the end of Satan's pitchfork:

"My husband isn't a bastard like the likes of you. You couldn't even polish his shoes. The pity of it all is this, that I can't get you to go out and work. I'd make you work so down hard the sweat would fall from your brow like the rain you keep talking about. That's the only thing that will save you, Work, Manual Labor. . . . I suggest that you try writing about real people like us and not jerks like Doctor Sax and his rainy nights. Don't ever call yourself a religious writer again, you don't know your ass from a hole in the ground about religion. You brought me down to your level, but that won't be for long."[16]

An angry husband was all Kerouac needed for an instant departure. Neal, Jack, Al Hinkle, and Luanne piled into the Hudson Hornet. Neal took the wheel.

While in New York, Bill mailed letters to Allen, wondering where they were. Although Helen Hinkle paid her way, Burroughs was still amazed that Al could be so callous. But Hinkle had only known Helen for a short time, having decided to marry her a few days after they met. Neal used Hinkle's rash union to his advantage. Combining the new-lyweds' need for a car for a makeshift honeymoon with Jack's need to return west, Neal told Carolyn that he was the one "ol' Cass," coming to "everybody's rescue." To ease Carolyn's anxiety, Neal kept the best part for last, as if it would vindicate his selfishness: Helen Hinkle was "loaded," making it a "free ride." According to Burroughs, Al Hinkle had married Helen at Neal's instigation to take her money.

The road was, by turns, formidable. Inspiring. Spirituality guided Jack: "God is what I love," he wrote on his first day on the road. Salvation was just beyond the horizon. He would keep moving.

Around this time, Kerouac was fixed upon the phrase "beat generation." John Clellon Holmes had written an essay, "This Is the Beat Generation." To Holmes, "beat" originally meant "spent": "bad or ruined." It suggested being "beaten down" or physically and materially exhausted. It referred to a generation who had come of age during the Second World War but could not polarize themselves as clean-cut white collars or dutiful militants. "Beat" metamorphosed into a conscious objection to straight but spirit-killing jobs, with its adherents preferring to eke out their existence on a dividing line between material comfort and bohemian poverty, at best, or in outright indigence, at worst. This struggle to survive often encompassed selling or using narcotics, promiscuity, a kind of restlessness, and sometimes spiritual bankruptcy.[17]

To this original meaning, Jack added a second meaning: "beatific." In this sense, beat captured the holiness of being among the oppressed, comparable to Prince Myshkin in *The Idiot*. In Jack's world, these masses included lost men, dusty hoboes, drunk and depressed husbands, disillusioned soldiers, truck stop diners, outcasts of color and religion, and that mythical man of the cowboy West. They were just the type he was about to meet on the road.

CHAPTER SEVEN

The Bebop City

ON JANUARY 19, 1949, A HUDSON HORNET CROSSED THE UNDER-ground Holland Tunnel from Lower Manhattan into Jersey City, New Jersey. It emerged into the raw drizzle. Twenty-six-year-old Jack Kerouac beat on the dash, haunted by something he had yet to remember. The road glistened. Rain. The rainy saga of the night. The car drove by a road sign. To go west, veer right. To go south, veer left. Jack and Neal talked. They spoke of the value of life. "Whither goest thou America in thy shiny car at night?" They stopped next to Otto's diner for gas. They continued. Bop played on the radio.

Why was he so haunted if he was so happy?

Luanne smelled nice. Her thigh touched Jack's. Neal was detached. He had pressing matters to reconcile. By dawn, the car reached Washington, DC. The nation's capital was silent and emptied of humanity. Truman was to be inaugurated on January 20. The war machines were in solemn display: jets, submarines, tanks, and jeeps. They wanted coffee. Neal was stuck on a rotary and made the wrong stop. They found a diner. Al stole a coffee cake for them to split. Though Jack's experience was authentic, he felt it less so under Neal's shadow. That's the way it was through the entire trip.[1]

By the close of February, Jack was in New York. It was a harrowing yet rewarding trip, for he had reaped an abundance of material. He was happy to be in Ozone Park by his mother's side and prepared to submit his manuscript to more publishing houses. Several rejection slips for *The Town and the City* had been mailed in his absence.

At his writing desk, he envisioned *On the Road* as a picaresque like *Don Quixote*. He wanted to merge scenes and people with spiritual overtones which he felt lacking in earlier drafts. His hero would emulate the gentle but impoverished "Knight of the Sorrowful Countenance." A month later, these notes developed into more definitive ideas. Ray Smith, the novel's principal protagonist, became the sole narrator narrating "the story with ravenous absorption, & with great beauty (naturellement)."[2] He likened his narrator to Melville's "Confidence Man," who dupes his fellow passengers on board the *Fidele*. Kerouac's mid-twenties "hero" of "many talents & personalities" winds up in jail. After lingering in New York City with his acquaintances (characters like "Junky" [Herbert Huncke] from *The Town and the City*), Ray Smith accompanied Pip, an "idiotic" boy with a gentle nature. He is regarded as being "too saintly for this world." The quest of Red Moultrie (an early manifestation of *On the Road*'s Dean Moriarty) was to find his father. On March 25, Kerouac extensively built his characterization. Red Moultrie is a veteran of minor-league baseball, an ex–seaman/truck driver/jazz drummer/college student from London University now imprisoned in a jail cell after being jailed for robbery. He earns a lost inheritance. He reads from the Bible and prays. The night before his release from jail, Red lies on his bunk and listens to the night sounds of other inmates.

As he meditates upon the sounds, his consciousness drifts further from the jail block to that of the outside world. It all blends into an indistinct roar of sound. The "sounds of the universe as we sleep." Jack inserts wordplay derivative of Whitman's "Out of the Cradle Endlessly Rocking" intended to evoke a lyrical, imaginative universe, ultimately appropriating Moultrie's external world. Upon release, Red ventures into New York and meets with some sordid Times Square characters. He meets Smitty and Pip; they travel west to rendezvous with Vern Pomeroy (an early prototype for Dean Moriarty). Kerouac intended to transform his 1947 road trip with Moultrie's characterization and merge it with Moriarty. Red locates his lost father in Montana; Vern finds his in Denver.

Jack wrote another story titled "Shades of the Prison House," a title lifted from Wordsworth's poem "Ode."[3] Jack's writing turns poetic. It was a new high for Jack, as he ebulliently weaved into the text a

Wordsworthian splendor of the world. This road story culminates in a long burst of experimental language:

"And finally it was the bejewelled night, dry, dusty, soft, and dark: with roads, fields, fences, bushes and flowers all around: and on the great spread plain beyond was the bebop city and all the lights a-yondering. California? Texas? Illinois? Whereupon, all the sheer night in names glistened suddenly in his brain as if swirling messages from his life were flashing on and off upon an incalculable neon sign in a rainy plain:— 'Frisco, the Embarcadero, Pier 59, Fillmore, Geary, Market street, Mission, panhandlers, winos; wild bop, Vern, Marylou, Richmond jazz-shack in the oil flats, lights, Allen Eager, Dexter Gordon, Wardell Gray, tenor, piano, alto, drums and bass, and beat, beat, beat, and Red Dot snouts the blues. . . ."[4]

This list continues for three more pages. Essentially, it conjures sights, sounds, places, and people mentioned throughout *On the Road*. He closes the story:

"It was a conversation fittingly and most sinister the last, spoken in the oldest and most serious and foreboding tongue on earth, while paler men no demons innocently slept unaware of the first that be, which were being spoken for now, in the final hours of dawn. Or if Red had known he could have answered in his own strange tongues, with edification and winks and counter-signification of hints, perhaps, but in any event the quivering earth turned again to the morning sun, as ever tranquil, and all the birds sang in city trees, and the Sunday bells at seven did begin to peal."[5]

Jack heeded Allen's advice by permitting Professor Mark Van Doren to read his completed manuscript and two chapters from *Doctor Sax*. With little mention of *Sax*, Van Doren was impressed by Kerouac's perseverance and quality. Van Doren (in allegiance with Alfred Kazin) telephoned Robert Giroux at Harcourt, Brace, and suggested that they should publish *The Town and the City*. By the end of March, Giroux sent Jack a letter of acceptance, offering a $1,000 advance against royalties. Giroux agreed to begin editing the manuscript.

Jack accepted their terms; not long afterward, writer and editor spent several evenings making extensive cuts and revisions. *The Town and the*

City's acceptance brightened Jack's dour outlook. Invigorated by his trip, Jack wanted to realize his communal ranch idea with Neal. However, Jack was unaware that Neal had spent all his money on a car. He had no intention of relocating. He had no job. Carolyn was forced to work as an assistant in a doctor's office. Two weeks later, she was pregnant again despite her efforts to practice birth control. Regardless of Neal's dilemmas, Jack was determined to move his mother and his sister's family to Colorado once his editing work for Giroux was complete.

In mid-April, Kerouac worked on another draft of *On the Road*. He structured it in three unifying concepts: American places, seasons, and Red Moultrie's inheritance. The inheritance had some implication meant to impart the loss of America's innocence. To focus his stylistic shifts, Jack read Dostoevsky's short story "An Unfortunate Predicament," noting the usefulness of developing an idea before arriving at "what actually happens in the story." During the first two weeks of May, he wrote eight thousand words, an itinerary of travels, and a sixteen-page outline. He put it aside and made preparations to leave.

He failed to finish his courses and dropped out of New School. Editing his book for publication would consume his time entirely. And, he was returning to the road.

Then there was the Shrouded Stranger symbolic of Jack's guilt dogging his every step. He felt its presence in the West until it followed him to the East. It loomed over his desk. He discussed the idea of it with Allen. Jack once dreamed of the Shrouded Stranger carrying a stave and kicking up billowy plumes of dust as he trailed him. To be saved, he had to reach the "Protective City." Prompted by Allen for the stranger's identity, Jack felt it may have been himself wearing a shroud. The shroud was given in darkness. It would be removed in that light only discernible at the hour of death.

Out west, Neal was trying to write his autobiography which he titled *The First Third*, with the last third presumably the remainder of a life not lived. He was miserable and disgusted. Changing baby diapers reinfected his thumb. He contracted osteomyelitis which infected his bone marrow. Writing to Jack, Neal itemized his misery: Carolyn administered daily injections of penicillin via a needle in his ass. He ingested pills for allergies because he was prone to hives. He became addicted to codeine. He required surgery on his leg for an inflamed cyst. He needed the services of a podiatrist. The bridge of his nose was collapsed. Finally, he anticipated that his thumb would need to be amputated. Despite his misery, Neal was happy for Jack who was now an officially published author. He must have felt disgusted with his own life as he thought that he had accomplished nothing at all.

Neal's misfortunes affected Kerouac, putting him into a "particularly stupid state of mind." Writing to Alan Harrington, he evaluated his life as it stood:

"I am no longer 'beat,' I have money, a career. I am more alone than when I 'lurked' on Times Square at 4 A.M., or hitch-hiked penniless down the highways of the night. It's strange. And yet I was never a 'rebel,' only a happy, sheepish imbecile, open-hearted & silly with joys. And so I remain. It is all ominously what you said about my 'innocence'—even though that Lucien business years ago, when everybody went unscathed except me (that is, me, & the actual pale criminal). But now (as I promised myself) I want to go on to further considerations."[6]

Jack envisioned a "new" life that treated him better than some "pale criminal." Perhaps he could live in Hollywood and adapt his favorite books into films. Maybe *On the Road* could be next. He could find a wife. Live on a farm. Part of his tension was relieved because his talent had found recognition. He had prospects. In the middle of May, he was ready to leave again.

* * *

In Denver, Jack's ranch-commune idea went bust. Thundershowers followed his bus into the Denver city limits. From then on, it was as if gray clouds forever dogged Jack's steps. He applied for a construction job to boost his lagging cash reserves. On his own time, he read Western dime novels and Jean Racine. He took long solitary walks over empty roads and abandoned fields to gather new impressions. Likening himself to Flemish painter Rubens, Jack jotted spontaneous impressions. He was the "Thoreau of the Mountains." In June, his family arrived with their furniture. They tried desperately to appreciate what Jack found so fascinating about these wide-open spaces. They saw otherwise, and so Jack kept his distance trying not to accommodate his band of pessimists. From May and into June 1949, Jack lived like a rural bachelor. He wondered whether *On the Road* would be any good. He predicted it would be "popular," and that it would differ significantly from *The Town and the City*'s traditional writing. He hoped to earn an early advance from Giroux for *On the Road*. He was scheduled to go to Denver to meet him at the train station on July 15. Jack was eager to work with Giroux, knowing the editor was too busy to be exclusive only to him in New York City.

By the Fourth of July, not more than a couple of weeks after her move, Gabe had had enough of Jack's Golden West. It was, according to Jack, "one of the saddest days I've ever seen," as he and Caroline watched their mother board the train at the Denver depot.

It had all fallen through. Caroline and Paul did not like Denver. They did not like living in the country. There had been no send-off. Instead, they sat in chairs while Little Paul's wailing resonated along the station walls. Jack watched the train roll away. The idea of his aging mother traveling east, alone, to continue her life punching a clock at a Brooklyn shoe factory tore at his guts. Caroline and her two Pauls followed her. Jack's grand effort to create a homestead of commune living had collapsed. Desperate for money, he wired Giroux for an advance against *The Town and the City* to which he was denied. He had signed a lease on the rented house, and so there was no getting out of that. Possibly he could sublet it and just leave, join Cassady in California. There, he could live as he saw fit. Maybe spend all of his days writing, listening to bop, and supporting himself as a fry cook.

In some ways, Jack was relieved. He was freed of his family. His eyes began to open to see the situation for what it was. This led to the "real import of the prayers" he said each day hoping for his situation to change for the better.[7] However, he was indecisive. Standing in the yard watching the Western plains flicker with heat lightning, Jack believed that the lightning of the West which to him personified Cassady was "strangely wild." The other was lightning "intense in the mystic east" where New York and Allen was. The dividing line was clear. Jack turned to Neal for kicks and Allen for poetics. Just as he divided his friends of childhood

Lowell by intellectuals (Sammy Sampas) and rowdies (G. J. Apostolos etc.), Jack had the luxury of going to one or the other depending on his mood. He renewed plans with Neal, and depended on potential money for *On the Road* and $105 a month for attending a G.I. school; they could then go to Italy and live inexpensively. He would recoup the $1,000 lost moving his family to Colorado. He would also travel to San Francisco to meet Neal and they could move cross-country to Gabe and Jack's new apartment in Richmond Hill, Long Island. Halfway there, Jack could reunite with Edie.[8]

Giroux suggested that there was no need for metaphysical writings like "Myth of the Rainy Night." Instead, he should write about people. He must guard his writing against too much symbolism.[9]

Over time, the Denver experience helped Jack appreciate the Western "myth" of the "great classless mass of Americans" unwitting of their American mythos. He watched family softball games played under the bright arc lights of gas tanks and felt silly for being too "longfaced" to join them: "I said to myself, 'What's the use of being sad because your boyhood is over and you can never play softball like this; you can still take another mighty voyage and go see what Cody [pseudonym for Neal Cassady in *Visions of Cody*] is finally doing.' Oh the sadness of the lights that night! . . . the great knife piercing me from the darkness."

Yet, as much as he admired honest, bold "classless Americans" from the Midwest, he missed conversations about books, jazz, philosophy, and art. In a letter to John Clellon Holmes, Jack encouraged the budding novelist to keep writing about New York City's social milieu and the characters who frequented the San Remo, a hipster hangout in Greenwich Village on the corner of Bleeker and MacDougal Streets that served beer, hard liquor, and coffee.[10] Jack suggested that the descriptions in Holmes's writing should depict "the bars, the mad parties, big swirling vortexes" as in Dostoevsky's novel *The Possessed*; he shouldn't concentrate on any one person but instead paint a "large impassioned portrait" as Charles Dickens had done. Already attempting a novel about 1940s New York, John asked Jack for an objective portrait of Ginsberg. Jack replied: "Burroughs is his father. Neal is his God-Bone. Lucien is his Angel."[11]

Though his dreams were collapsing around him, Jack remained calm.
Stoic. He read voraciously so as not to get too lonely. He found the locals
to be classless and illiterate. He was annoyed by tourists. He had a dog
that he took walks with; other times, he slept in alfalfa fields. He ate fresh
eggs and heavy cream. Attended ten-cent movies. He rewrote parts of *On
the Road* with the character Red Moultrie to make it more "Melvillean."
He received letters from Lucien (he had met a new woman from North
Carolina) and Allen (retorting about the tone of his poetry as a "dirty
ditty" that was phrased as such by Jack). Allen had been incarcerated at
the Columbia Presbyterian Hospital for psychiatric observation after he
became involved in a thief-operation (he was an innocent bystander yet
implicated in the crime). Jack told Giroux about Allen's poetry. In a letter to Allen, his advice was to "Be smart, now, and don't shit your pants.
The world is only waiting for you to pitch sad, silent love in the place of
excrement."[12]

To offset the Western dime novels he was reading, Jack devoured
Alain-Fournier's *Le Grand Meaulnes*, Cicero's *Offices*, Matthew Arnold's
Study of Celtic Literature, Keats's *Letters*, and Spenser's *Complete Poems*
(purchased for 50 cents in a Denver bookstore). Spenser whetted Jack's
appetite for using words for poetic power and wordplay. In a letter to
Elbert Lenrow, Kerouac described his method: "I conduct private phi-
lologies of my own in a notebook, concentrating mostly on tremendous
words like 'bone' and 'door' and 'gold' and 'rose' and 'rain' and 'water.'"
Through Spenser, Jack "kicked off" poetic insight to create "perfect bones
of images." Celtic poetry also contributed to this development.[13]

Through mid-June, he typed ten thousand words into *On the Road*.
He felt that he expressed that one does not begin "writing a book till you
begin to take liberties with it." One section of *The Town and the City* he
needed was still in Vicki Russell's possession. She was indicted on drug
charges; he feared that his "Levinsky and the Angels on Times Square"
was probably holed up in the evidence locker of the New York Police
Department. Even so, he wanted it returned.

On July 3, Cassady wrote Kerouac from San Francisco. The letter
served as a "case history" that Cassady, echoing Proust, called his "remembering of things past." In the letter, Cassady details his past incarcerations.

Neal had been arrested ten times and served fifteen months of his life on six separate convictions.

Jack was forestalled again. Giroux refused to advance him any more money. Jack had to work to be able to leave. In desperation, he found work loading and unloading fruit crates in a Denver food market on Larimer Street. He woke at two in the morning and walked four miles. He punched in at 4:00 a.m. and worked until 6:00 p.m. It was, as he wrote in *On the Road*, "the hardest job of my life." However, when asked not to return after a single shift, Jack assumed it was because he "was not as fast as the Japs."[14]

It was not difficult for him to decide which direction to take once he left Denver. His family had disappointed him; his $1,000 advance was thrown away. Allen's implication in a crime meant that somehow he would become involved.[15] He had no use for the East, as exemplified by his family. Instead, Jack invested his faith in the oppressed; the fertile ground of his emerging literature was to document the marginalized people that increasingly populated the landscape.

Instead, he focused on the immediate future, Neal, and the promises of the West. There was nothing for him to return to.

Jack drove to San Francisco by a travel bureau car. This would be his mode of transportation to the West and back east. At the Colorado state line, he saw a cloud formation "huge and massed above the fiery golden desert of eveningfall." He envisioned the "great image of God with forefinger pointed straight at me." The symbol was clear; to Jack, it was prophetic. He reached San Francisco just after midnight; by two in the morning, he was knocking on Cassady's door. Although Jack felt that his arrival made him feel strange and somehow evil, Carolyn and Neal welcomed him. Jack stayed for several days, but when he left, Neal again left behind Carolyn with a few dollars and nothing more. He did not indicate that he would be returning. He did leave a note: "Carolyn: Am leaving today. Won't ever bother you again. I won't come back in a month to make you start it all over again." He told her that he was bringing Jack back east. He would not be seeing Luanne.

Jack and Neal returned to Chicago and continued east, stopping in Detroit to see Edie Parker where they stayed overnight. By late August, they were back in New York.

* * *

On January 23, 1950, Jack finally received his first copies of *The Town and the City* and promptly mailed them to Beverly and Bob Burford, Burroughs, Ed Smith, and Ginsberg. Anticipating its imminent publication, he wondered if he would become wealthy or stay the same. He was restless for the first reviews. While he waited, Kerouac wrote another version of an opening for *On the Road*, stopping after four handwritten pages. He dated it February 1, 1950. The following month, his book was presented to the world.

Kerouac turned twenty-eight years old on the month his first book reached the marketplace. His portrait of his parents brought them to life in their joys and sorrows. They were simple people ingrained with an excellent work ethic. "George Martin" is a "man of a hundred absorptions." "Marguerite Martin" is reduced to a "superb housekeeper." Each are steely strategists. One a master of home and hearth, the other of the busy Galloway streets where he runs a small printing business. The Martin siblings are torn strands of Jack's personality. What emerges is a complex family drama of life before, during, and after wartime. Galloway is the town, New York is the city, the novel a Spenglerian meditation of fallen Western civilization. Two worlds serving two minds.

On March 5, 1950, the *New York Times* reviewed the book. *Times* book critic John Brooks appreciated Kerouac's technical and spiritual scope and compared the Massachusetts settings to Wolfe's descriptions of New York. He also sensed Kerouac's nod to Dostoevsky: "One gets the feeling that the author grew spiritually and improved technically while writing 'The Town and the City.' The early scenes in Massachusetts tend to be overly idyllic in content and wordy, even ungrammatical, in presentation. On the other hand, Mr. Kerouac's somewhat Dostoevskian view of New York City life is certainly exaggerated in another direction, but it is powerful and disturbing."[16]

Jack was optimistic that *On the Road* would be his break-through. He vowed to "express more and record less." He wrote a new three-thousand-word story for Jay Landesman, "Hipster, Blow Your Top." It paid him $30. Several days after that, before going to Boston, he typed another story, "Tales of the Mad Bop Night," to be retitled and revised as "Flowers That Blow In the Night." Giroux retitled it again as "Go, Go, Go" (to be used in *On the Road*). The story centered on Dean and Chad listening to jazz in a bar.

Despite Jack's publicity efforts, *The Town and the City* sold poorly. Plans for advance sales of twenty thousand copies, a $7,500 advertising budget, and the novel's acceptance by a British publisher (Eyre and Spottiswoode) were deemed too ambitious, though it was received positively in Ireland and England. Jack wrote London editor Frank Morley expressing gratitude that his book was being published there. He revealed to Morley that Giroux had rejected an early draft of *On the Road* and that, for now, he would be his "own editor." The London critics suggested that Kerouac move on and find a different style that was not so emulative of Wolfe. Such criticism hurt him and his spirits plunged.[17]

Bill Burroughs wrote to thank Jack for the book; he asked when he could expect him to visit. Bill had begun writing a new novel "about junk." Jack wanted to meet him there. It would be his first time, though he did not want to become an expatriate. Jack knew Mexico for what it was, his generation's version of "Lost Generation" Paris. The Mexico City slums replaced the Left Bank for affordability. There he could write with the little bit of money he had.[18]

One day he lit up a potent marijuana joint. It caused him to hallucinate. He saw Gerard. Over the next two weeks, the ghostly brother phantom advised him on immediate life issues. They had a conversation about the road which Gerard told him to leave. He called Jack a fool. Would he be always the constant wanderer? He prophesized Jack as a ragged, flannel-shirted phantom, a forlorn figure travailing beneath looming finger-pointing clouds. Jack became the embodiment of his guilt as personified by the "Shrouded Traveler."

Jack did not arrive in Mexico until June. He connected with Neal in Denver to accompany him south. Neal had his own reasons for agreeing to go to Mexico. He needed a cheap trouble-free divorce from Carolyn so that he could marry a woman from New York, Diana Hansen, whom Neal had impregnated the previous February. Diana phoned Carolyn asking her to divorce Neal so that they could marry. Carolyn agreed and appeared in court in June. However, their separation would not be final until a year later. This was not soon enough for Neal. By going to Mexico, he hoped to expedite the process. Though he eventually got the required papers, they were still no good unbeknownst to him because they were not legally binding. His marriage to Diana was bigamous.

Jack and Neal drove a worn-down beat-up '37 Ford. They brought with them another companion, Frank Jeffries. The passenger door hung from its hinges. The passenger front seat was broken. The passengers, Jack and Frank, sat dangerously close to the windshield. It was a road of perils prescient of the journey to come.

CHAPTER EIGHT

I Dedicate Myself to Myself

CASSADY, KEROUAC, AND FRANK JEFFRIES LEFT FOR MEXICO IN EARLY
June. The car drove straight through New Mexico into Texas, where Neal
planned to cross the border into Mexico. After San Antonio, the air
turned hotter. Drier. It baked the land like a brick oven. Jack imagined
he could smell the Rio Grande's muddy waters. When they reached the
South Texas Crossroads, that region of Texas that hosts three major
intersecting highways, they decided to put in at Victoria and visit a
whorehouse. Afterward, they turned the car west for Laredo, the Rio
Grande, and finally into Mexico.

They exchanged their US currency at eight Mexican pesos for a
dollar. They howled with delight. Their fat bankrolls encouraged them
to indulge freely in drinking and eating. They could take advantage of
the numerous Mexican sex workers hawking their trade in the market
district. They drove on toward Monterrey. At the higher altitude, the air
cooled. Snow capped the mountain peaks of Sierra Madre. Though Jack
wanted to stop and appreciate the City of the Clouds, Neal wanted to
keep going. There was no time to waste. He lied and told Jack that Mexico City had more exciting sights. What was really on his mind was that
he wanted to wed Diana before the baby was born.

Montemorelos. Nuevo León. The slow-moving Pilon River with
bright orange trees. The air became more humid. The car drove into the
lower altitudes. Dense. Relentlessly hot. Primal lands like before recorded
time. The native men bore machetes that they swung with tense wiry
arms. Thatched huts. Jack drove through Linares into Rio Soto la Marina.

Jack noted that he was, at last, among Oswald Spengler's *fellaheen*. The natives' dark features suggested strains of an ancient lineage. These were not from the Spanish ancestors who had decimated the indigenous people. In Gregoria, Jack solicited the services of a young prostitute from a young boy. The boy gave him some pot. Jack smoked it and instantly got high. It was the "great billowy trip of the world."[1] Later, they went to a brothel. Mexican police officers stood at the establishment's doors barely noticing the three horny gringos. Inside, a jukebox blared "El Tren" from Mariachi Vargas. Like extras from a Peckinpah western, dark-lidded mysterious women seductively enticed them. *Cerveza preparada*. Spiced meats wrapped in grilled corn tortillas smoked the air. Delicious. Through the clamor of smiling, happy people, Jack was the mysterious one hunched with a pencil in hand jotting all he encountered.

Church steeples. A looming crucifix, like the one in Lowell that his mother and he prayed at upthrust over the Grotto where they ascended on their knees up hard granite stairs. The Station of the Cross lit in mysterious yellow bulbs. Christ stumbling with the Cross at his tortured shoulders. Whipped. Bearing the cross again until he reaches the summit of Golgotha. These people were *his* people. Dark worshipers of ancient mysticism. Smoke another blunt, and then it will all make sense. The music whirled. The air grew denser. Claustrophobic. Neal talking, rapping a mile-a-minute spiel until the end of the night.

The next day they left, driving into a chaos of towering trees. Birds yakked high in its canopy. They had crossed the Tropic of Cancer north of Mazatlán. The land of ghosts and apparitions. Myths of women floating on the estuaries of La Estacada. In El Limon, Jalisco, located in central-western Mexico, they stopped to sleep. Neal slept outside. Jack, crushed within the car, was restless, wary of night insects sucking his blood dry. He despised the heat and so he remained awake most of the time. He saw a silhouette of a man approaching the car. It was a policeman who inquired of their intentions and then moved on. Unlike back home, the law made no complications for innocent people. Burroughs was right.

The deeper they drove, the more the country turned alien like a lunar landscape. Strange. Jungles dissipated to arid farmlands. They reached the

Sierra Madre Oriental, a chain of mountain ranges running from the Rio Grande to northern Puebla. They were deep within a pine-oak forest. The climate was drier. Pleasant. They heard the titter of a Mexican chickadee. The hammering of a Strickland's woodpecker. The piercing lament of a zone-tailed hawk. Beyond, the billowy white fog drifted its spectral tendrils through a cloud forest. They continued until they saw women in desert shawls carrying bundles of flax. Then they were in Mexico City. It immediately reminded Jack of Lowell. It was, he realized, a universal resemblance: no matter where he was in all the wide world, there were similarities. Humanity tied with a cosmic bond.

Burroughs's reasons for liking Mexico were altogether different. Here he could be left alone, no matter which nefarious enterprise he undertook. People minded their own business. Police officers were no more than civil servants, not billy-club-swinging thugs with tin badges. Any scofflaw among these relatively gentle people was handled where it happened. Bill could carry a .45 magnum in his holster without trouble. Even drug trafficking could be dealt with a payoff. And the only thing Mexican authorities seemed to frown upon was drug trafficking. Even this was subject to a payoff if and when one found the right person.

Bill prospered with his monthly allowance of $200 even though his morphine habit sometimes cost him $30 a take. A new acquaintance of his, the diminutive drug addict "Old Dave" Tesorero, and his junkie girl-friend, Esperanza Villanueva (whom Jack later used as the subject of his novella *Tristessa*), sold cheap faux silver crucifixes to worshipers. Bill and Old Dave schemed to take advantage of the legal government rations for drug addicts (fifteen grams monthly at the cost of $2 a gram), with Bill paying for half. This transaction assured them a constant high throughout the month.

Jack was high on the "large bombers" he smoked that made him see "the end of the night." His days were hazy in a stoned stupor. The world passed him by. His skin became tanned. He ate steaks and peasant food from street vendors. He shot morphine which induced visionary highs. He drew a fever and became delirious. Then he blacked out: "I looked up out of the dark swirl of my mind and I knew I was on a bed eight thousand feet above sea level, on a roof of the world, and I knew that I had lived a whole life and many others in the poor atomistic husk of my flesh, and I had all the dreams."[2]

On a Sunday afternoon, the Catholic day of consolation and prayer, Jack was high. He walked across the baking-hot plains of an ancient Indian village. He was among a circle of stone huts. Hallucinating, he squatted at the base of a shimmering pile of orange bricks (in his view, it appeared to be a makeshift altar). He saw God. His perception became distorted. At a bullfight, he saw the senseless slaughter of the heaving beasts. A bull vomited a stream of gore as it was dying. A team of horses dragged it away. Men shoveled the coagulated blood into buckets. Disgusted, Jack thought that Hemingway was a fool for writing about such gory spectacles.

Jack came down with dysentery and had a fever. Diarrhea drained him. In Jack's weakened state, Neal informed him that he was leaving. He had his divorce papers in hand. A week later, after he recovered, Jack left with a kilo of cured marijuana concealed inside a silk scarf tied around his waist. He boarded a *Ferrocarril de Mexico* Pullman car that took him to the Texas border. It was night. Jack stood on the hot tarmac under an arc light fluttering with hordes of moths. He heard footsteps, turned, and saw an energetic elder with long white hair walking by. He was a wanderer, too. He told Jack, "Go moan for man," and moved on into the darkness.

Jack boarded a bus in San Antonio that took him straight to Baltimore. Then he was home.

* * *

Jack's home life with Gabe was an uncomplicated respite from the rigors of the road. He was worn out by travel. Life was always better with Gabe fawning over him. She missed her "sweet boy." However, Jack wanted a wife. Having one meant that he could have maternal solicitude and everyday sex. He could have simplicity. The Cold War and the Red Scare meant nothing. His utopia of drugs and sexual hedonism as a portal to universal consciousness was all he cared for. Even when President Truman committed American arms to defend South Korea from communist North Korea, Jack's response was to believe in guardian angels.

Slowly, Kerouac altered the style of his writing to reflect his recent experiences. Cassady's writing helped stimulate Kerouac's creative drive, especially since he had purchased a tape recorder. Kerouac once recorded himself with Cassady during one of their stoned rap sessions and transcribed it faithfully for *Visions of Cody*. Cassady saw the possibility that such a device could save him the hassle of writing long letters. Instead, he could unwind a "5000-page" letter every day. Experimenting, Cassady bought a copy of *Of Time and the River* and read from it into a tape machine. Later he did the same with Marcel Proust's *Remembrance of Things Past*.

More importantly, for Kerouac, Cassady's letters from the fall of 1950 pointed the way to a writing breakthrough. High on pot, Cassady dispensed with mechanics and emphasized feeling over craft. He was writing his book at last, making progress after a period of stagnation. Jack's letters to Neal were also of great importance, assuring him that he was not alone in his "mental world," and that the two shared an affinity for pure abstraction in storytelling. Dwelling on details and sexual frankness often pointed the way to complete and honest liberation of the word. Depressed by his domestic conflicts, Cassady retreated into himself. To Kerouac, he described his writing as dropping into the "deepest parts of the mind until they are sunlit corners because one recognizes them so well because of the repetition and emotional strength of the deeper images." He felt it was best to vent in abstraction than to let the torments of his thoughts grow stale in the void of his heart and soul: "any thought, no matter how gone becomes so binded and cramped that the vegetation entangles itself endlessly and rots in jungle fashion of rot."

Neal was buoyed by Carolyn's acceptance of him into her life. When he wasn't tending to his numerous injuries and ailments at the Southern Pacific Hospital, he wrote. Crassly, he informed Diana that he spent what little else he had "fucking" his still-legitimate wife. Still, he was anxious to go on the road once again and maybe make the trip to Mexico an annual one. As he wrote on October 22, "Keroassady" was expected to return to New York in ten weeks. He intended to arrive with a new car and bring Jack back to Mexico. Jack, however, had other plans.[3]

Jack was depressed that *The Town and the City* had virtually sank without a trace. Allen was proud of his achievement and was equally incensed by Harcourt, Brace's lack of commitment toward marketing the novel. Because the book sales hardly brought in enough money to pay back Kerouac's advance, he would earn no royalties from it. Allen's attitude toward *The Town and the City* was as if he were its original author. He encouraged Jack to protect his hard work and to behave more assertively toward it. He must "man the lifeboats" before it was too late.[4]

By June 1950, however, it *was* already too late. After four months of floundering, the book sank into oblivion. John Clellon Holmes remarked: "I think Jack had to have *The Town and the City* published and had to go through the bad times of the editing of the book—the book was cut by a third—and get sick of it. Get sick of the scene, but also take a look at what he really wanted to do. I think if it hadn't been published, he would've been cranky and hung up on it. This way he was freed from it and he could look at it and say, as he used to say, "It's alive."[5]

On the Road continued through mid-to-late summer of 1950. Jack typed seven chapters and retitled it *Gone on the Road*. The aborted draft (begun on July 26, 1950, in Richmond Hill) opened with a chapter entitled "An Awkward Man." The "awkwardness" of the first-person narrator was utilized to impress upon the reader his temporary loss of identity. This feeling occurs when the narrator awakes in an old beat hotel with the shades drawn. He has no idea if it is day or night, and "in the space of five or six seconds . . . I completely lost every faintest, poorest, most woeful recollection of who I was."[6]

However, this style of writing was behind him. He floundered for several pages until he gave up. The bulk of the work was a sounding board to confront his self-deprecation: "I stared in the mirror to see the damage of the slob, grieving, all-grieving at the sight of it, astonished at the suffering face I saw, horrified by the drawn, hooded eye that looked at me."[7]

Jack submitted what he gleaned as the best sequences of *On the Road* to Giroux, who rejected them. Upset with their reception, Jack gave up on them and sent the manuscript to Farrar, Straus & Young. Although the company did not reject the manuscript outright, they advised extensive revisions to render it publishable. Taking the company at its word,

Jack tried to revise the text but decided to start over. He sent portions to John Clellon Holmes, who helped Jack acquire an agent, Rae Everitt, from MCA. This development left him with one responsibility: to write. Returning to the 1947 cross-country trip with Neal, Jack began again.

Meanwhile, Neal encouraged Jack to drop what he was doing and return west. His September 25, 1950, letter detailed a commiseration with a hallucinating hobo sunning on an S&P boxcar. Neal's charged letters would multiply over the coming months to usher in Jack's stylistic breakthrough. He was almost there.

Listening to the 1950 World Series on the radio in Richmond Hill, Jack noted the frantic banter of sports announcer Gene Kelly. He mined literary gold in what he heard. Jack was no stranger to sports talk. He was familiar with it as a boy after writing play-by-play imaginary baseball games. It wasn't necessarily the World Series itself that fascinated him, but the banter which sounded uniquely American in its frantic but focused delivery. He made a tentative plan to write an "American Times Series" narrated by various American voices: a ten-year-old Negro boy; the drone of English "sagas"; the original tongue of indigenous Americans; working-class vernacular; the sound of newly transplanted ethnic people; hobos, hipsters, westerners, and dilettantes. Jack told Neal that it was the "voice" that determined a book's pacing. It was how the narrative sounded in the reader's ear, that ultimately the "voice was all." A straight traditional description was insufficient for what Jack had to say. He tested various voices. There was the "effeminate" drawl of a Manhattan socialite, the New York lament of Herbert Huncke, the Western vernacular of hobos, and Neal Cassady sidling down Larimer Street.[8]

The first section, written on October 2, was "The Night of September 27." It begins as a commentary on war from "Uncle Ernest Boncoeur" in a Lowell cafeteria conversing on the current Korean War and the bombing of Hiroshima. He is having a reunion with an old school buddy, Charles Reilly. Reilly grips Uncle Ernie by the arm and admonishes him that he will grow old before his time by worrying "with every foolish thing that comes into your head." With Boncoeur is his fifteen-year-old nephew, Freddy Boncoeur.

"Even in the cafeteria, where they sat in a secluded corner by the tiled wainscottings and faced the street outside with all its Autumn-night lights and brown, blown leaves, there was for the boy this delightful sense of everything being ripe, rich, and golden-dark and all he had to do was love and enjoy till the day he died."⁹ Freddy's father, Smiley Boncoeur, somewhere in the West, occurs in a recurring motif as "the father never found": "Sometimes he thought he saw his father's face in the sorrowfullest day-dreams of the afternoon."

Jack continued with the next section, "Around the Kitchen Stove":

"The night of September 27 was an important night in the history of 20th Century America. Equally important have been some nights since, if we are to judge the history of a nation not by single large events, but peak intensities of an entire populace roaring its life beneath the skies, here, there, and everywhere on the bulk of its land—not small, everyday events as they are commonly called, but really the sparks from a gigantic flint of action. What is a continent, over which a single flag is understood, however casually, or sometimes with maudlin adulation of real idiots, but one giant organ breathing and moving within the shore of oceans; like an enormous animal prostrate on the face of the earth; a protective animal, that broods, like Milton's angel, upon the abyss of inhuman universes, protecting men, women, and children under its outspread wing for better or for worse, as is said of any marriage."

Freddy is to be sent home to his mother, but he pleads with his uncle not to let it happen. As they drive to his Little Canada tenement, Uncle Ernest opens two quarts of cold beer and pulls up his rocking chair by the warm wood stove. Napoleon, Freddy's eighteen-year-old brother, joins them. He discusses America as the last chance for "men to begin again." His companion speaks of the Last Chance Saloon, the last bar at the ocean's edge. Kerouac's exploration of French-Canadian Lowell as his centerpiece for *On the Road* was short-lived. He never returned to it.¹⁰

Jack remained interested in exploring pure Americana. He was intrigued by such common scenes like the intermittent silence between chatter around a campfire. Or old-timers drinking hot coffee at a truck stop diner. Within each Jack sensed an innate yearning for the frontier. He started another book he titled *Pic*. For this, Jack taped what he called "nigger dialect": "AIN'T NEVER NOBODY LOVED ME like I love myself, cept my mother and she's dead." It was a minor work with a crude understanding of African-American vernacular. He was attempting what others had already successfully rendered in similar Southern novels such as those written by William Faulkner and Thomas Wolfe. What Jack was attempting to achieve was to distill the pure locus of Cassady, rendering all of his mortal trappings into prose.

Jack urged Neal to keep writing the way he did. He was so taken with Cassady's spiel that he wished to type it verbatim to experience his mindset. "It was," he wrote Neal, "the best letter I ever received and the best letter you ever wrote in your life."[11] No longer did Neal hang himself up on miming a "literary" voice. He captured the magic of Shakespeare's *Hamlet*—when Hamlet spoke, it *sounded* like Hamlet's voice and not Shakespeare's. Neal's confessional words were ebullient, frank, and honest. The words moved with the discordant complexities of bop. Going forward, Jack could use Neal's voice and spirit as his dowsing wand.

Another aspect of his writing, most evident from a letter of November 5, 1950, was Neal's usage of sexual language. The pejorative "cunt" was followed by a string of adjectives strung before it ("juicy & ripe"). It was Neal as he spoke in the Hudson across America, unexpurgated and cut loose from convention: "but get a cunt & your cunt & us'll have a real orgy unless you want to go 'lonely fucker.'" Neal unabashedly captured "locker room" talk as a method of pure expression. Jack was enthused by such unexpurgated scatological talk. It was naked talk between comrades; its immediacy of unfiltered language made the commonplace divine. It was brand-new poetry. Neal's descriptions of his sex acts communicated a latent urgency of a predatory pathology:

"In fact, pal, if you love me, you'll do all in your power to find a girl, any girl (like em skinny) (for fuckin' that is, you see, skinny girls are all CUNT) & tell her I can fuck all night & blow them till their belly falls out & get their cunt inside out so I can fuck them to the real bottom, not that I can't anyhow, with a little cooperation."[12]

Though Jack was skittish about sharing his sexual experiences (except to Neal), he later incorporated similar graphic language into *Visions of*

Cody and admitted that his style of writing was discovered after "reading the marvelous free narrative letters of Neal Cassady."

The door had swung wide open.

CHAPTER NINE

What God Hath Wrought

JACK WAS IN DIRE NEED OF CASH. BAD.

He read more scripts for Twentieth Century-Fox. However, his excessive drug use made it difficult for him to maintain any concentration for such tedious work. Kerouac's "road to excess" did not lead to a palace of wisdom as much as it ran him ragged on the highway to exile. He welcomed the discomfort. He wanted to go to Mexico with Neal. He needed money. He had to sell *On the Road*.

Jack was drinking with Bill Cannastra, a Village fixture. He was, according to Norman Mailer, a "real hipster": "I never knew him, but I know a lot of people that did. He was tremendously handsome, a real operator. I know girls who still talk about him."[1]

One chilly autumn night, Allen was reciting a poem, "In Judgement," based on Cannastra and Huncke. They discussed "death" for several hours with Cannastra until closing the San Remo. A few nights later, after leaving a party with a friend, Cannastra boarded a subway. There was talk of going to the Bleecker Street Tavern, and so Cannastra, impulsively, made as if to leave by exiting through the train window. He stuck his head out into the labyrinthine depths of the subway and, reaching out even further, saw the supporting pillar of the tunnel racing toward him. He screamed. The support beam wrenched his neck, bashed his skull and yanked him out completely.[2]

Cannastra's girlfriend and roommate, Joan Haverty, was a San Remo regular able to match wits with her beau and Allen with relative ease (contrary to Allen's description of her to Neal as a "tall dumb dark-haired girl"). She seemed already a natural fit for Kerouac who was then ripe to acquire a woman who seemed to him to be marriage material.

* * *

By December 1950, Jack was ready to disclose the "full confession of my life" to "renounce fiction and fear." He felt courageous and filled with artistic conviction. His ill-fated marriage occurred when he had finally achieved a crucial peak in his artistic growth. One evening, Jack appeared below Joan's window looking for Lucien. From her loft window, Joan dropped her keys to him. Minutes later, he was at her door holding an attaché case. He withdrew a fresh copy of *The Town and the City* and gave it to her. She insisted that he autograph it. He wrote "For Joan" and told her, "When I know you better, I'll add something to that."[3]

Jack endeared himself to her from the start. A few days passed before he again called from the street. She let him in. That evening, he proposed.

In mid-November, Jack and Joan went for blood tests and bought a marriage license. Their wait for Jack's annulment papers from Edie delayed them. A phone call to Jack's attorney confirmed its legitimacy. They were waiting at City Hall for the justice of the peace to officiate when news that they were thirty-four minutes shy of the required seventy-two-hour waiting period delayed them. Incensed, Jack pleaded with the authorities at City Hall to stay open a half hour longer so their brief ceremony could take place. (The reception had been planned for that night.) His plea went unheeded. Joan suggested that they tell their guests they were married, an option he declined. He did not carry off deception well. They took the subway to Greenwich Village and found a friend of Jack's with a power of attorney under New York law to wed them. Judge Vincent Lupiano, from his Horatio Street residence, presided; Lupiano's wife and a secretary were witnesses. Joan wore Gabe's wedding ring, blessed by the pope. After the ceremony, Lupiano poured them a shot of booze and reminded Jack that he had never kissed the bride. "Oh yeah. That's right," he said.[4]

* * *

Neal planned on coming to New York in January 1951.

Agreeing with Allen that Joan had made a morbid shrine of Bill Cannastra in the loft, Jack felt uncomfortable with her persistence in leaving things the way they were. He had wanted to move his writing desk to a specific space. He felt that they did not need to keep Bill's possessions or the loft and wanted to move. Joan thought it was best to keep things as they were before he died. Jack, however, was persistent. In the process of moving, he found several twelve-foot-long rolls of paper in one of Cannastra's cabinets. Asking Joan to brew a pot of coffee, Jack fed one end of the roll into his typewriter, arranged some preliminary notes and outlines for *On the Road* beside an ashtray, and began typing. "It just about guarantees spontaneity," he assured Joan. He filled four feet of the new paper before putting his work aside.[5]

They rode a bus upstate to Poughkeepsie to visit Joan's mother. They returned in dire need of rent money, thus setting off a predictable trend of unrelenting dire straits. Because Jack slept all day and entertained his friends at night (he claimed such socializing was necessary for composition), he was unable to ever earn any meaningful income. They had no choice but to move. They would live with Gabe until Jack could sell a book.

Standing in a floral-print housedress and fuzzy slippers, Gabe wept with joy that her sweet boy had returned with his bride. She called her "little Joan." Though Joan found Gabe to be a persistent busybody (as did Jack and Caroline), Gabe was fond of her. She once wrote to Jack: "Be good to little Joan she's a very sweet little girl."[6]

Jack returned his writing desk to its original spot. Gabe placed his slippers beneath it. She surrendered her bedroom and slept in Jack's twin bed. The den was refashioned into a sewing room for Joan. Gabe was mindful of her domestic duties and her dressmaker career. Though tiny and unheated, the room confirmed her worst fear. There was no space for her. Although Jack promised such a room, Joan had to remove the accumulated clutter, clean, and move her things in while Gabe was working. Jack slept. No doubt, she had begun to regret her choice for a husband.

Jack was happy, seemingly oblivious to Joan's concerns. Under one roof, he had both mother and wife—caretakers to his needs. To help ward off extreme poverty, Joan took a job in a department store for the

Christmas rush. No longer counting on *The Town and the City* for his fortunes, Jack needed to complete his "REAL BOOK," to earn an advance. He wrote some potential titles: *Souls on the Road, Home and the Road, In the Night on the Road, Love on the Road,* and *Along the Wild Road.* Perhaps wanting more hands-on experience to kick-start his ideas, Jack anxiously awaited Neal's arrival, now postponed to February. Should that fail, he would resort to "plan 2" and move himself and Joan to San Francisco so that he could get a job at a newspaper. Joan could continue her chosen career as a clothing designer.

High on pot, Jack sat at his typewriter and wrote as Joan showered. Gabe watched the news. That was how most days went. Joan remained an outsider no matter how much she wanted to involve herself between Gabe and Jack.

In December 1950, Jack received Neal's latest letter, and perhaps the most important for Jack.

Jack left the house with it in his pocket. He went to a cafeteria. For two hours, he read it repeatedly. He returned and gave Joan the letter. She read it and was enthralled by Neal's misadventures. Jack showed it to Alan Harrington and John Clellon Holmes; neither was impressed. Neal's rambling prose did not suit everyone. Yet this correspondence was a crucial catalyst in Jack's transformation. It was when he went from "John" to "Jack."

Jack had found the first ingredient for his writing breakthrough. The thirteen-thousand-word letter was a rambling scattershot narrative that assaulted its reader with reckless verbosity. The door to Cassady's demons had cracked open. Jack placed the story of Cassady's 1946 Christmas in Denver in the same league as Dostoevsky, Joyce, Wolfe, and Céline. He perceived that its honesty would spark an "American Renaissance." Excitedly, he showed Allen, who also sensed its merit.

Cassady's writing had cracked the code for the final manifestation of *On the Road.* That night, Jack wrote:

"Just a word, now, about your wonderful 13,000 word letter about Joan Anderson and Cherry Mary." Cassady's technique, Kerouac explained, would be published. "It was a moment in lit. history when I received that thing & only sweetwife & I read it & knew. Ah man it's great. Don't undervalue your poolhall musings, your excruciating details about streets, appointment times, hotel rooms, bar locations, window measurements, smells, heights of trees. I wait for you to send me the entire thing in disorderly chronological order anytime you say and anytime it comes, because I've just got to read every word you've got to say and take it all in. If that ain't life nothing ain't."[7]

Jack wrote Neal that his letters bore traces of Joyce, Louis-Ferdinand Céline, Proust, and Dostoevsky—all of these merged within Neal's "muscular rush" of prose. Two days after receiving Neal's epic letter, Jack wrote a series of confessional missives to his high priest of modern prose (though he never mailed them to Neal). In his process, Jack reached back to his birth, beyond his "falseness." To be truthful to himself, he must "renounce" any prospects of writing for profit. Jack mirrored Neal's letter in style, spirit, and conviction. During the process of writing them, Jack had hoped that he would finally come to the "actual truth of my life."[8]

Jack broke from his confessional spill-out by going into the city. He went for a long walk. He sought shelter from the bracing cold in St. Patrick's Cathedral. He watched the dusk darken the huge stained-glass windows. As he listened to the novenas, his mind returned to Lowell and Gerard. Miserably, he agonized that he was Judas. Gerard, the ethereal "do-no-wrong" older brother, was his Jesus. There was a shawled woman knelt in prayer who looked like his mother. Two priests spoke in winter-hoarse voices. He wept over Joan and their dysfunctional home life. After three months, his marriage was irreparably damaged.

Although he was peeved by Joan's unhappiness, he refused to blame himself for it. Before they married, she knew who he was, and that his writing came first. He was self-absorbed and preferred to be alone. It was why the Navy booted him.[9]

Joan was a mere sexual convenience for Jack. Since she would not mother him, then she was less vital to have around. In her bedroom alone, Joan felt like a child under Gabe's watch. Jack did as his mother asked because he was indebted to her. She provided the physical and emotional comfort that Joan felt was impossible to compete with. Gabe's firm resolve was that Jack's work as a writer was more important than being a husband. Her belief mirrored how Jack felt. Jack was used to this attitude toward his mother. He felt that a woman's jealousy was because of her "possessive feminine instinct."[10]

Though Jack could be generous and kind, he was also mercurial in temperament. The high-spirited extrovert Jack became when he was drinking quickly turned into a cynical drunk. He was a mess of contradictions. When he wanted something, he expected to have it.

Jack continued writing through the new year. He demonstrated renewed confidence in his narrative writing through writing long letters. His narrative was punctuated by personal asides and flashbacks that defied linearity. Allen viewed Jack's letters as a "long confessional of two buddies telling each other everything that happened, every detail." On January 9, 1951, Jack finished the last five letters (approximately 22,500 words totaling over twenty-nine pages) and signed off with a quote spoken by Horatio in Shakespeare's *Hamlet*: "Goodnight Sweet Prince."

CHAPTER TEN

Beat Fellaheen

IN JANUARY 1951, JACK WROTE A STORY TITLED "BEN BONCOEUR." ITS opening lines became *On the Road*'s closing. Some of *On the Road*'s most famous lines find their genesis here. "Ben Boncoeur" is about two brothers, Roland and Anthony Boncoeur, that arrive in New York to collect their sickly older brother from a hospital and return him to New England. Jack describes the brothers as having the "same souls." They drink from "the same simple fountain of satisfaction."[1]

"One night in America when the sun went down—beginning in the East at dusk of the day by shedding a lovely gold in the air that made the dirty old building look like Rembrandt's temples of golden darkness, then out-flying its own shades as it raced three thousand miles over the raw bulge of the continent to the West Coast before sloping down the Pacific, leaving the great rearguard shroud of night to creep upon our earth, to darken all of the rivers, cup the peaks and fold the final shore in, as little lights twinkled + everybody mused—two young brothers came riding down to New York City in the fast Colonial Express from Boston with meditative faces."[2]

Ben was recovering from dysentery. Jack, who had been afflicted with the same, piled on the details as he remembered them:

"His illness had been strange. Passing through N.Y. with only a dollar left after traveling all the way from Mexico City by Mexican bus, and Laredo, Texas by thumb, he suddenly had a recurrence of feverish tropical dysentery; but something else unnerved him, his nerves shook, a sharp throbbing took up in his head precisely in the part of his brow where those dull nails seemed driven, in his eyeballs too and somewhere in the quivering nerve-disk at the top of his stomach. The throbbing in his head radiated a ragged burning X across his face, but in his fever and sorrowful pain it seemed that in the middle of that X there was a palpitating organism with a life of its own that kept beating against 2 unalterable sides, from pain to relief, at first, and then from humility to pride, humility to pride, ceaselessly. It was only a notion he had about it but his very bones shivered with the terrible intelligence of it."[3]

By story's end, Jack brought in Dean Pomeray for an appearance. He was desperate to find any potential direction for the road novel. "Ben Boncoeur" lacked the kinetic energy he needed to muster to bring conviction to his prose. Frustrated, he abruptly ended it without resolution.

Later that month, Jack and Joan moved out of his mother's house and into a Chelsea apartment at West 20th Street. Gabe had left with her movers to live with Caroline. From North Carolina, Gabe dispatched letters to "Jackie and little Joan" sorely missing both. Over the next several months, Gabe also came to miss her independence, job, and her friends in New York. She was peeved because the movers had damaged her chairs. She was suffering from back pain and could hardly sleep in her bed. She also found that Caroline and Paul were using her as a live-in babysitter for Paul Jr. She had no television, which for Gabe was the most deplorable bane of her existence in North Carolina.

Over time, Jack mailed separate batches of his papers for Gabe's safekeeping, perhaps sensing his unstable living conditions with Joan. When Gabe could afford it, she mailed Jack spending money she had from cashing in her Vacation Club check.[4] She had hoped to one day use it for a trip to New England to visit her family in New Hampshire and friends in Massachusetts. Gabe hoped that Jack and Joan would fly to North Carolina to visit her. She offered to pay for their airfare.[5]

Neal was due to arrive in February. His visit had a purpose: he had a son, now a year old, with Diana Hansen. When he arrived, Jack was out somewhere. Joan offered him a beer. She drew a pan of hot water for him to soak his sore feet. She enjoyed his presence. She admired how he could speak on several planes of thought without losing track of them. One thing she did not feel toward him was any physical attraction.[6]

Jack was still disgusted. Four years of his life was sunk into *The Town and the City* only to have it slip into oblivion. Still, he knew that it must be written to put that experience behind him. He had the discipline to write a book from start to finish. Now, he must write what he wanted to say. It did not have to be a novel, memoir, or diary. It could be any book. The writing did not have to be "good." It only had to have feeling.

Some time in March, Jack and Joan went to North Carolina but did not stay long. The heat was unbearable though it was barely springtime. They left Gabe with Nin. Not long thereafter, her constant letters shot north like arrows complaining of the relentless heat and the unsavory treatment by Nin and her son-in-law. Over ten days, there was no rain. Caroline's yard was all burned-out grass. Nothing grew. The sand burned brilliant white to the eyeballs. Gabe thought it looked like a desert. She was always crying. She only saw Nin and Paul at dinnertime. The only relief she got after keeping Paul Jr. out of mischief all day was when he fell asleep: "I'm just about ready for the grave." Like Jack, she was restless and wanted to keep moving. She wanted to return to New York. She was envious of Joan, addressing her by letter:

"Joan Honey, I hope you don't think I'm crazy for acting as I do. I should have done like you did, do what I wanted to do. You made up your own mind to get your home for yourself and did it or bust, and me I should have stopped crying and feeling sorry for myself and stayed put and kept my job. Gosh Honey I'll never learn."[7]

Gabe made up her mind by letter's end to apply for her old job skiving shoes. For her, hell in a shoe factory was a better option than the one she was living in now.

* * *

On April 2, 1951, Jack took the sheets of paper he found among Cannastra's possessions and taped them end to end. He fed the single roll into his typewriter. Following Allen's vow to avoid amphetamines for serious writing, Jack, this time, followed suit. His drug of choice was caffeine. He was utilizing what he called a "stream of perceptions" to write the book, a technique he learned in Kinston, North Carolina,[8] the previous month. During that time, he used what was had at hand, a red ink pen and some paper. He focused on a chicken coop to lock his vision and wrote what he saw and felt:

"It used to be that many chicken coops were built against a tree, and the chickens scratched in the shade with chicken dumbness not realizing the bark was part of the trunk of a tree, and anybody waking up in the morning saw the pleasing shady scene of rickety coops instead of in the new America where they now build small block-houses on flat sandy land outside town and if you want to build a chicken coop it will have to be in the open hot yard and not leaning on any great tree of life."[9]

Jack strung these long sentences together like sheets hung along a washline. He wrote as if he were speaking breathlessly. He felt his way into any sequence, belting out enthusiastic spillways of language as if a great dam had burst.

"This is an example of the 'stream of perceptions' that flow through the mind but are never utilized by the man who dreams of fabricating a continuity-tale, and can be compared to the signal of a television transmitter which flies too high to be picked up in a fringe-area unless a 65-foot tower is erected to catch it as it tangents over the curvature of the earth, whereby the only image without a tower that can be made is what you might fabricate in your mind. Or if you had a partial antenna that only picks up the force of the signal and not the signal itself, and you tried to make something out of that. This stream of perceptions, which is in the trace of waking-consciousness and not the 'subconscious,' is the most important level of any artist's mental endeavor, but because it is removed from the moral continuum which constitutes the image of a tale,[10] no one knows what to do with it."

Jack knew what to do with it. By way of example, he referenced Faulkner and Joyce for employing a similar technique in their books. Faulkner, he felt, did it most successfully. However, each suffered from what Jack described as an "over-density of the mind." The function of this method was not to "imitate nature" but to "create our own images in the image of ourselves." Jack wanted to write as he saw it, "as it travels in waves through my brain, as in a dream": "I imagine then the tale would be of least significance, and there would come into existence, the form of the natural story." This feat required a "tremendous trancelike discipline."

Lastly, "stream-perception can only be used as the mine of images from which but a portion can ever be lifted—fished out, as befits the old fashioned fisherman of the deep."

This, for Kerouac, was his significant breakthrough. He would take it with him to New York, where he was living with his unhappy wife in their Chelsea apartment, to his desk where a taped-up roll of paper was fed into Leo's old Underwood. He would belt the book out within the next three weeks as described in a little North Carolina town during the raw muddy month of March.[11]

Jack was at rest in "mystery and uncertainty." He permitted ideas to float through his mind without "seeking through after fact and reason." He possessed an intuitive appreciation for all that was beautiful. Lastly, he abided by Keats's third tenet of negative capability, which is to be interested in everything, to empty oneself of a "fixed identity so that you can be better sensitive to the world."[12]

* * *

Jack had created an outline to guide him so as to write nonstop, spewing a single continuous paragraph to break it into single pages afterward. For now, he wanted to get it all out. Desperate for money, he tried to demonstrate by way of example what his craft could earn by writing alone. It was his last make-it-or-break-it defense to Joan. To simplify the task, he used real names. This kept the story straight. Knifing the narrative edge to coincide with real-life events made it more accessible and fit in with his emerging "Legend of Duluoz." He could hone closer to the events of the last several road trips. His "Self-Instructions" were vague descriptions to riff from: "Talk about Neal with Hal"; "Thieves and socialites"; "Description of Hank," etc. Jack's strategy was simple. He glanced at his "self-instructions," closed his eyes, fingers poised to strike and typed. The "spontaneous flow" of the month before permitted him to move through his narrative like space and time. By now, he had committed every sequence in his head and on various drafts, so it became second nature to write about it. For now, all he had to do was to tell it all straight and naturally.

Though Jack was a central protagonist of *On the Road*, he realized that his "Sal Paradise" character alone would have flattened the story out. Paradise, as the recipient, even remaining external to the story, became an adequate participant. The novel belongs to Neal Cassady through the moniker of "Dean Moriarty." *On the Road* moves toward forbidden areas through a method disallowing divulgation. Moriarty arises out of shadows, labyrinths, and caves. The physical presence of Moriarty is not as crucial as the textured shadow of the man. His troubled persona ("the sideburned hero of the snowy West") is a mythical avatar. He is the forbidden, the tabooed object, the nasty myths made flesh. His presence dominates the novel less than one-third into the story. Moriarty hovers over the entire book. While the book doesn't seem to be only about him, in actuality, it is almost always about him.

Jack wrote for hours at a time. His tremendous athleticism pushed him through a physically arduous task. He sat straight, hands attacking the keys like a piano virtuoso. He did it trance-like, his mind freed from narrative constraint. He was detached from external realities. He broke through from the New Vision and dispensed with Self-Ultimacy. For now on, he need only to contemplate truth and beauty. He had achieved Keats's "fine verisimilitude":

"would do well to break off from his relentless search for knowledge, and instead contemplate something beautiful and true ('a fine verisimilitude') caught, as if by accident, from the most secret part ('Penetralium') of mystery. The experience and intuitive appreciation of the beautiful is central to poetic talent and renders irrelevant anything that is arrived at through reason. Keats ends his brief discussion of negative capability by concluding that 'with a great poet the sense of Beauty overcomes every other consideration, or rather obliterates all consideration.'"[13]

Jack knew in advance exactly how his book would turn out. He centered each section upon different stages of the road trip, sometimes combining them to avoid a pendulum effect in the narrative. Ten days in, he had accumulated eighty-six thousand words. He was exhilarated: "I don't know the date nor care and life is a bowl of pretty juicy cherries that I want one by one biting first with my cherry stained teeth."[14] By April 22, he finished a typescript approximately 125,000 words in length.

Three weeks later, it had expanded to 120 feet, consisting mostly of a single paragraph. In appearance, it resembled that novel, *120 Days of Sodom*, handwritten by Marquis De Sade on a single scroll stretching to approximately thirty-nine feet.[15]

* * *

A new novel wasn't the only thing Kerouac conceived. One night as he was working, he appeared behind the screen that separated his desk from their bed and had sex with Joan. By June, Joan knew that she was pregnant. Expressing doubts, Jack sent her to Caroline's obstetrician. When it was confirmed, Jack remained in denial. The baby couldn't be his. He was convinced he was sterile.

Furthermore, he had seen her in their apartment with a young Puerto Rican dishwasher from the restaurant where she worked. She told him that he was her friend. Jealous, Jack did not believe her. He denied paternity and said he was infertile (which he had failed to tell her before they were married). It was the final straw. She kicked him out.

Jack's version of these events was later written in Tangier in March 1957. In it, he claimed that he married a woman "that just didn't love men."[16] The fact of his incompatibility with her failed to strike him. He had taken his chances with love at first sight. He had gambled on marriage. Both failed him. He lost a wife but gained a masterpiece.

Lucien arrived and helped Jack move out. It was raining. Jack was limping from the onset of phlebitis. He loaded the rolltop desk into Lucien's car. Lucien was talking to Joan while Jack placed his possessions in the vehicle. Afterward, Lucien tried to get to the bottom of what Jack had done.

"Kerouac, methinks you tried to marry with your head."

"What you mean?"

"Boy, you tried to improve your lot with what I guess you thot was a fancy doll." Jack felt that Lucien spoke with "inexpressible sadness."

"Ah, Kerouac."

"So, what do I do now?"

Lucien shrugged: "You can move into my loft and stay as long as you want and I spose the Good Lord'll let you stay on earth long as you want but boy that fucked up psyche of yours is not an enviable thing to see, Jack."

Jack carried his belongings up four flights to Lucien's loft. His papers, stacked from desk to ceiling, towered over Lucien. Lucien was drunk. He told Jack, "I should knock all that down and then there wouldn't be nothing left of you, boy." Jack thought: "Truer words were never spoken."[17]

* * *

Jack brought *On the Road* back to Bob Giroux. Giroux was astounded. He told Jack that he couldn't accept the manuscript this way. Furious, Jack rolled it up and left.

He had shown Lucien the scroll. Lucien read some of it and called it "shit." Before Jack moved away from Joan, he wrote Neal:

"Now I sit here, with sore phlebitis foot, my book finished, handed in, waiting for word from Giroux, a book about you and me, I sit here, my wife's not here, she's at her mother's, presumably tomorrow I move out and we part, I don't know what to do, where to go, on June 20 I may have a thousand dollars or more, meanwhile I stay with Lucien and Allen in loft."[18]

Holmes suggested that Jack bring the manuscript to Rae Everitt, his agent. She declined to accept it in its current form. For now, he ignored her advice to retype the entire thing. She suggested breaking it up into paragraphs and forming a traditional structure that could be more easily sold to a publisher. To write another book like *The Town and the City* was impossible and unwise. Everything he had written before was a pack of "lies." He was not about to start creating new ones. What he needed to do was rely purely on his own instincts. To alleviate Jack's anguish, Neal invited him to stay with him in San Francisco. Neal had reconciled with Carolyn (now pregnant with their third child). He offered Jack his attic space.

This option gave him the time needed to polish *On the Road*. He would be freed from financial duress. He didn't have the money to go to Mexico as he wanted; the Guggenheim Foundation had denied his grant application. He also knew that, before long, Joan would be after him for child support once the baby was born. He lacked the means to go to San Francisco. Again, he was reliant on the charity of others.

Gabe was growing impatient. She was clueless to the state of Jack and Joan's marriage for Jack had written her that he was in love with Joan and that she made a superb "little wife":

"Only Joan I am terribly lonesome for you both for I love you dearly and it breaks my heart too that I cant see you more often, God bless you dearly girl for being such a good little wife to my only boy. . . . "

Again, she pined for her old job "dirty or not" because the money was decent: "I could buy myself some damn good steaks." She apologized for her restlessness and dissatisfaction. She wanted her own home. Her own things. For either, she realized "I'd have to find myself a man, and that I'm afraid it's too late." Like her son, she did not find herself at home anyplace. She was dislocated and exiled from nowhere to anywhere.

Joan Burroughs had written Jack from Mexico. The last time he had seen her, she was a wasted figure withering on the dying vine of her life. She had noted that Bill's South American travels were a failure. She encouraged Jack to come. They had a three-room apartment. They only occupied one. All it would cost him was $10 a week. She hoped that maybe he could bring Lucien with him. The last time he saw her, her teeth had blackened and began falling out. She was exposed to polio and struggled with alcoholism.

It was the last time Jack heard from Joan Burroughs.

* * *

In August 1951, Jack was in North Carolina. Being there kept him at a distance from Joan, who was seeking money to help her during pregnancy. He was still suffering from his limp, which had gotten progressively worse. Gabe and Caroline tried to care for him, but he needed serious medical attention. It had been his fifth phlebitis attack since 1945. Caroline was frustrated and would remain that way for the next several years. Gabe was always lonely and sad. When she was with Nin, she missed Jack; when she was with Jack, she missed Nin and her grandchild. Caroline urged Jack to get a job so Gabe could live in a stable environment without having to move frequently. Caroline blamed

Jack's prolonged absences for Gabe's frequent bouts of physical paralysis, which would find their nadir in the late 1960s, when she suffered a partial stroke. Caroline saw no logic in Jack "roaming around" the country with so little money in his pocket. Though she was supportive of him once *The Town and the City* had been accepted, Caroline's enthusiasm had waned when she witnessed the sadness Jack's absences had wrought upon their mother. For now, they were both flustered at Jack's ailing health. To them, he was wearing himself down. Gabe suggested he return to New York, where he could be treated for free using his VA benefits.

On August 11, Jack was in Greenwich Village. He saw Allen's physician, Doctor Hector Perrone, notorious for only charging $5 per visit. Perrone gave Jack a penicillin shot and told him he had a severe thrombophlebitis attack. He suggested that Jack should quit smoking and sent him to the VA hospital that night. Perrone wrote up the necessary referral papers and sent Jack on his way. Mexico would have to wait.

In Kingsbridge, Jack lay in his bed and stared at the ceiling. He listened to the "silence of the sick sleepers" and realized, "God intended I stay and be quiet instead of mad trips, again and again to nowhere—I have nothing to do but rest and remember the folly of my life and maybe something will come of it & I be reborn in repentance and recall." That first night, Lucien's message came from Allen: "Leaving for Mexico tonight—be a good angel." Jack folded the letter up and listened to the rain "gurgling in the gutters of New York." His recovery wasn't just for his leg. He needed a mental break. The rain helped "silence the fury" within.

Jack's bed was in the corner of the room with a view overlooking the hospital yard and the Bronx. A war veteran named Kaiser came to Jack's bed for idle talk. Another patient lying across from him was suffering from brain cancer. He was praying to Jehovah. He gave Jack his dessert off of a tin tray. "Go," he told Jack, "go on and eat it. I'm old and dying." Another patient reminded Jack of his father. His belly was swollen and tapped regularly.

Despite his physical discomfort, Jack was pleased. He was drugged, fed, and cared for by dutiful nurses. He vowed to stop smoking, drink more tea and less coffee, and moderate his calorie intake. It was here that his creative life would take a decisive turn. In a 1956 notebook,[19] he wrote that this hospitalization made all of his subsequent writings possible, most of which became published books: *Visions of Neal, Doctor Sax, Maggie Cassidy, The Subterraneans, Tristessa, Visions of Gerard*, and "October in the Railroad Earth" among others.

On the Road lay dormant, rolled up like a medieval scroll in Lucien's apartment. Jack intended to forget that version and rewrite it using a character named "Victor Duchamp" utilizing the same traditional structure as *The Town and the City*. Perhaps he believed that he could more easily make money that way. It was, after all, a proven method worthy of repeating. Giroux's refusal to even read what he had so passionately typed out was discouraging. He was in desperate need of money. He thought of William Faulkner's novel *Sanctuary*, populated with bootleggers, rape, and murder. Maybe he could write such a "potboiler." On August 25, Jack attempted to write his own titled *Hip*.

Hip was to capitalize on John Clellon Holmes's success with his novel, *Go*, by borrowing its theme and subject matter. Holmes had received a sizable advance, which made Kerouac highly envious. His solution was to write something fast and sensational. It was to be a "potboiler" novel written in the vein of Faulkner's purpose for *Sanctuary* which was to capitalize on the then recent fad of utilizing gangsters and bootleggers as his main characters. *Hip* told a story of a single night on 42nd Street in the "fragrant dark American westward land." It was the "Last Chance Saloon" of America's rebellious youth. The plight of the juvenile delinquent was the new social pestilence, the post–World War II fallout of absent parent figures during the war. In Kerouac's evocation, this new brand of youth was drawn to the rebelliousness of bop. This new youth energy was inclined toward unleashed sexual freedom, observing women cutting sexily through the night: "where are they going? What will they do? What? What?" It was girls in tight slacks "cleaved like a peach" that drew their restless paramours like moths to a flame. Bohemian girls were out to marry a millionaire or to shack up with a poet. A slick young cat named Buddy Black wearing pegged pants and clutching a Ronson lighter for his marijuana cigarette served as *Hip*'s first-person narrator. Black is a wayward dishwasher who seems (like Kerouac) to never settle at any one place. He is a scholar, thinker, and writer working eight-hour shifts by pushing racks of dirty dishes through a mechanical dishwasher. He spends equal time reading at a city library and lives in a $4-a-week Brooklyn Heights rooming house where he cooks his supper on a hot plate. Buddy aims to live frugally so that he can exist the way he wants. As he listens to bop, he writes a book about "Cody Deaver," a character he met in New Jersey pulling Coca-Cola bottles from an ice machine. Jack ultimately switched perspectives in *Hip* by focusing on a character named "Sal Paradise" whose Italian father is a "ghost on Times Square." Paradise works a freight elevator in the garment district. Several days later, Jack revised his narrative when Paradise meets Buddy Black and Cody Deaver and a "very sharp cat" that was on the scene.

"He was about thirty five, or more or less, you couldn't tell because he was one of those gliding graceful spades who look like they're oiled low to the sidewalk. He came floating up to us with a 'Hey now daddy' and just stood beside us, facing the street, cool. He had a pencil thin mustache, drooping brown eyes full of sadness, an expensive low drape jacket, the new kind without lapels that bop musicians wear. It was just a split second till he said 'Put this in your pocket and keep it.' He shoved a small package in Cody Deaver's pants pocket and was gone."[20]

This potboiler lasted three pages before stopping. For Kerouac, writing was sacred. He wasn't equipped to write in such a hackneyed style.[21] Determinedly bent on earning, he drafted a five-tiered plan to earn money. The first was to return to his mother's apartment and write the first half of a road trilogy. Secondly, he wanted to return to sea (this could earn $150 a month). This he would do for at least a year. Possibly, he would go on another road trip before spending the next two and a half years writing his entire road epic without distraction. Thirdly, he'd draw $300 from an expected advance in October 1951—though it never came—and go to Florida where he'd live on his winnings from betting horses. After that he would save money to buy a house in Long Island for himself and his mother. Or, he could buy a less expensive house in Mexico, where he hoped to earn as much as $9,000 a year. All of these, for the time, were a far-fetched fantasy.

The fourth part of his plan, which he ultimately went with, was to live rent-free in Neal's attic. He could work part-time on the railroad as he rewrote his road novel.

For now, he had $360 in his bankroll. Discouraged, he thought back to 1941, when he imagined himself as wealthy and famous. Instead, he was broke and sick. Furthermore, he was hiding from Joan, who was five months pregnant and who was trying to serve Jack some legal papers.

Jack read Melville's *Pierre: or the Ambiguities* and was most impressed by Henry A. Murray's foreword. Murray, a Jungian professor of psychology at Harvard, had written *Explorations in Psychology* in 1939. However, the focus of his writing was a planned Melville biography. He amassed thousands of pages of notes. After reading *Moby-Dick*, Murray was swept up by Melville's masterpiece, whom he found as psychologically compelling as Jung or Freud. Murray was researching, writing, and accumulating from this tangle of information a foreword for *Pierre* published by Farrar, Straus in 1949. Murray's approach toward understanding Melville's complex novel was to delve into his "unconscious mental processes." Jack read:

"Since his mind had come of age in 1845 Melville's experience had been one of continuous unfolding, until one day his questing spirit encountered a barrier which, so far as he could see, was insurmountable. The presentiment of his personal defeat sat heavy, and in the spring of 1851 Melville wrote his literary colleague Nathaniel Hawthorne that he had 'come to the inmost leaf of the bulb, and that shortly the flower must fall to the mould.'"[22]

Startled, inspired, and energized, Jack immediately rejected Murray's Jungian associations as "crap." He sensed a kindred spirit in Melville. Through this kinship, Jack felt capable of completing *Doctor Sax*, which, like *Moby-Dick*, relied on symbolism. In *Doctor Sax*, Gabe (as "Ange") is prophet, seer, and mystic. Leo becomes disembodied. Emasculated. He is a ghostly presence shuffling through the hallways of their Lowell home and through downtown. Gerard is the Snake of Snake Hill tormenting Jack through life.[23]

Jack stayed up late through the night thinking about his writing. He felt it had to be inspired from the bottom of his mind without reservations. The one thing that held him back was his fear of death. Gerard, the Snake, represented his thanatophobia. He dreamt that he was sitting in a deserted pub in Mexico with Carr—or a Lowell bar. He was in the hospital, waiting to get well and return home. He woke up the morning of September 3 with a vision of Neal racing east in his Hudson. The car was the perfect metaphysical representation of twentieth-century America. So intoxicated was he with this sudden vision that Jack pictured the Hudson cruising through an ever-changing panorama of backdrops. A Roman chariot symbolized progress. Christopher Columbus and his ships. It was a pioneer wagon rolling west, epitomizing manifest destiny.[24]

The automobile symbolized youthful rebellion, sorrows, kicks, fast and fleeting thoughts, sexual cargo, and a whorehouse on wheels. At 70 miles per hour, it was the climax of youth, bending, arching, and ultimately releasing. Putting the tedious matter of *On the Road* aside, he worked on *Doctor Sax*. The sun warmed his skin as he lay under the trees on the cool green lawn. He daydreamed of Snake Hill, where he could hear the heart of his dead brother beating. The questions were forever wrestling inside of him: "What should he do? What should he write?" He felt the universe's mysteries outside his window. The Hudson River sparkled. He intuited Melville's "ungraspable phantom of life." He sensed a man, solitary in misery, writhing in pain. There was a November in his soul. Jack brooded over his death that afternoon until he went to see a Yankees game. He got drunk. When he returned to his room with a newspaper, he was shocked—but not surprised—to read that Bill Burroughs had killed Joan. Jack had personally witnessed trigger-happy Bill and listened to his morbid yarns of death. Joan's death seemed a logical conclusion.

Reading the news, Jack was unable to sleep. His affirmation of life increased. He lay outside. The sun glowed through his eyelids, inducing "visionary tics" like ecstatic charges of mental energy that floated images like a movie screen before him. After several seconds, they were gone. How could he capture this sensation into his writing? On September 12, he was discharged from the VA hospital. He returned to his apartment with new ideas. He felt a new ambition to write, a desire to sequester himself while he was immersed in reinvention. He knew that he wanted to write a grand mythology of America. Among others, he wanted to describe the antics of "Hot Lips" Page, Old Bull Balloon, Dean Pomeray, Artie Shaw, a few Lowell buddies, and a host of New York City locals that he imagined could populate his road saga. A day later his ambitions departed him. He was drunk, crying in the arms of his friends.

The week after his discharge, Jack rearranged his possessions in his mother's apartment. He still had his desk and typewriter at Lucien's house. Days later he was trudging through a grassy field at four in the morning lugging the old typewriter home. It was important to him. It had belonged to his father. It had supported their family at Spotlight Print. *The Town and the City* and *On the Road* were written with it. When he arrived that morning, there was a knocking on his door. Joan and her attorney were trying to serve a summons. Bristled by their appearance at his home, Jack left for a walk. When he returned, he wrote "Dean and the Poolhall":

"Have you ever seen anyone like Dean Pomeray?—say on a street-corner on a winter night in Chicago, or better, Fargo, which is a mighty cold town, a young guy with a bony face that looks like it's been pressed against iron bars to get that dogged rocky look of suffering, perseverance, finally when you look closest happy, prim self-belief, with Western side-burns and big blue flirtatious eyes of an old maid and fluttering eyelashes; the small and muscular king of fellow wearing usually a leather jacket and if it's a suit it's with a vest so he can prop his thick busy thumbs in place + smile who walks a mile a minute on the balls of his feet, talking excitedly gesticulating poor pitiful kid actually just out of reform school with no money, no mother, and if you saw him dead on the sidewalk with a cop standing over him you'd walk on in a hurry, in silence. Oh life, who is that? There are some young men you look at who seem completely safe, maybe just because of a Scandinavian ski sweater, angelic, saved; on a Dean Pomeray it immediately becomes a dirty stolen sweater worn in wild sweater."[25]

This prose style suited him better. There was immediacy. Its candid nature suggested a conversation between two men at a pub. Jack had unbottled his creative prowess. This wasn't just "Dean Moriarty," "Red Moultrie," or "Cody Pomeray," but a man symbolic of all men. The epitome of the Brotherhood of Man. This man bent over the pool table, steadying his cue with a keen, knowing eye, like a hunter drawing an arrow on a deer. He was a man of the Snowy West and the East.

Faced with the prospects of moving forward with his new prose, he was still faced with distractions, mainly Joan. She was incessantly telephoning the house. By September 19, she had endured enough and made clear her intentions through her lawyer. Police arrested Jack and he was jailed for ten minutes before being bailed out by his mother. Death-haunted, Jack underwent a massive drinking binge. He gasped great gulps of air. He realized he was becoming a drunk. He wrote in his journal that he did not want to take on the same habits that killed his father.[26]

In Jerry Newman's recording studio, Jack recorded himself reading passages from *On the Road*. He was enthralled by the sound of his voice and the eloquence of his prose booming through the speakers. Later at the San Remo, Jack, Jerry, and Allen ran into Maxwell Bodenheim. Max returned to the studio with Jack and Allen to record poetry. To Allen, old Max was "too beat." Max's eyes were red-rimmed, his hair long and unkempt. Whenever Allen ran into the haggard sage, Max always had a battered briefcase with him filled with typewritten poems. He was a familiar sight around the Village, sometimes sleeping in Washington Square or in alleyways with Ruth Fagan, an ex–mental patient who had now taken on the role of common-law wife. Bodenheim was proto-beat, possessing the spirit of the Beat Generation, though he had little in common with them. To Burroughs, Bodenheim seemed to be a "lost soul," though he couldn't figure out why. At Minetta's Tavern, Bodenheim had appeared. Burroughs heard him shriek, "I'M MAXWELL BODEN-HEIM!" as he made his way out the door.

The hapless trio recorded their poems in Newman's recording booth. Bodenheim then passed out. Jack suggested that Allen should read in his stead. Allen recited "The Shroudy Stranger." Afterwards they escorted drunken Max back to his cold-water flat on MacDougal Street, where a landlady refused to allow visitors after 10:00 p.m. They were booted out for being too loud. They talked in the empty street and then left Max behind. Jack and Allen walked to Allen's father Louis Ginsberg's house in Paterson, New Jersey. Dazed by whiskey, they ate a big breakfast and walked some more. Jack ended up in Times Square where he saw two homeless men wrestling in the street. The other men were just watching. Jack threw his briefcase filled with books and manuscripts down on the sidewalk and tried to stop the fight. However, the daunting size of the men and the fact that nobody bothered to help made him stalk away in disgust. He felt that if this was how they wanted the world to be, let them have it.

Back home, he aimed to finish retyping *On the Road* on separate pages by Christmas. On October 6, he barely typed eight hundred words before he was interrupted. He was restless, unable to sit for long periods like he used to. He went to Birdland and made an extraordinary discovery this time. Watching Lee Konitz play "I Remember April" on his alto sax, Jack sensed the musician's internalized process. He was merging innovation with an old jazz standard. Konitz played with a method that Jack was trying to find in his writing. In Birdland's dark interior, he wrote on the first page of a new notebook, "ON THE ROAD / A MODERN NOVEL." Then he scribbled a vow to himself, stating his first essential component of spontaneous prose: "BLOW AS DEEP AS YOU WANT TO BLOW!"[27]

He tried it:

> . . . but actually choking over
> love he missed and growing
> old & growing old for no
> reason but broken
> loss, and to go and die
> die and be dead and
> gawk in graves.

That wasn't quite it. He crossed it out entirely and did it again: "—choking over loss, and love, he missed & growing old." He was almost there. The best way to do it was to go out on the street and write it on sight. Write in flashes of sensory impressions, like an artist with a brush and watercolors catching birds on the wing. He went to an old diner and tried again. He would confine each to the length of a notebook page:

There's nothing like the old
lunch cart that has the
oldfashioned railroad car
ceiling and siding doors—
The board where bread
is cut is worn down fine
as if with bread dust and
a plane; the icebox is
a huge brownwood thing
with oldfashioned pull-out
handles, windows, tile walls,
full of lovely pans of
eggs, butter pats, pile of
bacon—old lunchcarts,
always have a dish of
sliced raw onions
on hamburgs—

Then he focused on the grill and stools of the establishment.
"Wooden drawers" holding loaves of bread. Countermen with "big red
drink noses." Flip the page and continue: the coffee is served in "white
porcelain mugs." An old pot is filled with a "half-inch of black fat." He
continues with fresh impressions on the next page:

the marble counter is
ancient, cracked, marked,
carved, and under it is
the old wood counter
of late 20's, early
30's, which had come
to look like the bottoms
of old courtroom benches
only with knifemarks
& scars & something suggesting decades of delicious

greasy food. Ah![28]

Having seized his bounty, Jack continued walking on the New York streets. He sketched his impressions, how it made him feel to walk into a diner, like those he remembered in Lowell where his father once ate: "Makes the guts of men curl in October. . . . " This was his answer. Writing of America as a whole did not suffice. America wasn't just seen from highways, mountain passes, or the Western plains. It was there in diners, old vaudeville theaters, and dime-store cafeterias with their desserts and deli meat. It was a lost America, swallowed by emerging consumerism and gentrification. Neal first saw it when he came to New York with Luanne in '47. Neal was Jack's avatar for America. These sketches were Jack's "Visions of Neal." But were they Jack's visions of Neal, or Neal's visions of America? They can be read either way. It was Jack's "vertical study" of the road. It was the land of "young American hipsters." He excitedly wrote Neal, floundering for a sympathetic eye that could dig where his mind was at: "I'm sending you these 3 now-typed-up-revised pages of my re-writing ROAD . . . to show you that 'Dean Pomeray' is a vision—and also my finally-at-last-found style & hope; since writing that I've come up with even greater complicated sentences & VISIONS. . . . "[29]

Almost despite editors and publishers, Jack continued with this unconventional prose. It lent itself well to spontaneity. By absorbing commonalities and shedding light upon them, he was transmuting them with his artistic sensibility. He blazed through each page, not with a character study of Cassady, but of New York City scenes, cathedrals, women, masturbation in public toilets, stained sidewalks, rank weeds between sidewalk cracks, the bottom of the world. It was his "metaphysical study" of America. This was his road novel, and once it was completed, Jack considered it his masterpiece. He titled it *Visions of Cody*.

Scattered about what to do next, he had to earn cash. His current writing would not guarantee a book contract. He wrote Neal about a brakeman's position on the railroad. His current earnings[30] from script synopsizing were not enough. He had to pay $5 a week to Joan and $10 a week to his mother. Also, Gabe wanted to leave New York and live with the Blakes to be closer to her grandson. Jack had no money left to buy a coat for the winter.

On the Road was typed onto separate pages. Begrudgingly, he had to commodify it for publishers (he would retype it twice between 1951 and 1952). He made annotations, added typesetting suggestions, crossed out passages, and proposed textual insertions. Jack realized that the vast pendulum swing of his trips crisscrossing across the country had to be brought into tighter focus so as not to discombobulate his readers.

Rewriting the April 1951 draft was not where Jack's heart and soul were at. Sketching had hit Jack "full force." The technique only required no more than fifteen minutes of a sketch. At first, he thought they were the scribblings of an insane person. Upon re-reading them the next day, they read as masterful prose. He suggested to Allen that he should choose selections from his notebook, type them up, and send them to his publishing contact named Carl Solomon. However, Allen was not impressed. He failed to see what Jack was attempting. None of it seemed publishable. The notebooks wrought several visions at once. They contained no narrative. No characterization. They were vivid yet unassembled prose descriptions. Yet, Jack was still encouraged, and through his agent, Rae Everitt, he contacted Solomon himself. Solomon was an editor for publisher Aaron A. Wyn, who edited and published pulp paperbacks. Maybe *On the Road* could serve his readership? Jack typed one thousand words to show Solomon on behalf of Wyn how it could be done. Based on what he offered, Solomon promised an advance of $1,000. Upon signing, Jack would receive $250. However, the signing never took place. Jack was hesitant to return to *On the Road*. He wanted to show them instead some prose sketches he had written and not what he had promised.

On November 8, Jack showed Carl Solomon his latest writings. Solomon advised Jack to write a thorough synopsis for his uncle to read. Wyn wanted to see the entire novel arc.

Then he withdrew his offer.

And then Joan was back on Jack's case.

Jack went on a three-day drinking binge. He told Allen that he had no interest in God. Later, after Allen and his girlfriend, Dusty Moreland, fell asleep, Jack shit in his shorts. He slipped into a severe depression.

Advance or no advance, "the unspeakable visions of the individual," would deal only with "the source of the mind." It would become one of his central tenets for "Belief and Technique for Modern Prose": "write what you want bottomless from bottom of mind." He had "no time for poetry but to tell exactly what it is. . . . " Rather than reassess his publishing chances, Jack continued his writing. Except, it was no longer an experiment. It was a proven method. He "tranced fixation upon an object before me." At 4:00 a.m. he sketched a bakery window and a "bleak rectory" across the street and was frightened yet jubilant at the results.

The next day, Jack sketched people passing by Stewart's Cafeteria at 89 Christopher Street in the Village. However, his despondency made this a miserable outing. He was irritable, empty, and lost. He lost an assigned script from Twentieth Century-Fox in the subway. He could not sleep. He was sore from phlebitis. Constipated. He lacked money for a haircut.

By mid-November, Jack had decided to write his "Neal book" without linearity. A "dream prophecy." He sketched Saint Patrick's Cathedral from a pew. He was unshaven and disoriented: "I'm lost but my work is found." He took a long midnight stroll through Queens. Gabe was concerned. She encouraged him to go to sea, thinking it might do them both good.

Jack borrowed $60 from Henri Cru, who was to arrange another gig on a merchant ship. He bought a bus ticket. A week later, Jack was in Southern California. In San Pedro, he missed the boat and then went to San Francisco and knocked on Neal's door.

Neal showed Jack his attic room. He had free reign over the rest of the house. Neal even offered him Carolyn like a piece of meat, which Jack accepted. He bedded her by his count at least thirty times. In return, Jack helped Neal to finish *The First Third*. In return, Neal got him a railroad job. He hauled mailbags into boxcars. It was long, arduous work. His muscles were tired. He was annoyed. The men called him "college boy" and "Jack Carraway."

Neal bought a reel-to-reel recorder, and they read to each other. Sometimes Carolyn joined in. Once Jack replayed the tapes, he typed "completely verbatim" from what he heard. In total, Jack had transcribed five nights of rabid conversations.

In the attic space, Jack typed from his *Visions of Neal* notebooks through the winter and into the spring of 1952. His stay was not without problems.

In Carolyn's memoir, *Off the Road: My Years with Cassady, Kerouac, and Ginsberg*, she tells a story about Neal's birthday. She baked a cake and cooked him a steak dinner. Neal unwrapped some gifts. However, they were puzzled by Jack's absence. After the celebration, the children went to bed, as did Neal and Carolyn. Later, the phone rang eight feet from the bed. Neal sprang up to answer it, as he often did. Sometimes he received late-night phone calls from the railroad. But, it was Jack. Neal told Carolyn that Jack was drunk and in jail and needed to be bailed out. Carolyn paced the house restlessly and in pain from an attack of Bell's palsy that had erupted earlier that day. Neal did not return.

The following day, after the children woke and Carolyn had taken care of their needs, she washed her hair. While rolling her hair under a towel, she noticed Neal going up the stairs to the attic with Jack, who was escorting a young woman. Appalled, she followed Neal into the kitchen and asked where he had been. Neal admitted that Jack had not been in jail. The lie had been Jack's drunken way of getting Neal out of the house. Carolyn insisted that Neal should return upstairs and evict the strange woman. A few minutes later, Neal, Jack, and the woman came down the attic stairs to pass through the Cassadys' bedroom. The woman suddenly lunged at Carolyn. She picked up Neal's keys and insisted on being driven home.

On their return, Jack sheepishly returned to the attic and did not come down for over a day. Carolyn's concern overrode her anger. During the last few months, and at Neal's urging, Carolyn and Jack's platonic relationship continued to be mainly sexual. Before long, Neal became uncommunicative. Although Carolyn was delighted with Jack's attention, the open affair made Jack a part of an increasingly awkward triangle. It was time to leave. He wrote Burroughs in the spring of 1952, asking if he could visit. Lonely for companionship, Burroughs consented.

On February 16, 1952, Jack's daughter was born. Joan named her Janet Michelle Kerouac. Jack firmly denied paternity. Gabe and Caroline also believed that Joan's infidelity had conceived the child.

* * *

Neal dropped Jack off in Sonora, Arizona, where he hopped the wire fence over to Mexico. He bought bus tickets south. On the bus, the passengers sat on wooden benches on both sides. Some of them had animals. Others put their children on the roof. The long passage drove through starlit deserts and dense jungles; the bus crossed a shallow river. Water surged to the wheel-tops. In Jack's enthusiastic assessment, it was a "tremendous journey."

From his journey through Mexico, he wrote a short travel piece, "Mexico Fellaheen," that would be published as part of a collection of travel stories titled *Lonesome Traveler* (1960). He swallowed a pellet of opium. The Mexican darkness loomed strange and hot. Grilled tortillas. Little pigs: "And O the holy sea of Mazatlan and the great red plain of eve with burros and aznos and red and brown horses and green cactus pulque."

While there, he experienced an epiphany:

"I pray on my knees so long, looking up sideways at my Christ, I suddenly wake up in a trance in the church with my knees aching and a sudden realization that I've been listening to a profound buzz in my ears that permeates throughout the church and throughout my ears and head and throughout the universe, the intrinsic silence of Purity (which is Divine). I sit in the pew quietly, rubbing my knees, the silence is roaring."[31]

After Joan's death and Bill's release on bail, Bill had remained under suspicion by the Mexican authorities. If the ballistics experts found any evidence of foul play, he could face considerable prison time. One alternative was to flee. The other possibility was to be forcibly deported to the United States. He warned Jack not to roll any marijuana cigarettes in his presence lest he risk another arrest.

Bill spent most of his time typing his second novel, *Queer*. He may have thought—as Neal did when writing his autobiography—that Jack's experience as a novelist could shape his manuscript into something publishable. He noted a dispirited air about Jack and rightfully assumed that it stemmed partly from the rejection of his writing. Even Allen remained stoic that Jack was not being serious about his work. In July 1952, Allen wrote to Neal, "He was not experimenting and exploring in new deep form, he was purposely just screwing around as if anything he did, no matter what he did, was O.K."

He called *Visions of Neal* a "holy mess":

"It's great all right but he did everything he could to fuck it up with a lot of meaningless bullshit I think, page after page of surrealist free association that don't make sense to anybody except someone who has blown Jack. I don't think it can be published anywhere, in its present state. I think this is an awful hang-up for everyone concerned—he must be tired too—but that's how it stands. Your tape conversations were good reading, so I could hear what was happening out there—but he put it in entire and seemingly un-unified it so it just skips back and forth and touches on things momentarily and refers to events nowhere else in the book; and finally it appears to objective eye so diffuse and disorganized—which it is, on purpose—that it just don't make."[32]

Allen wrote Jack with a total breakdown of his typescript before loaning it to John Clellon Holmes. He informed Jack that the book "just drags itself exhausted over the goal line of meaning to someone else." In short, there was little he could do to sell it to anybody. He was begging Jack to budge, just a little, to make it an easier sell.[33]

Jack replied by comparing *Visions of Neal* to *Ulysses*. He would allow no editor to cut the story up. "Intelligibility" didn't figure into Kerouac's grand design; he knew that his current writing would define him as a serious artist.

Jack liked to walk around Mexico City after dark. He ventured as far as the slum district and encountered packs of vicious dogs. Sewer rats slinked between trash cans. He went into the sex worker district and paid a single peso for a teenage prostitute named Luz and accompanied her to a low-ceilinged hovel. He waited there as another woman played with the penis of a Chinese man. Afterward, Jack and Luz lay on a curtained-off cot where he enjoyed his purchase.

Jack went with Bill into the mountains of Tenancingo with "Old Dave" Tercero and Esperanza Villanueva to attend a Mexican fiesta. Bill shot at targets with his .38 Colt. Jack and Bill parted for an hour before meeting in Tenancingo. They went to the Ballet Mexicana and had a Turkish bath. Bill was everything a host could be, gracious and willing to spend his time and knowledge on Jack. In return, Jack helped type pages for Bill's novel *Queer*. Jack was handwriting *Doctor Sax*. The synthesis of Mexico City and Lowell in his imagination invigorated the story. Following Allen's advice, Bill urged Jack to focus only on his road chronicles and not to be distracted by any other books. Only then, he felt, would Jack be published again.

But Jack could not be deterred. Excitedly, he wrote John Clellon Holmes that he was riding a new crest of fervent creation. His "discovery," which began in December 1951, was an explosion of "wild form," taking him beyond mere description into "revealed prose." His sketching technique freed him from the narrative constraints of linear form. He had made it, he thought. He only had to get stoned and write.[34]

Jack sat on Burroughs's toilet, rolled some bombs, and wrote *Doctor Sax*. He was high. Hallucinating, almost. Lowell and Aztec Mexico swirled together into a diorama of myth and memory.

After a while, Bill became annoyed by Jack's rabid food consumption and incessant drug abuse. He had overstayed his welcome. Writing to Allen, Bill had made his position clear on how he regarded Jack when they parted ways. Jack left owing Bill $20 that he promised to repay once he was home:

"I have never had a more inconsiderate and selfish guest under my roof. I certainly would not consider making any jungle expeditions with Jack. If I had not received the $180 I would have become a public charge."

Bill was shocked by Jack's behavior. He was on bail, and so the presence of narcotics on his premises posed a danger to his freedom: "I simply cannot get along with Jack." Bill thought that unless Jack underwent a "radical transformation," he would not see him again. Jack needed intervention beyond his scope and limited means. Jack was paranoid. If Bill was out of money, he could count on Jack to consume what was left. Jack got angry after Bill ate his half of the two pats of butter they had left: "If anyone asks [Jack] to do his part or to share on an equal basis, he thinks they are taking advantage of him. This is insane. He simply does not see the facts correctly."[35]

On Jack's final day in Mexico City, he went into a little colonial church called Santa María la Redonda in the barrio of Guerrero.[36] At its outskirts, low-income people were buried in its sanctified ground. Jack had been walking all over the town delivering packages and letters. He had eaten only fudge candy for breakfast. Now he was in the church, "contemplating the void," beneath the rotunda especially constructed in such a way to permit different lighting effects throughout the day. He sat on the floor enthralled by a colossal statue of crucified Christ. "Mon Jésu," he implored, "priez pour moi."[37]

He left Mexico on July 1 and thumbed to North Carolina with only $5 in his pocket by the time he reached Texas. He hitchhiked to Houston and met up with a drunken construction worker who invited Jack to shower in his hotel room. When Jack emerged still damp from the shower, he found the man nude on his stomach, "begging me to screw him." Jack left once the man started crying. Shortly after that, Jack was in North Carolina, where his mother and Nin nagged him for not having a job and taking such a wasteful trip.

Allen's stinging criticism[38] of *Visions of Neal* infuriated Kerouac, as did the lackluster reception by publishers of his "spontaneous prose pieces." Kerouac answered months later:

"My heart bleeds every time I look at *On the Road* . . . I see it now, why it is so great and why you hate it and what the world is . . . specifically what you are . . . and what you, Allen Ginsberg, are . . . a disbeliever, a hater, your giggles don't fool me, I see the snarl under it. . . . Go ahead and do what you like, I want peace with myself. . . . I shall certainly never find peace till I wash my hands completely of the dirty brush and stain of New York and everything that you and the city stand for . . . and everybody knows it."[39]

Nin and Gabe were confident that Jack would meet an untimely end in Mexico. They were suspicious of Bill. Gabe was alone in Richmond Hill. Caroline wrote Gabe on May 16 asking if she had heard from Jack:

"Well I don't suppose you've heard from Jack yet if you had you would have written. Where did he say he was going? Mexico City? Isn't that the city where Burroughs lives. Why don't you write him and see if he has seen Jack. Or write Cassady and ask him if he knows where Jack is located. Like you say no news is good news—but I know you're worried and nervous. You better watch the nerves too, cause if you don't stop worrying you're liable to get the paralysis back again. We can't have you alone and sick in N.Y."[40]

Caroline urged Gabe, once she heard from Jack, to go to Rocky Mount and get a job. She wanted Jack and Gabe with her so the family could be together again. Jack had not written his mother. Instead, his letters were written mainly to John Clellon Holmes, one of the few of his friends that understood what he was trying to achieve:

"I am starving to death. I have no more money, not one red cent. I weigh 158 lbs. Instead of 170. Bill thinks I am mad at him because I was writing when he got up and retired to the bathroom with my tea and pencil pads, so he's gone, has only money, nothing to eat in his house, it's cold. . . . I sit here yearning to get back to food and drink and regular people."[41]

Miserably, he assessed his life's progress thus far and again wrote to Holmes, this time evaluating his situation more gravely. For the first time, he reconsidered his responsibility for fathering Jan:

"What have I got? I'm 30 years old, broke, my wife hates me and is trying to have me jailed, I have a daughter I'll never see, my mother after all this time and work and worry and hopes is still working her ass off in a shoe shop; I have not a cent in my pocket for a decent whore."[42]

As Jack faced his realities—his indigence, unpublished books, the failure of *The Town and the City*—he predicted a dire outcome if something did not change soon. As if to taunt his sour luck, he wrote even more experimentally in the coming years. His inner resolve was a brutal taskmaster.

Jack wrote to Carolyn in June complaining of his poverty: his sea bag had a hole in it; his raincoat was stolen; he had 60 cents to his name; and, as usual, he thought that he was getting "fucked" by his publisher. He was convinced that there was a conspiracy of silence in New York against him.

He wrote Carolyn knew there was no future between them after she had written to inform him that Neal was bothered by her and Jack's physical relations: "he has been very hurt by my loving you and very jealous."[43] Carolyn wanted Jack close to her, but she didn't know how to "play the game." She was of two worlds: one with Neal, the other with Jack. She had to force herself to "resist delicious dreams" with him. She pleaded with him not to stop corresponding despite the awkward manner in which he left.[44] Jack replied that "eternity" was the only thing on his mind and encouraged them all to come to Mexico. He could continue helping Neal with *The First Third*. This arrangement, in his view, could only yield positive results. He questioned Neal's feelings, that he was not actually "jealous" but "just didn't know what we expected him to do, and we didn't either." For Jack, there were no consequences except "life and death."[45]

Denigrating everything New York City stood for, Jack reduced his situation to an "almost humorous chronicle of a real dumb Lil Abner getting taken in by fat pigjaws." He lashed out at Giroux and Cassady, who he claimed had stolen a book from Giroux's office back in 1949. Such was the depth of his despair that he wrote Stella Sampas in December that he had been experiencing "long, dark depression with thoughts of suicide sometimes." He was hostile to New York: "The rich homosexual literati of New York at first offered me alluring scholarships and then withheld them when it became apparent that I wouldn't be famous—This includes my own editor, Robert Giroux."[46]

In Stella, Jack had a grounded and objective correspondent to whom he could open his heart completely. In return, she tolerated his mercurial temperament and rejoiced in his accomplishments. Stella was of a strong fiber having suffered many hardships. She was well-read and she was intelligent. To Jack, she epitomized the idealism of his youth.

Jack wrote Carl Solomon in August 1952, comparing his present situation with those of Dreiser, Hemingway, and Joyce, all of whom had works deemed "unprintable." He derided Solomon's hasty readings and remarked that he personally read difficult books like *Finnegans Wake*, *Under the Volcano*, and Marcus Goodrich's *Delilah* by understanding the writers' "intellect," "passion," and "mystery." Jack assured Solomon that *On the Road* would eventually find its publisher.

Furious still with Allen, Jack was also still jealous of Holmes's success with *Go*:

"Everybody knows he has no talent . . . and so what right has he, who knows nothing, to pass any kind of judgment on my book—He doesn't even have the right to surl in silence about it—His book stinks, and your book is only mediocre, and you all know it, and my book is great and will never be published. Beware of meeting me on the street in New York."

Despite the criticism, Jack was convinced of the worthiness of his writing method. He started a new series of notebooks (fifteen in total) that would be completed in 1957. He called these prose poems *Book of Sketches*.[47]

Neal wrote a letter of recommendation for Jack addressed to J. C. Clements, the captain of police in Rocky Mount. It was Jack's goal to secure a position as a brakeman with the local railroad. Neal wrote that "no man has all the superlative virtues I seem to be attributing to Mr. Kerouac, nonetheless, he is the only man I know into whose hands I could entrust the use of my saxophone, fountain pen or wife and would rest assured that they were honorably and properly taken care of."[48] Despite Cassady's recommendation, Jack was duly passed over. Financially strapped, he seemed to owe money everywhere. He put the finishing touches on *Doctor Sax* and put it and some clothes and rations into his seabag and left North Carolina. He was going west to San Jose where Cassady had arranged a job as a brakeman for the Southern Pacific. The Cassadys had moved from Russian Hill to a rented one-story house in San Jose with nut and fruit trees on the front lawn. Neal wanted Jack to live there. After Jack left, he missed Neal's letter with instructions on how to beat a new Southern Pacific ruling prohibiting the hiring of recruits over thirty years old. Without this news, Jack left feeling optimistic, hoping once again for financial stability.

CHAPTER ELEVEN

The Shrouded Traveler

CAROLINE WROTE GABE WONDERING IF JACK HAD MADE IT TO SAN
Francisco: "Five dollars was mighty small money for such a long trip."[1]

The night before, Jack wrote his mother explaining that he needed to
roam. Nin could not understand how he could do so without money or
a job, "at least have enough money to eat properly and try to take care of
one's health. If he keeps up that pace, he'll ruin his inside completely. I
don't imagine he'll be sensible about anything he does."[2]

Jack stopped in Denver. From there he mailed a postcard to Neal.
After receiving it, Neal posted an extremely urgent telegram with $25
from his pocket so that Jack could arrive ahead of Southern Pacific's
deadline. Thrilled to have him back in their home, Carolyn prepared
a room. Days later, Jack had reached the West Coast. He called Neal
from San Francisco. Neal arranged passage on the *Zephyr* (nicknamed
the "Zipper" for its barreling, straight-through passage to Los Angeles
and back). Neal and Carolyn drove their Model-A Ford to the train
yard to pick him up. Leaving his wife to sit alone, Neal left the car to
meet Jack. After waiting a few minutes, she could see their two familiar
outlines illuminated by the glare of the train light. Jack got into the car,
and Carolyn immediately sensed his warm presence next to her. Because
Neal had to work in Watsonville that evening, Jack was alone with her on
his first night back. After taking a hot bath, he met Carolyn in his attic
bed. When they finished, she returned to her own bed. Her rule was that,
should one of her children wake during the night, she should be found
in her own bed.

Jack played with the children the next day at a nearby ball field. Carolyn noticed how relaxed he was with them. Around adults, Jack was self-conscious and had to rely on alcohol to be convivial. Around children, he became childlike. One of them told him that "God is Pooh Bear" and he notated it in his notebook for later use.

Jack's status as a trainee lasted for only two weeks. Each night, Neal and Carolyn encouraged him to return to his training, but he was tired of the process. Nonetheless, Jack stuck it out, and after completing the training, he faithfully showed up for work. It took all of Neal's enthusiasm and Carolyn's persuasion to make Jack stick it out. For more reasons than pay, Jack had other motives for staying. He was thrilled to dress like Neal, to physically experience his friend's occupation from the inside looking out. It inspired new material to write about. Squatting with the workers over their lunch pails and kerosene lanterns caused him to become privy to their world. The sounds and sights of the railroad was authentic. However, he soon discovered that writing about railroads was more appealing than doing the actual work. His sturdy frame, more suited for football than for chasing railroad cars, was not advantageous when he had to rely on swiftness to execute the job correctly. There was a problem with his legs, a layover from his phlebitis attacks that left him prone to long spells of discomfort. Besides, he was discontented and wanted to return to Mexico.

Then he felt unwanted again.

Neal's assessment of Jack became harsh. He did not like that Jack wanted to be alone with Carolyn. He refused to engage in a three way. Carolyn felt the same. In a letter to Allen, Neal called Jack out on it:

"Jack's the lonely fucker of Carolyn, who blows him; he was almost capable of going 3 ways, but hope for that is about given up since he's so morose all he talks of now is moving from up here to way down there on skid row 3rd street, to be near work (he brakie now too) and write."[3]

Jack revealed to John Clellon Holmes that he did not like Neal anymore. Jack called Neal an "asshole." He was through being conned by Neal, though the con jobs were symbiotic. Through Neal, Jack had free room, board, and Carolyn.[4]

These multiple complications prompted Jack to make good on his promise to move to Skid Row. Relieved and fed up, Neal drove him to San Francisco, where Jack took to a seedy flophouse on the corner of Third Street and Howard near Little Harlem. Jack compared himself to the winos and hoboes in the alleys and doorways. To Holmes, Jack declared himself to be a "true hobo" who lived like an "indian." Neal told Jack that people who lived on Skid Row were haters of life. Jack, limping along the Row, tried making eye contact with these haters of life. Four transients refused to oblige him, avoiding eye contact from the dark swarthy stranger limping along with a sea bag on his back. It was a cold hostile world for all of them.

Jack was able to live up to the image of being one with them when he was laid off from the railroad that December. His brakeman job, which he had been working for seven days a week, had earned him $600 monthly. His frugality made that income last. His cold hotel room cost him $4.20 a night.[5]

The flophouse's shabby hallways and thin walls did not bother him. He dug the sordid scenery for the prose sketches he was writing. He notated his expenditures: 35 cents for a fifth of wine, 20 cents for coffee, and 25 cents for breakfast (two eggs with toast, coffee, and oatmeal). Despite his careful budgeting, he still went hungry. The misery of it wasn't squandered; it made for excellent poetry. Evoking Mallarmé's dictum that poetry was a language of a state of crisis, he wrote:

> The rat of hunger
> Eats at your belly,
> then dies &'s left
> to rot & bloat there.[6]

Jack made entries in his notebook of sketches. He wrote little "pomes." His drug of choice was cheap wine. He often joined the Third Street winos to drink from their fifth bottles of Tokay. On that rough high Jack wrote a spontaneous prose piece titled "October in the Railroad Earth," a meditation of the railroad, the Little Harlem streets, and Southern Pacific train yards:

"The sweet flesh intermingling, the flowing blood wine dry husk leaf bepiled earth with the hard iron passages going over, the engine's saying K RRRROOO AAAWWOOOO and the crossing it's ye famous Krrot Krroot Krroo ooooaaaawwww Kroot—."[7]

This writing method permitted him to record every impression and sensation as it struck him. His keen senses caught the sounds of all people, young and old, rich and poor, Black, Indian, white, Mexican, and Chinese. Jack juxtaposed hobo conversations alongside manual laborers. "Neverthefuckingless" merged the words exactly as they sounded to him; "your" was changed to "yr"; "nothing" to "nathing"; "Mom" to "Mam"; "the" to "de." Kerouac evoked the Western lexicon as accurately as Faulkner's Mississippi dialect in his Yoknapatawpha stories. Then there were train sounds, slamming boxcars, and klaxon horns written out in the spirit of *Finnegans Wake*. Most tellingly, "October in the Railroad Earth" became Jack's first complete, mature work written in spontaneous prose. It is also the first not steeped in the spirit of Neal Cassady or Lowell.

One day Jack had fallen asleep on his ratty couch. He woke; Neal was standing over him urging him back to his home. Short on cash, Jack obliged. He was soon back in his makeshift bed and Carolyn's warm embrace. It was a short stay. Neal was restless again. He wanted to drive Jack to Mexico.

Jack took him up on his offer.

* * *

It was late fall 1952. Neal sped down to Mexico through San Diego and Yuma, Arizona, with Jack nervously sitting in the passenger side of his "gray ghost Nash." Jack tried to drive for eight miles but was unable to properly work the clutch. Neal promised that he would not touch any woman while he was in Mexico. When he reached Mexico City on December 2, Neal sat in the car outside of Burroughs's place. He wrote Carolyn by the light of his brakeman's lantern.[8]

Neal bought some marijuana and left. In Mexico City, Bill's life had become a shambles. After the arrest of his lawyer for shooting a boy in the leg, Bill's bond was increased beyond his means. Not wishing to be imprisoned, Bill jumped bail and fled from Panama to Rio de Janeiro shortly before Jack arrived. Jack was alone and assumed residence on Bill's rooftop at 210 Orizaba. He adjusted to his preferred simple lifestyle. From this vantage point, he could observe the people and the "Mexico Thieves Market." With his familiarity with Spengler, Jack saw them as not only genuine denizens of their country, but of the world.

Jack swallowed Benzedrine and roamed the streets alone. Burroughs would not have him because he was already having a guest over and perhaps was still stung by Jack's behavior the last time Jack visited. Garver would not let him sleep on his couch. Jack wrote into a notebook:

"Okay, I may be a mooching hipster—I paid for everything but not everything like that peso and a half 18 cents tonight for the benny tube. But a man has no friends. I have the literary illusion that B. likes me because once we talked about books & wrote books together,—Well screw it up his ass, I'll go live by myself & wont bother nobody. Of course—N. put me out of the car into B's, & B. put me into the street, & now I'm really alone."[9]

Jack felt dejected, unwanted, and lost his "sense of reality." The darkness swirled in the light of flickering kerosene lanterns. He was alone in an alien swirlscape of poverty and sickness. He had nowhere to go. Burroughs had company. Garver had denied him his couch: "Everything's already happening, we're only waiting to die." He was pinged by misery. He thought of his mother. His childhood:

"Here I was in baggy pants, at the end of the road, the down dark road down to further dark roads down there, below, all of it friendless—like a streetlight in Bayshore Frisco, friendless. Not very inviting the world. I flew along like a bat and I suddenly began to speak with my mother & to hear her voice counselling, berating, & as always, consoling me in the end, the throatchoking end when you want more of salvation & eternity than you were made to carry, but you want to cry because tho you're lost you still love love."[10]

He could hear his mother speaking as clearly as if she were next to him:

"'Ti Jean,' she said, up in the darn trees near Insurgentes, as quiet middleclass Mexican fathers & daughters came in & out of chocolate store beneath my feet, 'poor fool, there you are caught again. You never know what to do, or do it right. You saved yrself a little money to come to Mexico to write your book, youve been here 5 days, and you're still caught at B's, you havent moved, youve done nothing—drunk, smoking drugs—and there you are in the street all dirty for five days, sleeping in yr. clothes—.'"[11]

Jack's notes, "Benzedrine Vision," spilled out his anguish over eighty-four pages with a yearning to be freed at last from his suffering. In the same notebook, Kerouac wrote "Memoirs of a Bebopper." Writer Ben Giamo explains that Jack was walking in his homeless state in the city streets, and "begins to lose his sense of reality, soon becoming a pitiable homeless figure in the Mexican night":

"In this state, he has a vision of his mother, offering consolation and help. The bebopper, overcome with weariness and exhaustion, eventually finds his lair and, with a flimsy roof over his head, the rain of disturbing thoughts turns into two visions. The first vision is of heaven, in which 'everyone was simply a level higher than they are on earth,' and the second is one of madness, which he witnesses when looking at his reflection in the mirror."[12]

Another notebook from this period and later reworked into a larger novella is "Mary Carney" and then, at publication, *Maggie Cassidy*. In the same notebook, Kerouac wrote what he originally titled *The Happy Truth*, crossed it out, and titled it *The Blessedness Surely to Be Believed* (which would evolve into *The Scripture of the Golden Eternity*). He began with a pencil-written page and then crossed it out entirely before continuing.

"This immeasurable happiness of your original perfection is already there because it has always been there. You've been like a person who thought north was south, and south was north, and was going exactly the wrong way. You believed in the absolute realness of the circumstances that contributed to your unhappiness without realizing absolutely equally that they were as real as they were unreal which would have given you pause to reconsider the scenes of your grief. There is a blessedness surely to be believed."[13]

Despite his suffering, Jack was peering through his misery into the happiness that could be had in life: "Under stress of harsh circumstances smile and think deeply, there is a sudden center of enlightenment that has nothing to do with what you're experiencing in life."[14] On the verge of delving into Buddhism, Jack reigns in his Catholicism to achieve Original Essence, or what he called the "Sea of Mind." The "Blessedness Surely to be Believed" preaches that we are all united through suffering and joy.

He also wrote *The Ecstasy of Life and Death* and *The Happy Truth*. The latter was translated from a piece originally written in French. This translation, completed over six days from December 16–21, concerned the relationships between a wino named Dean Pomeroy, his son Dean Pomeroy Jr., and a stepson named Rolfe Glendiver. Like much of his work, it was set in October. As with his road novel, the characters were heading east from Denver to New York in a Model-T Ford. The stepson, Rolfe, was a cowboy from Gunnison, Colorado, who worked at the Robeson Bar Ranch breaking broncos and castrating bulls. Like Kerouac, Rolfe had blue eyes and a movie-star-handsome face and was preoccupied with his thoughts. Rolfe's kin back home did not understand him. Dean Pomeroy Sr., modeled after Neal Cassady's father, was an old wino carrying a bottle of port and stumbling around Larimer Street in Denver. Together, all three meet "Old Bull Balloon," a composite character based on W. C. Fields and William S. Burroughs about whom Kerouac wrote at greater length in a French novella of forty thousand words. Unlike his other writing, *The Happy Truth* was written in a linear structure. The French novella *Old Bull Balloon* was written in five days. As described in a letter to Neal, it featured Neal and Kerouac as children in 1935 and was much like *The Happy Truth* in both setting and narrative. Against the noisy backdrop of Chinatown, they meet Old Bull Balloon. With their fathers and some hot blondes for company, the two boys take off in a Model-T for an adventure that ultimately was planned to tie *On the Road* with *Visions of Cody*. Jack left the piece untranslated.

Life was easygoing in Mexico, though Jack was lonely. He wrote Carolyn, wishing she could join him. To pass the time, he called upon Bill's junkie acquaintance, Bill Garver. But even Garver did not plan to stay in Mexico City for long. Kerouac's $12-a-month, two-room apartment was tiny. He decorated it with handmade native pottery sold from street stalls. A peasant woman did his laundry. He ate glistening oysters fried in butter for 35 cents and chased them down with cold Chianti.

In the morning he ate steak and eggs for 30 cents. It was just what he wanted, living in luxury for next to nothing. Also, he had stocked up on an array of narcotics despite the threat of the Mexican government and the depressing junkies with festering sores skulking through the ghetto.

During this time, recipients of Jack's letters were reading them under his chosen moniker, "Señor Jean Levesque," a combination of his first name (in French) and his mother's maiden name.

Jack returned home for Christmas. During the holiday, he stayed with friends in New York. Although he was glad to see them, Jack had moved on. Past talks of the New Vision, of goofing and smashing bottles with Lucien, and all-night rap sessions were in the past. Each poet was set to their respective destinies.

* * *

On January 12, 1953, Jack returned to his adolescent Lowell years to focus on his first true love, Mary Carney. He already had writing that he had started in Mexico. Now he wanted to expand it into a novel which he was writing into several notebooks. There is a printed line separating the notebook page into two columns. Jack wrote from the left column up to the right, and continued page after page over five notebooks. He begins in English and reverts to Canadian French to tell his story: "In winter-night Billerica street dismal, the grounds frozen cold, the ruts and pockholes have ice, thin snow slides over the jagged slack cracks. The river is frozen to stolidity." Within the scope of the Duluoz chronology, the "Mary" project continues where *Doctor Sax* leaves off in Pawtucketville. While *Doctor Sax* was narrated through flashes of memory and dream, *Maggie Cassidy* is recollected via crystal-clear imagery which embellishes Jack's romantic reveries. Kerouac dispensed with his sketching style in favor of a straightforward narrative.[15]

In February 1953, Jack joined famed editor Malcolm Cowley (representing Viking) for lunch to discuss his books. Though Ace was interested in publishing him, Kerouac sensed that their interest was lackluster and was hopeful that Cowley would have opened more doors for him. But Cowley had to agree; he felt that all of Jack's latest work required extensive revision. For example, *Doctor Sax* may have earned Kerouac upwards to $50,000 if he would only excise the fantasy portions. However, Jack resisted Cowley's advice to write a bildungsroman narrative, preferring to wait out the next tide. Kerouac felt that if William Faulkner had written *Doctor Sax*, it would have been published even if it was a critical and commercial failure. Cowley retorted that if Viking opted to publish it, they would indeed do so at a loss. Faulkner, after winning a Nobel Prize in 1949, had earned his clout. Kerouac only had a single published novel, a definite commercial failure, to make his case.

Ace had firmly rejected *Springtime Mary*. It was too bland. Too juvenile. *Springtime Mary* wasn't a book about juvenile delinquents as Ace wanted, but a story of a lovesick teenager whose love remains unrequited. There was no money in romantic nostalgia. In fact, none of Jack's writings were selected for publication. Allen mailed Jack a draft of a press release for Ace Books' imminent publication of Burroughs's *Junky* (written by "William Lee"), a novel about a drug addict which was more to their liking because it catered to their young demographic. Jack denied Ace Books permission to use his name in the book. He also prohibited the use of his name for any publicity purposes if his book made reference to drugs. If Burroughs's real name could be concealed with a pseudonym, then he had no reason to permit his own name to be associated with such a book.

Jack was resisting *any* association with his Beat contemporaries. As he came into his own, he had less need for them. He resented that his publishing prospects were tainted by the belief in some circles that he was heavily into drugs. He believed that his own agent thought he was a "dope addict." Gabe advised Jack to drop his friends and start off new. Besides protecting his name and reputation (nascent as it was), he was also trying to avoid the possibility of gaining the attention of Joan Haverty or her lawyer.

Then, Neal was in touch. He had an offer for Jack to return to the railroad. He could live at their home again. Carolyn was uncertain whether Jack's presence would lessen Neil's estrangement or worsen it. That spring Neal had become injured as he was setting the brake on a boxcar. The car had collided with a bumper and threw him from the roof. He landed on the toe of his boot. Neal's foot bent backward. He broke the bones of his ankle and foot. He was hospitalized, and his foot was placed into a cast. He faced lengthy physical therapy. For now, he had to sit with his leg elevated to ease the pressure from his healing bones. When Jack arrived, he decided against staying with them. Neal was still in the hospital. Jack felt awkward staying alone with Carolyn. Instead, he rented a $6-a-week hotel room in San Luis Obispo.

His California stay was for practical reasons: he needed to earn money to take him through the next phase of his journey. He wanted to move his mother to New York. Caroline had her own problems with Paul and wanted Gabe, who often interfered with their squabbles, to live with Jack. Jack wrote his mother that he hoped to have earned $2,000 by Christmas. For now, he itemized every purchase he made through April with the efficiency of an accountant. A coffee with cream: 30 cents. Rent: 90 cents. Groceries with a steak: $2.10. He could write something. Anything. Maybe sell to magazines. Dourly, he wrote: "But why write narrative when what makes you mad is that Giroux changed T & C from a great poem into a publishable novel?" He could keep sketching, but he now felt it was not "artistically absorbing" enough: "like making jerky or building a fire or writing a Dean Pomeray in the Poolhalls or sketching from the mad mind itself." He was undecided. He had to "get away from 'myself' into a great epic poem of America." Just the freedom of writing was no longer enough: "my life so lonely & empty without someone to love & lay & without a work to surpass myself with, that I have nothing to write about even in the first clear joy of morning." Maybe, he thought, he could buy a trailer in San Luis Obispo and move his mother in, if he played his cards right.[16]

Jack cooked food on a hot plate in his little room and gazed dreamily at the California mountains. Work was within short walking distance. At night he slept soundly. He felt good. Revitalized. The move back west brought him back to life. New York had worn him down. It made him more depressed than usual. Jack was not fond of San Luis Obispo, preferring San Francisco. At a loss for either, he wondered how it would be to live as a roaming ascetic. Or maybe he could live like John the Baptist, roaming in a robe eating milk and honey. Or, he could go back to Mexico. He listed off his life decisions:

Get rid of pride

Get rid of sorrow

Mix with the people

Go among the people

The Fellaheen not the American Bourgeois middle-class world of frustration, sex, neurosis, not the Catholic French Canadian European world—The People—Indians, Arabs, the Fellaheen in country, village, or city streets—an essential world. . . . [17]

He should not care if the other men laughed at him as they did at the railroad, he could just challenge them: "Fuck, drink, be lazy, roam, do nothing . . . Get out of America for good, it's a Culture holding you, not Life. Go to the People of No Good & Evil—of No Culture no prophets—nothing but essential politics & literature as tales of the people." He could live like Gauguin, he wrote, who lived among the "primitive fellaheen people."[18]

With some difficulty, he resumed writing. He had grown used to writing with drugs. Now he had neither Bennies nor pot. Without them, he was disinterested and uninspired. He felt alone. He regretted his refusal to live with Neal and Carolyn. If only Neal were there!

Then, he was tired of working full-time. The itch to write full-time and to hope for the best struck him again. He felt like life had sprung a trap on him. He was disenchanted. His prayers brought him no respite. He didn't even like books anymore. He doubted his convictions. He doubted himself. He was a "healthy man imitating an invalid—me imitating Gerard—men imitating Christ Cockless Christ—."[19]

Allen remarked to Neal that Jack should "lay down his wrath." He needed to reveal his true self and shine through "untroubled and tender." Yet, he was already doing that. Jack was alienating even his closest comrades.

All's I want'
Cunt when I want it

Rest when I want it
Food when I want it
Drink when I want it
Drugs when I want it
The rest is bullshit.[20]

At San Luis Obispo, he meditated in the grass of San Luis Creek. He heard stories from hoboes. He lay in the sun. He worried about where his soul was going and what to do about it. He no longer had any use for radios, televisions, newspapers, or education. He only wanted a "sombrero, a Mujer, goats, weed, & guitars."

Allen was pursuing Jack through the US postal system. He could not keep track of his address changes. Allen required Jack's approval for Allen as power of attorney. The forms needed to be signed before Allen could sell Jack's manuscripts (*Doctor Sax* and *Springtime Sixteen*—previously called *Springtime Mary*). According to Allen, Jack's agent wasn't even sure if he wanted to publish *Doctor Sax*. Sterling Lord demanded a note from Jack confirming his intentions. Nothing about anyone's professional dealings with Jack was easy. In Allen's estimate, Jack could publish all of his works if he only tried. However, Jack showed no sign of letting up. He was still exploring his "first thought—best thought" mode of composition. On May 11, 1953, he started *Book of Daydreams*. In his "Editorial Explanation of Various Techniques of the Duluoz Legend," Kerouac described *Daydreams* as a "prose description of daydreams, wish-dreams during waking hours, example: 'Wearing top hat with black cloak with red lining, with T. S. Eliot, walking into the premiere of DOCTOR SAX, through crowd of queers, handsome.'" Throughout the work, Jack interspersed passages about friends, a New Orleans prostitute, and Neal and Carolyn using experimental wordplay. In the notebook, he began:

"Neal & I are in Mexico City buying weed off a bunch of young Mexican 'court-dancer' queers—we're in our Hotel room like The Hunter Hotel about $10 peso a day fairly expensive with gray furniture & beds, 2 rooms, 2 baths but we're only there a week—just to get weed & gin & few Organo St whores—then boys are La Negra & his lover—La Negra 14 went out & got a kilo for 300 pesos—Neal is now rolling, blasting, turning everybody on, batting, talking, 'Dig these cats—think of their life on that old Organo St & all the shit of this crazy town.'"[21]

For Jack, daydreams, dreams, tics, and visions were his sole solace from depressing reality. He blamed God "for making my life so boring." There was drinking. Jack declared why he drank, confessing in his notebook, "Drink is good for love—good for music—let it be good for writing.—This drinking is my alternative to suicide & all that's left." He blamed nobody for his boredom. He blamed time. It dragged on hour after hour. He felt that he would rather commit suicide than be bored.[22]

Neal no longer had confidence in Jack or his writings. He felt betrayed that Jack had bailed on another job that required Neal's vouching to their employer. Jack quit the railroad in late May 1953 and signed on to the SS *William Carruthers*. Al Hinkle, who had visited Neal with Jack, went there alone one afternoon to tell Carolyn that Jack had gone to sea. Al Sublette, a mutual friend of Jack and Neal, had been with him on his last day ashore. They celebrated with an all-night bar crawl.

Jack woke with a start with barely enough time to make the ship. Hoisting his sea bag over his shoulder, he hurried to catch the "A" train across the bridge to the army base, where the ship was already turning its screws. Up the gangplank, Jack sprinted twelve minutes late. He was immediately assigned to the officers' pantry.

The vessel passed under the Golden Gate Bridge until the coastline was a thin wisp. In the officers' quarters, Jack wore a white jacket. He swallowed some Bennies smuggled in his knapsack. The sea had its customary boundless joy and freedom. However, the ship itself was "one vast new iron nightmare." As it steamed south, Jack glimpsed the Mexican coast. It passed by like another ship. The warm balmy air felt invigorating. It awakened a Melvillean passion. He wrote:

"The Loves came to New England in the summers and stayed in the old 10-room house, under pines. The backyard was a sandbank connecting them to the French Canadian Bretagnes who lived in a white frame cottage. That was how the socialite New York Love children grew up like brothers and sisters and had fates intertwined."[23]

The story falters. His handwriting is quick and sloppy as if he were jotting ideas between duties, or, the Bennies were making him jot his ideas down hastily. He wrote about two families: the Loves and the Bretagnes, an idea that seems to have vanished after this voyage. He continued with another approach: "Gaby Bretagne came home from work. It was Friday, a coolness had come into the air at 4 o'clock, high blue light of the supper universe was mixing with the low oranging sun. . . . "

Jack wrote "Gerard Avenue" and drew a page-high X across it. He did so for the following five pages and started anew:

"The mother brought breakfast to the helpless child: it was on a tray, steaming oatmeal, with milk, sugar, and buttered toast. The red sun synonymous with oatmeal time flooded the curtains & a corner of the room in golden pink—a moment almost sweet enuf to make rhapsodies sing in that rich & innocent heart who'd waited for the ritual with a nurturish profound & passionated care."[24]

And there, his story stopped. It was as if he were making preliminary stabs at writing a novel about Gerard but somehow could not bring himself to do it. Instead, he dashed out a quick poem titled "The Waves Are Chinese." There were some descriptions of the topside of the ship and another sketch of a sort titled "Gnashing Phantoms & Hot Ports."[25]

Jack calculated *Carruthers*'s progress. It was sailing at 350 miles per day toward Panama to pass Yucatán and the island of Cuba. Each day was structured by routine. A grapefruit every morning by the ship's rail. Porpoises dipping in and out of the warm ocean waters. The bow knifed the water in half through the open sea. He thought of how uselessly heavy rain drove into the jadestone-colored waters: "Tragic as driving rain on the sea." He turned it into a haiku, its message the same; one essence the same as another. We are all linked by a singular spirit. If there was a place to lose himself from the woes and worries of the world, this was it. He disembarked in New Orleans. His discharge date, June 23, 1953, left him a free man. He earned some money and experience to write a short story, "Slobs of the Kitchen Sea."[26]

On June 28 in Richmond Hill, Jack wrote some short reflective prose entitled "TICS"; a "tic" was a "vision suddenly of memory. The ideal, formal Tic, as for a *Book of Tics*, is one short and one longer sentence, generally about fifty words in all, the intro sentence and the explaining sentence."[27] On one page, he typed out several:

"A bunch of people sitting on a screened porch in Rosemont on some cool golden afternoon & there's a garden hose—children—I have a little girl friend—There is joy unrememberable, a dream of some kind of lost whatnot what tic recall it? I must find out what tics recall—what visions, how, how many, where—This is the book of Tics."

And:

"Cold Fall mornings with the sun shining in the yard of the St. Louis school, the pebbles—the pure vision of world beginning in my childhood brain then, so that even the black nuns with their fleshwhite faces and rimless glasses & weepy redrimmed eyes looked fresh and ever delightful."[28]

Tics, described elsewhere by Kerouac, are "involuntary shivers of memory" that acted for Jack like a flashbulb after-image, a sudden recollection. The memory resurfaces upon a visual or spoken cue. A dew drop on a verdant leaf oscillates as the wind stirs it. It differs from a sketch because it depends on memory instead of what is in front of him. It differs from a "Daydream" because it is not conjured from the subconscious as a fictional encounter but is an actual recollection from different points of his past. Though he had written "tics" in other notebooks, this attempt in his mother's apartment spans forty pages.

Life took on Jack's customary routines under the rule of Gabe. He avoided her incessant nagging by staying in his room and writing. If it was late, he lit his brakeman's lantern and wrote by that. When he tired of staying home, he went to Greenwich Village.

In the Village, he had made the acquaintance of a new woman, Alene Lee. She was unlike all of the other women he had known. She was young (about ten years Kerouac's junior) and beautiful. She was as intelligent, if not more, than any of the Beats. She would not be taken for a fool. She was Cherokee and African-American. She was a writer.

In Kerouac's depiction of this period in a novella titled *The Subterraneans*, Alene Lee is thinly veiled as Mardou Fox. Lee was a native New Yorker raised in poverty. She suffered the scourges of racism. In her hand, she writes:

"I began reading a great deal. I had never belonged to any group, I had no friends, my family was my enemy, and the neighbors with their incessant fighting during the summer nights made morning light become shame. I began to withdraw from the intimacy and familiarity of neighbors, and became more conscious of the world around me. I began comparing. And, I always came out second best. I envied everyone."[29]

Now she was living in the Paradise Alley section of the East Village in a tenement building located at the corner of East 11th and Avenue A. Burroughs was there with his South American loot, dried ayahuasca vines. Allen was, too. Jack had arrived on the scene after his trip, intending to help Bill type more of his pages. Bill also had letters he had mailed to Allen, which they would collate into manuscript form and ultimately publish.[30] Ultimately, Alene left Jack and their relationship failed. She remembered him as "insecure and paranoid to the point where if I went into the hall, he imagined I was sleeping with someone in the hall. If he was outside the door, I was in bed with someone." His paranoia may have been somewhat justified in the case of poet Gregory Corso, who had successfully wooed Alene. To Jack, it was a crisis, even though Alene did not take her relationship with him seriously. For all his amorous pursuits over her, Jack was left with nothing but the idea of a book.

That fall of 1953, Jack wrote his next book. He gathered enough from this brief fling to write autobiographical fiction. So much did he revere Alene that *The Subterraneans* centers on their relationship, a tribute paid to only three other women in his life (Gabrielle, Mary Carney, and Esperanza Villanueva). It was a neat multi-ethnic triumvirate revealing Jack's disregard for race. This did not bode well for Gabe, who enclosed in one of her letters to him a newspaper clipping about a subway rape. She scribbled on the clipping: "There's your damned niggers!" Her patience with Jack was conditional: "So you want to roam & leave—well don't you dare do anything that will dishonor your father's name!"[31]

From October 21–24, he typed the entire account of the Village Subterraneans. Benzedrine fueled his stamina at the typewriter. Bill admired Jack's athletic stamina and determination. Allen was impressed with the work, although he felt once again that Jack was deliberately thwarting any chance for success. Alene Lee also read it: "Jack showed me *The Subterraneans* probably four or five days after he wrote it. He sent me a telegram: 'Have soul surprise! Wait for me. See you Friday.' Like a child who was going to receive a magical gift, I waited." When Jack walked in, he sat down at the fireplace and handed her the manuscript. She started to read it and was immediately shocked by Kerouac's version of their time together:

"I could look at it one way and feel it was like a little boy bringing a decapitated rat to me and saying, 'Look, here's my present for you.' These were not the times I knew them and the people, except his friends, were not as I knew them."[32]

Jack offered to toss the manuscript into the flames but resisted his dramatic gesture.

* * *

Jack had experienced rejection. Now it was seeping into his dreams. In a dream of October 14, 1953, he was back in spectral Lowell. He was a boy. It was sleeting in Pawtucketville:

"The fine sleet white strengthens my belief in the unreality of the older 'snow dream' of Moody but the thinner (more believable therefore) realities of this one-Kid Gringas in the sad dusk has that same sharp and humangrieving reality I saw in the 'moonlight bum caps of Amsterdam' and many other dreams where figures stalk cleanly and sharp in soft gloom clouds of poor nap (H horror) brain."[33]

He was dream-haunted by Leo and Gerard and wrote isolated prose fragments without linearity or symbolic meaning into a notebook. For Jack, his dreams did not represent Freudian keys to his psyche. They were living pieces of the past, present, and future. They were "the core and kernel written on the awakening." In another dream, he returned to live with his father. He was "closer than ever" to him. They shared "profound absorptions." Leo was jobless and homeless, still living in Lowell. He was the Hooded Wayfarer. The Shrouded Traveler. In another, Leo ignored Jack in a Pawtucketville 1930s pool hall: "So different than he was in real life—in haunted life I think I see now his true soul—which is like mine—life means nothing to him—or I'm my father myself and this is me." His attitude toward dreams was that they were keystones to his neuroses. Much of what he had dreamed in the early 1940s was influenced by how he treated his parents. It could have been as slight as neglecting to say goodbye because he wanted to avoid the emotional strain of leaving them once again. However, the guilt stuck; it manifested into his dreams. Kerouac's published collection of dreams, *Book of Dreams*, is a document of guilt. He recorded a dream he had sometime in September 1943 aboard the SS *George B. Weems*. "I caught sight of my father's face coming toward me over the shoulder of the friend in front of me. He looked at me in a very pained way, and appeared weary with care and distraction"; a different dream: "I dreamed that my mother had died while pining for me, died in sufferance. . . . " Despite how they impinged his psyche, he thought of them as "stark beauty."[34]

The dejection felt by Jack over Alene Lee was profound. He felt suicidal. In a later essay written in Mexico City (August 19, 1955), Jack reveals that he was contemplating "painless suicides." He stared angrily at his wall feeling helpless to change his real life. Only through literature could he do it. He picked up a volume of Thoreau he had checked out of the library ("He is magnificent"). Jack walked through the late afternoon into the Long Island Railroad yards. He watched the shadow of youths dancing along boxcars under the starry night. He had a bottle of wine with him and drank it on some discarded railroad ties. He felt the "something from the outside" referenced by Thoreau, "the Other." He was gripped by his understanding. He understood Thoreau's reference to "Hindoos" and their "philosophy from the other side of the sunrise where you put a stop to everything and everything stops with you." He crossed the railyard and into a small library. He checked out books on Oriental religions and philosophies. Later, in his room, he was absorbed by Asvaghosha's *Life of Buddha* (translated by Samuel Beal). He was stopped in his tracks.

"'Rest beyond heaven,' in effect it said. Buddha says you don't have to struggle to go to heaven, all you have to do is rest beyond heaven. There is no heaven, and no no-heaven either. All that is to be done, has long been done. Saved, sweet hero. Sufferer, your suffering is stopped. All life is suffering. So ignore life. The cause of suffering is ignorant craving. Grab no more at pretty girls. The suppression of suffering can be achieved."[35]

Jack did not think this could ever be possible, that his suffering could be subdued to set him on the right path. Suffering did not exist as he knew it. They were mind illusions of thinking. He knew the answer. He must find a quiet place in the forest, sit under a tree and "slip into Nirvana." This new understanding dazed Jack. He then read the *Surangama Sutra*, translated by Lin Yutang in *The Wisdom of India*. Jack first read Yutang's "The Monkey Epic" from *The Importance of Living* (1939) sometime between 1939 and 1940.

Excitedly, Jack swallowed some Benzedrine to stay up all night. He read the first paragraph about the Five Defilements: attachment, aversion, ignorance, pride, and jealousy. Jack experienced his first flash. Enlightenment.

"Go away, stop, purify your mind. Remember that everything that happens has a form, if you ignore form it doesn't happen; ignoring form, you don't go through the process of discrimination, of picking-out, of thinking-it-out. Not thinking it out, naturally there's nothing to grab. Not thinking of roast beef au jus, your mouth doesn't water. Not grabbing means not aching and aching to grab. Not aching to grab, not suffering decrepitude and decay. Not suffering decay, you never change. Not changing, you never were one way or the other and can never change to something else. Everything's all right inside. Always knew it."[36]

He went to the New York Public Library and walked out with a copy of Dwight Goddard's spiritual anthology *A Buddhist Bible* (1932) tucked under his belt. He stole the book intending to return it within five to ten years once he had learned all it had to offer.

Goddard intended *A Buddhist Bible* to teach the essence of scripture without bogging the reader down with "matter not bearing on the theme of the particular Scripture," interpreting only what was "necessary" and "advisable." He intended to create an *anatta* (no soul) doctrine, thus illuminating the "unreality of all conceptions of a personal ego." The anthology contains selections from Pali, Sanskrit, Chinese, Tibetan, and modern sources and concludes with a summary of the dharma of the Buddha. Goddard sought to awaken a new faith from self-doubt. Jack had come across the book at precisely the right moment. He hoped Buddhism would be the key to correcting the negative traits he felt were affecting him.

At home, Jack sliced off the front and back covers and held the book together with rubber bands. It was "as holy and as soft as a foodstuff to my reverent touch. All of the instructions were in there that he had to follow. He planned to leave New York for the open country where he could read the Word and meditate it in solitude.[37]

Alene Lee was a "past dream."[38]

* * *

In November 1953, Jack received a letter from Viking editor Helen K. Taylor (who later edited *On the Road*) through Malcolm Cowley. She felt *On the Road* had "stirred" her for two reasons: his "bold writing talent" and that Jack "did not seem to exist as an outside agency of creation." Secondly, *On the Road* depicted a "raw sociology" of the "hipster gener-ation." It was "a life slice so raw and bleeding that it makes me terribly sad." Though her perception of the characters was harsh ("There is no redemption for these psychopaths and hopeless neurotics, for they don't want any"), the portrayal of Dean, the antihero, was "gargantuan but believably pitiful." Taylor's suggestion to Cowley, should Viking accept it, was "large-chunk cutting" to reduce the length and the "lightly touch-ing pencil, for refinement has no place in this prose." Though she wasn't alarmed by what she deemed obscene, she felt it was a challenging read. She recommended publishing it quietly "with no touting, previewing, or advance quotes from run-of-the-mill names."[39]

At the meeting, Cowley offered to show Kerouac's work to Arabelle Porter, editor of *New World Writing*. Kerouac considered the option and replied mid-November, assuring Cowley that if she wanted his work, he would send excerpts for consideration. Cowley's parting advice to Ker-ouac, whose publication prospects were bleak, was to get a job.

* * *

With his head in the Buddhist clouds, Jack made amends to give up drinking and abstain from sex. Drinking was perhaps the hardest one to curb, "the hardest part for a lush" he wrote in "On the Path." His mother was an enabler. Though she criticized Jack's excesses, she also liked him to have a drink with her. On New Year's Eve, they sat in their living room drinking dry martinis. She toasted him: "Happy New Year and good luck this year." Jack knew what she was referring to: his sicknesses, depression, unlucky love affairs, lack of money or a career, and "really ecstasy sitting in a trance of spastic anxious actually silent unconcerned near-catatonic thoughts all day." He tried to meditate. He waited until his mother went to bed. He set pillows against the wall and put his back on them.[40] Crossed his legs. He found that his muscled thighs were hard to bend. After a few minutes, they began to fall asleep. He felt needle pricks when he shifted them. He thought, "the Holy Saints forget their legs—they dont consider their legs as private property." Outside, the snow had fallen. He fixated his eyes upon that.

"I knew that though my eye-organ said it was snow, it might just as well be elephants for all the accuracy that conveyed. I thought of Helen Keller, the perfection of her Rosy Hope before the evil teacher drew her out to the darkness of our world. I was conscious that no one had ever thought of HK that way, but I didn't know yet that it was because of a stubborn and universal ignorance prevailing in our conditional world of cause and effect. Cause, birth; effect, death; condition, suffering."[41]

Jack had issues with Gabe's Christmas tree. They clashed with his Buddhist thoughts. He argued that "A life is suffering." Gabe told him that she was not brought up that way.

"Real is real—you've got to work for your living—enjoy what you can—then you die."

"And you die," Jack yelled, "and then you come back lookin for more, not any more enlightened than before—"

"I don't know those big words lighten—"

"Enlightened. You become awake to the fact that it's all a big ignorant dream, and that all the powers on earth and education are behind it—"

"Whattaya wanta do?"

"I wanta go away and do nothing in the desert."

"Why?"

"That's how you find the Holiness—it's bright, it's empty, it's your own mind, you can save yourself by doing it yourself, to stop, stop—"

"Why?"

"To understand that it's all the same thing—all poor sufferings—make people know how to stop all this—it's all in their heads—Heaven! You go to heaven."

"Why don't you go to heaven when you die?"

"When you die is too late—If you don't stop now—You gotta stop right away."

"Well," she'd sigh, "I always said you missed your vocation. You shoulda been a priest."

"I don't wanta be a priest—I am not a Catholic—I'm a Buddhist."

"Buddha, Buddha, weyondone—"

"I want to be a monk in the desert—"

"Go ahead—make your trip—You'll starve to death—"

"It's all that continual eating of food all day long—"

"Don't you like anything anymore? And why did you act so sassy when your sister was here?"[42]

Nobody would budge. Not Gabe nor Caroline. Jack sat dumbly watching the television, playing out his path to the road where he could pursue his Dharma Ecstasies in peace.

* * *

Jack was in financial duress. Neal offered Jack a job as a parking lot attendant. He accepted the offer and was prepared to board a bus to California after Christmas. He had $30 to his name. He hastily wrote the Cassadys that he expected to leave by the first week of January. Neal was now in the lurch, expecting Jack to have arrived earlier. Jack asked Neal for railroad passes. This option would provide free fare to Nogales, Arizona. Jack sweetened the deal by offering to get some marijuana in Mexico while he was near the border. Neal spat to Carolyn that he couldn't get any more train passes. By the end of January, Jack was still a no-show. Finally, he packed his raincoat that he bought for $5 in the Bowery. Maybe he could use it for a mat to sleep on. However, it was too thin. It got damp. He packed a bag: rope, an Army blanket, and Noxzema for shaving. He wore railroad gloves to keep his hands warm. He kissed Gabe goodbye and left. It was the 29th of January.

He took a bus to frozen Washington, DC, and arrived by midnight. He waited in the bus station until dawn to walk toward the Long Bridge crossing the Potomac River into Virginia. At a lunchroom, he ate Cream of Wheat and toast. He walked out without paying the check. Buddha has to watch his pennies; Christ has got to eat. The snow was disgusting to look at. Dirty. Brown. It was rush hour. Thousands of cars farted exhaust in a commuter-horror nightmare. They hardly gave him room to walk across the bridge. Jack was starting to regret leaving his quiet, warm room back at home. Then a car stopped. The driver was talkative, but it beat walking in the cold.

"All is well—realize your own essence of mind—be quiet—there—sleep—sleep with me—in God's Ecstasy—in—the pure snowflakes—in Transcendental Empathy—in Universal Brotherly Shivering Joy—rest."

The driver dropped him off at a Howard Johnson. Jack looked strange in the mirror. He combed his hair. Then a Black truck driver picked him up. This one was a little better than the last. He knew something about jazz. Most of the time, they sat in long silences. Jack looked out the window. Dharma America was passing. The Land of the Fellaheen. The driver took him to Richmond. It was a little warmer: "In search of peace, I am going through hell."

The following driver complained about ulcers. He could have lived in Florida, but he stayed where he was for the twenty extra cents per hour he was earning. Jack wanted to tell him that he got the ulcers because he worried about those extra cents. Instead, Jack said, "Quiet down your belly, sit still, think nothing."

"Hell, I'd go crazy thinking of nothing."

It was all a dream. One big illusion. The guy was at least sixty-five. He bragged about all the women he laid. Jack was dropped off at the James River Draw Bridge. He was 425 miles from home.[43]

Jack converted $50 worth of traveler's checks. The sun was warm. He got another ride right away from a car dealer. He was headed for Sanford, North Carolina. When he got there, Jack got a room in a railroad hotel. He thought railroad hotels were the best. Clean. Cheap. The only problem was the noise. All night long. Smashing and clanging, metal to metal. It had its music.

Jack lay in bed. He supped from a half pint of brandy. He had a dream of a brunette and Eddie Fisher. When he woke, her kiss was still on his lips. His loins ached from the thought of her. His legs ached from the journey. He had a lot of baggage to dispense with before he could become a big Buddha Saint. He had a long story behind him. College boy made good, then the war came. The boy leaves school to become a big-shot writer. He marries not once but twice. Both wives end up not loving him anymore for being true to what he believed. Local boy made good of leaving it all behind and staying poor. Now, even all of that was an illusion.

Jack slept. He has many more miles to go before burning campfires by the track, drinking brandy and meditating under the prairie stars.

"lights out—fall, hands a-clasped, into instantaneous ecstasy like a shot of heroin or morphine, the gland inside of my brain discharging the good glad fluid (Holy Fluid) as I hap-down and hold all my body parts down to a deadstop trance—Healing all my sicknesses—erasing all—not even the shred of a 'I-hope-you' or a Loony Balloon left in it, but the mind blank, serene, thoughtless."[44]

All Jack ever lost will return to him.

Jack paid his bill and left. The road was long and formidable. The whooshing of cars passed him, never ceasing. A mass commuter frenzy heralded the age of modernism. He wore his raincoat, so maybe he looked like a gangster packing heat beneath all the folds of fabric. But it wasn't a gun; it was a railroad lantern. America was no longer the joyous road for boyish hitchhikers. This was a new age of sinisterism. The Atomic Age. Who would ever pick him up?

Jack's feet were hurting. But it did not all amount to this. He was on a new road. A new path. The Path to Purity. He took off his cap and combed his hair. No rides still.

Then there were two hundred miles on an open flatcar. Jack only had a thin blanket between him and the night. Then he ran out of money. He felt like Siddhartha leaving his palace. How many more travels did he have in him? How many restless nights worrying his heart to sleep? Where was he going? He pictured himself going off the road down a "secret forgotten path through rocks and bushes and trees" to rediscover the Law of Old.

Then his money was gone.

In Watsonville, California, he ate grass.

Jack had little experience parking cars and proved to be an inept attendant. He fared no better than when he had the same job as a teenager in Lowell. Jack was not surprised. He knew he would eventually lose the job and end up begging door to door like a monk. He only needed buttered bread and beans. Simple.

Neal was now immersed in American clairvoyant Edgar Cayce's teachings. He urged Jack to read him. Neal felt Cayce had successfully integrated Hindu and Buddhist beliefs with Judaism and Christianity. Jack did not see the appeal. With both Carolyn and Neal as devout readers, it was an alienating force that shied Jack away from their home. Instead, Jack went to the local library to avoid this latest turn of events. In Buddhism he remained a firm believer. Later he would look back to December '53 as the time when he was perhaps wisest and began his faith in earnest.

"That whole dream of life, stop it, that's enough I said in the armed forces, in work, schools, frets, jails,—roads—leave me alone to forget your false 'realities' and remember the briefness of this dream and snarling delusion, stop it in eternity now—I want no more of it. And that's the gist."[45]

Jack had attained transcendental understanding through no singular text but as an intuitive understanding of it as a whole. His introduction to Buddhism in November 1953 was not his first. He had been reading from the fifty-volume set of the *Sacred Books of the East* in Lowell and New York in the 1940s. He was also well-versed in the *Bhagavad-Gita* after reading *Walden*. This time was different; he meant to devote himself entirely to Buddhism by reading translated texts, to obtain enlightenment directly without a mediator.

Jack was having a rough time of it with the Cassadys. Despite their promises of hospitality, they had had enough of him. Neal even forgot that he had invited him. The job wasn't worth a damn, and Jack lost it anyway. Now Jack was broke, and Neal thought he was a freeloader. He ate all the food. Smoked all the weed. He even took Carolyn. Neal had no more use for Jack Kerouac. There was a pile of pork chops on a dinner platter. Neal reminded everybody that what was on their plates was there because of him. Enraged, Jack vowed to buy a hot plate and eat alone in his room. Pork and beans and a hot plate were all that he needed. The breaking point happened after Neal and Jack had split a pile of marijuana. They got into a fierce argument. Neal told Jack he owed $20 for the pot. Jack presumed that the cost would be split evenly. Jack had had enough and told Carolyn that she should have "one husband at a time."[46] That night he went drinking with Al Sublette and did not return. It was March 1954. A room at the Cameo cost $3 a night. No bedbugs. Jack rented the room by the day.

Then Jack turned thirty-two. On his birthday, he felt radiated by the Pure Joy of transcendental understanding. His arguments with Neal did not seem real now that he was away. The night sky was lit dimly by a half-moon. He saw the "rhythmic torment of the sun vibrating for balance in Wholeness" with the moon. He never slept better.

Jack did not lament his separation from Neal. He was awash in insight. On March 25, he "attained suddenly the Diamond Samadhi, which is the buzz of my intrinsic hearing."[47] By day, he remained in his room. It had a rocking chair. Jack sat with an open notebook over his crossed leg capturing the sounds of the universe. He observed 3rd Street people down below: a Black boy, an older Black man, little girls, a fatter one, a sad old bum, and a man in a plaid work coat. There came a beautiful Indian girl, a "furtive whore" with her pimp. Jack followed each, jotting quickly, as Ginsberg later wrote, "tracing his mind's thought and sounds directly on the page." Jack was in love with the sheer physicality of writing and the words forming beneath his pencil, capturing his mind's drift. The conversations of people, distant yet audible, rose to him into the sacred bread of his composition.

Jack was writing everyday words of people which read like the prophecies of a divine oracle. There was no hierarchy. The smallest voice was treated equally as the "most heroic chunk of matter,"[48] poet Michael McClure had written. As Jack continued, he divided "San Francisco Blues" into eighty choruses. He explains that his "system" was to confine each chorus to a page: "It's all gotta be non-stop ad-libbing within each chorus, or the gig is shot." He was no longer just blowing prose as in his sketches and dreams but summing up meditative gems of observation into few words. He was distilling a moment of eternity onto a single page.

Jack did not stay at the Cameo for long. Carolyn secretly met with him before he left. Jack tucked his Skid Row poems into his knapsack along with the *Buddhist Bible*. He returned home without money to eat for the entire trip.

* * *

On the bus trip home, Jack had written another poem: "Bus East." As the bus bumped and shook along the road, he studied the land outside the window. It was a comfort to him. He had studied this land back and forth several times. But that seemed like a votal piece of his youth that had been severed from him. It was yet another shore that he was drifting further away from: "Society has good intentions / Bureaucracy is like a friend." Yet, Jack detected a dreamlike deception beneath society's veneer of "good intentions." Cars sped impatiently and recklessly. Traffic had steadily gotten worse in the past ten years. Many of these roads were previously the trails of Indian nations before they became the westward paths for oil speculators and Gold Rush pioneers. Now they were bland and sinister highways. The highway system was built to accommodate cars owned by nuclear families and not thrill-seeking hitchhikers, though this culture would become a fixture by the 1970s by sign-holding hippies. Some of these families owned more than one car. Homes were built with two-car garages. Now these anxious roadsters took to the highways with the same restless peripatetic movement that fueled Kerouac, but seemingly without purpose other than to keep moving. Consequently, the highways became choked by congestion. It was a commuter frenzy that Kerouac was unable to comprehend and he sensed this onslaught was an unstoppable force that would one day imperil the nation: "America's trying / to control the / uncontrollable / Forest fires, / Vice." For Kerouac, it seemed that the Earth was dead: "the ground / Vast and brown / Surrounds dry towns / Located in the dust / Off the coming locust / Live for survival. not for 'kicks.'" The poem was written not in choruses like his blues poems, but in free verse. It moved along as the bus rode east through wildflower prairies into Chicago railyards. By the time he reached home, Jack had 35 cents in his jeans pocket.[49]

* * *

Once Jack was at his bedroom desk, he wrote Carolyn. He sensed their tensions, especially the conflict between Cayce and his Buddhist studies. Jack noted that he had made a mistake. The world was not "empty" as he told them, but that it is "neither IS, or, IS NOT, but merely a manifestation of mind, the reflection of the moon on a lake, so the next porkchop you eat, remember, it's merely a porkchop reflected off water, and your hunger, and you the hungerer, Narcissus you. . . . "[50] Neal did not care what Jack had to say, and so did not write back.

Jack wrote Allen (who was then leaving Mexico to visit the Cassadys) that, despite his battles with alcohol and depression, he had found his "path."[51] Buddhism had taught him that his sufferings were not meaningless. He acknowledged the Four Noble Truths (or, in Pali, *Ariya Satta*): all life is sorrowful; the cause of suffering is ignorant craving; the suppression of suffering can be achieved; the way is the Noble Eightfold Path. Through knowledge of these four truths came the Noble Eightfold Path, which guided the way toward "Holy Ecstasy." This, however, was difficult to attain when he was lost in his alcohol, drug, and sex addictions. Jack's list that stated that all he wanted was women, drugs, and alcohol and that the first was shit was for now obliterated by a new quest for Truth. He gave Allen a reading list of Eastern texts. Allen thought Jack was wasting his time. All of the promises of his writing talent were being squandered by his eccentricities. Jack, it seemed to Allen, was too hung up on Buddhism and that all of life was a dream. Jack had stepped across the Holy Stream to the other shore.

Because he was officially laid off from the railroad, Jack was receiving unemployment checks. He worked as a yard brakeman on the New York Dock Railway two days a week before he was let go. This earned him $18.35 a day. Now he could collect and write.

His phlebitis returned. He needed medicine. Any notion of abstaining from alcohol was lost when he got bored and went into the Village.

He was smoking cigarettes and pot, phlebitis be damned. He was seeing an NYU student, Mary Ackerman, who had befriended artist Iris Brody. She was a junkie. Each of them enabled the other out of the depths of their addictions. When she overdosed, Jack split.[52] Another time, he caroused with "Ramblin'" Jack Elliott. They "banged two colored sisters all night." Elliott had first met Kerouac in 1953. He was friends with Elliott's girlfriend at the time. "He'd come to her apartment and read to us his manuscript of *On the Road*. Over three days sitting on the floor and drinking six big bottles of red wine, we all took turns reading from it. That stirred my desire to hit the road myself."[53]

Jack tried reconciling with Alene Lee. She had telephoned him, and they walked down the street holding hands. He later spied on her at her job at a restaurant where she was waiting tables. He had loaned her his *Subterraneans* typescript, to which he later had to bust down her door to get it back: "The things I could tell that little cunt and wont."[54] It was clear that New York continued to be his downfall. He was drunk and unhappy.

The unemployment agency felt that Jack was not trying hard enough to find a job. They stopped sending Jack his checks. They could go to hell. It was all irrelevant. He had read enough holy scripture to equip him with these failings. But he also felt that life was not worth living. For now, he gave up women, writing to Carolyn that he had offers from women and that he shunned them. He heeded the *Surangama Sutra*:

"When anyone becomes inflamed by sexual passion, his mind becomes disturbed and confused, he loses self-control and becomes reckless and crude. Besides, in sexual intercourse, the blood becomes inflamed and impure and adulterated with impure secretions. Naturally from such a source, there can never originate an aureole of such transcendently pure and golden brightness as I have seen emanating from the person of my Lord."[55]

Jack wrote Carolyn that they were being "duped" by Cayce. He recommended that she read *Jataka* (or *Stories of the Buddha*) instead. While Cayce taught that life was perpetual until perfection is attained, the *Surangama Sutra* stated that "the lives of human beings who are always being troubled by worldly attachments and contaminations" cause "their perception of sight to become inverted and unreliable," thus "seducing their thoughts and causing them to wander about ignorantly and uncontrolled." At a time when "control" was beyond Jack's grasp (except in his writing), this insight must have struck him hard. It is no wonder that he dismissed the cessation of his unemployment checks as unimportant.[56] He had seen another world. He was asleep in "the golden light again, deep within the womb of the mind." His Buddhist teachings did not abolish Catholicism. Instead, he synthesized them. Jack reasoned to Carolyn that if Christ had reached India, "one dab of Buddhism would have wiped clean from his mind that egomaniacal Messiah complex that got him crucified and made Christianity the dualistic greed-and-sorrow Monster that he is."[57] The difference between Christ and Buddha was that Buddha never claimed to be God or the Son of God but merely a man who had attained enlightenment.

Another summer arrived. Jack was restless. He had money to spend for once. He imagined cooking hot dogs over a campfire. Or, he could live an ascetic life and leave the sorrowful world behind. But, he had his mother to worry about. It was always his mother. And she had no understanding of what her son was experiencing. It was lost to her. She was a constant audience to Caroline's incessant complaints against her brother. He was a grown man. He should have a job by now, a "career." He should have a house with a family, and then he could also care for the welfare of their mother. Jack had a persecution complex: "Everybody is getting mad at me for knowing the truth now." He could have told them otherwise, of how he felt, but he was afraid of the consequences: "Please cease calling me Jack and thinking that I exist, that I am anything but a ghost in a dream, and please cease telling me anything about your 'selves' in this world."[58]

Jack stayed put until October.

* * *

In October 1954, Jack was in Lowell. Nobody recognized the disheveled lonely figure shuffling through the dead sidewalk leaves. He sketched as he walked. He noted its changes. He walked through the doors of the house of his birth and stood inside. Jack summoned memories of himself as a baby in a wicker basket staring at the fluted light of the porch.

"Dawn—The single switch track with deadhead block in the yard across canal from pa's shop—when I thought many (usta be)—The forgotten redbrick plus gray concrete of Bridge St. Eternity Warehouse—."[59]

He felt out of place. A stranger at home. Not a "soul recognized me in the streets." He walked over twenty miles over the three days he was there. On the second day, a quiet Sunday morning (October 24), he walked past the home of long-dead Sammy Sampas. He knew Sammy's younger sister, Stella, but was too afraid to knock on her door (though they were correspondents). Instead, he followed the Boston & Maine train tracks to South Lowell, where Mary Carney lived and knocked on Mary's door. She let him in.

They spoke in her parlor, but she felt Jack was too deep for her. He was afflicted with a lostness that she could not place. She would not know until *Maggie Cassidy* was published five years later that he had written a novel about their relationship as lovelorn teenagers. By then, he was too far gone ever to reach.

They had little privacy. When Jack left, Mary imagined running after him. She sensed him to be a changed man from when she knew him. He was a world apart. He walked a short distance away to a railroad bridge crossing the Concord River. A dead cat floated down the slow-moving stream. He immediately sketched it: "here down on the stain of earth the ethereal flower in our minds, dead cats in the Concord, it's a temporary middle state between Perfection of the Unborn & Perfection of the Dead."[60]

A tumbleweed bounced along the bridge. Bright ribbons of colors from the autumn trees reflected on the slow-moving waters: "What we call life is just this lugubrious false stain in the crystal emptiness." He concluded that what he perceived to be, smelt, saw, felt, and thought, were all arbitrary conceptions of reality and therefore false. He did not feel sorrow for the cat. In his mind, it wasn't even really there:

"But I'm too sad to care that I understand everything. Lowell is a happy dream but just a dream. All's left, I must go now into my own monastery wherever it's convenient. My life went from culture of Town, to civilization of City, to neither of Fellaheen."[61]

He walked through downtown Lowell, across the bridge, and through Pawtucketville up Crawford Street, where he and his family had lived only a little over ten years before. He prayed on his knees in church, peering up at Christ on the cross as he did at Santa María la Redonda. He fell into a reverential trance. Later he remembered this vision in an article written for *Playboy* in January 1959, "The Origins of the Beat Generation":

"I went one afternoon to the church of my childhood (one of them). Ste. Jeanne d'Arc in Lowell, Mass., and suddenly with tears in my eyes and had a vision of what I must have really meant with 'Beat' anyhow when I heard the holy silence in the church (I was the only one in there, it was five P.M., dogs were barking outside, children yelling, the fall leaves, the candles were flickering alone just for me) the vision of the word Beat as being to mean beatific. . . . "[62]

The next day, he caroused with his old Lowell friends. But they could not keep up and soon grew tired of him. It seemed to them that Jack wanted to be a child again. He was carefree with no obligations. Jack became disappointed. He sat in Ouellete's Lunch near Moody Street and wrote a French sketch: *"rien plus pire qu'un enfant malade."* ("There's nothing worse than a sick child.") Though the trip was tiring, he was revitalized. Lowell was his "Universe Canyon of mystery." The next day he was back in New York.

CHAPTER TWELVE

Lake of Light

IN THE SUMMER OF 1954, BEFORE JACK LEFT FOR LOWELL, HIS AGENT, Sterling Lord, convinced Malcolm Cowley to reconsider a short prose piece, "Jazz of the Beat Generation," which documented Jack's year with Neal in 1949. To Cowley, the essay was impressive, perhaps the best he had read of late, which best documented the post–World War II generation. Its language was astonishing and sincere: "Out we jumped into the warm mad night hearing a wild tenorman's bawling horn across the way going 'EE - YAH! EE - YAH!' and hands clapping to the beat and folks yelling 'Go, go, go!'"[1]

Cowley brought the manuscript to Arabelle Porter, who had been impressed by the work (and trusted Cowley's judgment). She scheduled it for the April 1955 edition of *New World Writing*. For his efforts, Jack was paid $108.

Nervous that Joan Haverty might see that he was at last published, he requested that it be credited to a one-name pseudonym: Jean-Louis, actually Kerouac's real first name. Cowley, however, was not happy with the name change. He had been plugging Jack's real name in association with *On the Road*.

On July 28, he attempted to write a "Book of Samadhi." He meditated in his yard (on one occasion, it caused him to faint): "I cant write my visions of the Dharma except as I write my dreams, swiftly, surely, undiscriminated, purely from my mind—So I hereby end this book SOME OF THE DHARMA."[2] He appended the "Book of Samadhi" as a postscript. It was his first extended piece of writing that incorporated Buddhist texts:

"Only if at death my body vanished into thin air—for its destruction among worms or in fire is only a vague rearrangement of atomic worlds infinitely empty in all directions moving about in imaginary hassle inside vast universes of worm cell or in universes of empty fire gas—in no sense vanishment of the primal mistake of false-existence—Is it all in the mind, the escape? the breakthrough? As I lay unconscious it wasn't 'I am dead,' it was 'mind essence is mind essence.' (This is why, when walking at night on my favorite sidewalk going under low trees I say 'Bend the head, your low branches wont hurt')—Nobody dies; there is nothing to die except aggregates of imagination that is not real in the first place but we cling and call it 'ego- personality'—Where is the escape?"[3]

Unable to sleep on the night of July 29, Jack began Book 3 of *Some of the Dharma*, apparently unsatisfied that he had exhausted everything he wanted to say in his previous notebooks. It was easier for him to project his writing through what he described as "Bliss Screen of Movies." It was easier to spill it all out on to blank pages than to discuss it with his mother, who felt that he had lost his mind with an unnecessary distraction to his Catholic faith. She saw no worth in Buddhism. To her, his Buddhist writings was a display of pagan blasphemy, but she was unable to convince her son of this. She had no choice but to wait it out. On August 24, Gabe may have gotten her wish when Jack plunged into the "lowest point in my Buddhist Faith" since commencing his practice from the previous December:

"Here I am in America sitting alone with legs crossed as world rages to burn itself up—What to do? Buddhism has killed all my feelings, I have no feelings, no inclinations to go anywhere, yet I stay here in this house a sitting duck for the police who want me for penury & non-support, listless, bored, world-weary at 32, no longer interested in love, tired, unutterably sad as the Chinese autumn-man. The silence of unspoken despair, the sound of drying, gets me down. I MUST GO AWAY ALONE."[4]

By the fall of 1954, Jack had written five significant works. After watching Alfred Kazin's televised roundtable discussion on Melville,

Jack wanted to send him *Doctor Sax* and *The Subterraneans*. He tried to impress upon Kazin the advancement of his prose since *The Town and the City*. Kerouac explained his writing method to Kazin: "The main thing, I feel, is that the urgency of explaining something has its own words and rhythm, and time is of the essence—Modern Prose." A response from one of New York City's leading literary critics would validate his techniques.[5]

Through December 1954, Jack was furiously typing deep into the night. He wanted to send a manuscript of *The Beat Generation*[6] for Knopf, which rejected it in January 1955.

His nighttime despair, often felt during his sleeplessness, brought him to spiritual heights or depths of self-loathing. Three nights before Christmas, he wrote "Night Dhyana," in which he realized that his father's death eliminated all human manifestations. That realization contained concepts of "Beginninglessness" and "Endlessness." The understanding of Mind Essence could be achieved by rationalism, whereas an animal (Kerouac uses a frog in his example) knew it by "mere sensation." When he prayed on the floor with his legs crossed, the throbbing ache he felt in his ankles was different from that of the "pain of Western Praying in the knees." He found coping methods: "There were tics of memory of Lowell long ago that I ignored, letting them bounce off the Universal Mirror." The following day, Jack wrote a "Morning Dhyana." He succumbed to a "useful realization of the triviality of the activities of people in civilizations." This continued through Christmas Day until midnight when he finally attained "at last," a "measure of enlightenment."[7]

Allen rescued Jack when he gave him some legal aid. His brother, Eugene Brooks, was a lawyer. In January 1955, they went to court to contest Joan Haverty's child support suit against Jack. Brooks's defense was that his client was too disabled from phlebitis to work full-time. Jack's physician advised him to remain in bed until his condition subsided. Brooks had neglected to bring the letter to the court. Jack demanded a paternity test. He felt for sure that he would be jailed, and so he got a manila envelope of his Buddhist writings and a tattered copy of *A Buddhist Bible*. Joan wasn't buying Jack's conversion to Buddhism. It was all a part of his "little game," she told the court. Jack was confident that Joan had learned about the test and so she left Jan at home. Joan asked if she could sit with Jack. He was pleased to hear that she converted to Catholicism. She brought up Jesus, the Virgin Mary, and her search for inner peace. She showed Jack photos of Jan that she kept in her wallet. Writing to Allen, Jack admitted, "She looks like me, especially frowning square-browed photo, so may be mine."

Despite his feelings, Joan did not want Jan to be in contact with the Kerouacs. Brooks and Joan's lawyer met in the judge's chambers. Somehow, the medical records turned up from the veterans' hospital in the Bronx, and the judge decided that the case had to be set aside if the defendant couldn't work. The case was suspended for a year.

By the spring of 1955, he was still studying Buddhist writings and recording dreams. Soon, Gabrielle was tired of her job in the shoe factory and decided to move south to stay with Nin. On February 13, Kerouac escorted his mother to Rocky Mount and stayed there because he did not have the money to maintain an apartment in New York. Again he slept in the room with a desk and typewriter. Two days after arriving, he hiked into the woods with Bob, one of the Blakes' two dogs. He sat at the base of a pine tree and meditated in the heat while the dog rested at his feet. Another time he walked with his nephew, Paul Jr., to an old sharecropper's farm, empty save for a crying puppy chained to a porch. Kerouac asked, "What's the use of all this suffering? Why was he born?"

Despite going "bugs in the cottonfields" of his sister's oppressive household, he stayed productive. He completed a seventy-thousand-word, colloquial-written biography of Buddha. He gave it different titles: *Your Essential Mind*, *The Story of Buddha*, *Buddha Tell Us*, *Buddahood: The Essence of Reality*, and *Wake Up*. He began writing it on February 18. Basing the piece on Buddhist readings, he merged actual biography with his perceptions of the rise of Siddhartha. It was to be, according to Kerouac, a "handbook for Western understanding." Opening the work with an aphorism by ancient Sanskrit poet and scholar Ashvaghosh, Kerouac begins:

"Buddha means the awakened one. Until recently most people thought of the Buddha as a big fat rococo sitting figure with his belly out, laughing, as represented in millions of tourist trinkets and dime-store statuettes here in the Western world. People didn't know that the actual

Buddha was a handsome young prince who suddenly began brooding in his father's palace, staring through the dancing girls as though they weren't there, at the age of twenty-nine, till finally and emphatically he threw up his hands and rode out to the forest on his war horse and cut off his long golden hair with his sword and sat down with the holy men of the India of his day and died at the age of eighty a lean venerable wanderer of ancient roads and elephant woods. This man was no slob-like figure of mirth, but a serious and tragic prophet, the Jesus Christ of India and almost all Asia."8

Kerouac continues Prince Siddhartha's story with his marriage at sixteen to Yasodhara and the birth of his son, Rahula. At twenty-nine, Siddhartha encounters three stages of suffering: old age, sickness, and death. Subsequently, he leaves behind his wife and child and departs on his horse in the middle of the night. Siddhartha also leaves behind the opulent palace to pursue a life of asceticism. One of the first things he does in preparation for his vow of homelessness is to shear off his hair. He trades his vestments for the robe of a beggar. He then sits under a bodhi tree and vows not to rise "until, freed from clinging, my mind attains deliverance from all sorrow." Siddhartha is ultimately liberated due to discovering the Four Noble Truths and the Noble Eightfold Path. He achieved full enlightenment and became known as Shakyamuni Buddha. However, Buddha delays his entry into Nirvana until all sentient beings are freed from suffering. He gives a sermon in Benares, forms his first sangha, and delivers his Fire Sermon in front of a thousand fire worshipers. His sermon addresses the nature of reality and the inconstancy of the self. By the close of Kerouac's story, Buddha is eighty years old and, to his assistant Ananda, proclaims his preparation to enter Nirvana:

"Now I have given up my term of years: I live henceforth by power of faith; my body like a broken chariot stands, no further cause of 'coming' or of 'going,' completely freed from earth, heaven and hell, I go en-franchised, as a chicken from its egg."9

In April 1955, Jack typed his manuscript.

Frantically, Jack wrote his agent. He didn't have 5 cents for a Popsicle. He returned to New York to retrieve his mother's belongings. In the city, he went out with some friends, who bored him, so he did what he always did—he got drunk. Guiltily, he was all too aware of how he was breaking his Buddhist vows. His abstinence was short-lived. The feeling of abandonment tossed him into despair. Jack wanted to put aside any differences with Neal. He turned to flatter Neal to convince him into writing back, proclaiming that he was "the greatest writer in America." He was ready to go west. However, Neal had changed. He was not the same person as he was in the past. He no longer needed kicks with Kerouac. Cassady did not write back.

Perhaps appropriately, given his mood, Jack wrote more blues poems: "Macdougal Street Blues" and "Bowery Blues." In "Bowery Blues" he began with a spontaneous sketch: "Cooper Union Cafeteria—late cold March afternoon, the street (Third Avenue) is cobbled, cold, desolate with trolley tracks—Some man is waving his hand down No-ing somebody emphatically and out of sight behind a black and white pillar, cold clowns in the moment of horror of the world."[10]

Jack's portrayal of New York reveals a humanity that has become broken: "A yakking blonde with an awful smile"; "A funny bum with no sense"; "Unutterably sad the broken winter shattered face of a man passing in the bleak ripple"; "a Russian boxer with an expression of Baltic lostness"; "the sickened old awfulness of it like slats of wood wall in an old brewery truck." Jack's "guts weep." His "brains are awash / Down the side of the / blue orange table." All of humanity, to Jack, is a pageantry of lostness. This time, Jack did not break his blues poem down into choruses. Instead, he continues page after page, writing as he sees it, without enumeration: "The story of man / Makes me sick / Inside, outside / I dont know why / Something so conditional / And all talk / Should hurt me so." Jack writes out of his loneliness and abandonment. No longer was he distressed by the state of America, but by the state of himself.[11]

In a feverish frenzy, perhaps to balance himself, Jack transcribed *Vajracchedikā Prajñāpāramitā Sūtra* (*The Diamond Vow of God's Wisdom*) on a typewritten forty-foot-long scroll. This Buddhist text, known as the "Diamond Sutra," relies on the diamond metaphor, that it is hard enough to cut and shatter illusions to get to ultimate reality. It contains the discourse between the Buddha and a senior monk. Traditionally, in Chinese cultures, the *Sutra* would have been printed on a pocket-size folding edition (like an accordion) to accommodate the entire text. Jack's replication was on a scroll he typed from a primary translated source. This is not the only time Jack would take the time to type sacred text. He edited 120 pages of Sanskrit texts for his improvement, which he titled *Bodhi (God's Wisdom)*, which is a selection of sutras.

He was too broke to go anywhere. At Rocky Mount, he was considered a layabout because he meditated under the trees. When meditation didn't help, a potent cocktail of ginger ale, orange juice, rum, and white lightning did. Locals called him a drunk.

That spring, Jack returned to New York for further discussions of *On the Road*. He was sick of talking about things. Meetings. Procrastination. He lunched with Malcolm Cowley and Viking Press editor Keith Jennison. Kerouac asked for a monthly stipend to support him while writing in Mexico. He showed Jennison the twenty-seven pages of *On the Road* that Cowley had requested. He was impressed with his writing but still turned him down.

In New York, he had no place to sleep. Lucien offered him a place to stay while his wife was gone. He was now married. A changed man. He was no longer the young Rimbaudian rebel of the New Vision that would chew glass just for the lark of it. He was sobered and dutiful to his job at UPI. Despite his seemingly stable lifestyle, Carr was capable of bouts of physical and verbal abuse. He was opinionated and blunt. He thought Jack and Allen's writings were shit. They were living in a fantasy world that he wanted no part of. While Lucien was working, Jack stayed behind in his apartment and typed letters. He began to place matters into his own hands, sending short stories and prose to magazines. He sent a note to poet William Carlos Williams asking him to pen a recommendation to Random House (he declined). Not giving up on *Beat Generation*, he submitted it to Dodd Mead. All of these efforts led to nothing.

* * *

The apartment was quiet. Lucien was working. Jack toyed with the idea of writing a sequel to *The Town and the City* to reflect his new interests. He had started one before, *Galloway Rolls On*, which he included in a typescript of *Visions of Neal*. Now he wanted to try it again, writing one of its main characters, Peter Martin, with a Buddhist spin. Martin, who had turned to the road at the end of the book, has found himself in Mexico. Peter is a "religious hermit" living outside the hills of Tenancingo, Mexico, a tiny village at the "end of the road," southwest of Mexico City surrounded by forests and mountains.

Peter lives simply. He takes water from a stream, strains it through a towel, and boils it in a clay pot. Once a week he walks six miles into the village for groceries that he buys by using $5 worth of traveler's checks. He has been doing this for six months. Peter lives in accordance "with the ancient rules of the homeless disciples of all the Buddhas of old." He has been meditating toward the true attainment of emptiness but still feels afflicted by a "bug." The bug is his former self; "a stray memory of life past in the town and the city in America." He has a fear of desert scorpions though he realizes that the creatures are One with himself and all other sentient beings. He hears a voice in a dream: "you've entered the Golden Stream of Awakening! Rejoice!" Peter has one weakness.

Drinking mescal inflames his desire for women. His concupiscences drive him with desire. He wishes to attain "Highest Perfect Wisdom" but struggles with his temptations. He meditates. When he does, the images of his dead father and Alexander Panos (Sammy Sampas) "or anything to which he'd ever been attached which was now extinct, destroyed, exterminated, following the law of things born that they may die" arises before him. He is relieved to know that all things must end, "all things begotten from a cause, die from a cause." Afterward, there is nothing but emptiness and a dream.

One Sunday morning, Peter is awakened by the peep of a bird. He glimpses the horizon to see that it is at one with the sky. A thought flashes: "It's all the same thing." He recalls his past life and the "eerie sensation of many other past lives, the endless sadness that he had undergone, his kind, his brothers, his kin, all because of pitiful ignorance and the false deception of space and sight." He hears bells tolling for Sunday church mass: "he suddenly saw everywhere the perfect crystal clear of emptiness of his enlightened intuition." Time is but a "burden on his back." Excited, Peter adds a postscript to a letter written to Leon Levinsky then living in New York City. Peter has a sudden desire to rejoin life.

To find his friends in New York, or San Francisco, anywhere, to be the bearer of the Dharma like a hipster prophet.[12]

* * *

Lucien's wife, Cessa, returned. Jack had no place to stay, so he returned to Rocky Mount. Hoping to escape from his sister's side eye, he wanted to buy a sleeping bag and go to Mexico. Jack thought he was missing something when he wasn't in the city. But after he did, he realized that it was all the same thing. It was the same as staying home and doing nothing: "all the same empty nature."[13]

On Independence Day, in sweltering North Carolina, Jack lacked the money to buy even a beer. He earned money helping his brother-in-law load televisions for 75 cents an hour. He received $25 from his lawyer, Eugene Brooks, and the same amount from Ginsberg's West Coast crowd to entice him west. Not that Kerouac needed enticing; all he needed was the money and the opportunity. On July 4, he noted in his journal that he would have to leave "home" and its comforts to eke out a "homeless" existence in the California riverbeds or in a Mexican hut to live like Thoreau.

Making a last-ditch effort to take care of business before leaving the States, Kerouac sent *Doctor Sax* to Sterling Lord to replace his missing copy. Now heading his agency, Lord was busy with other clients but still attended to Kerouac's affairs with unwavering devotion. *Buddha Tells Us* was submitted to the Philosophical Library in New York for consideration. While the company agreed that the work warranted publication, they offered to publish only if he would guarantee the sale of six hundred copies for $3.50 each. To Ginsberg, Kerouac wrote in September that he did not know "600 people with $3.50."

During the summer of 1955, Jack had to reappraise his life. He had made a list in 1954, which thus far he had failed to follow: "Modified Ascetic Life—For Temporary & American Responsibilities Followed By Final Austerities." In it, he had projected up to the year 2000 to attain Nirvana. He would stop chasing after women; no more alcohol, "no more sickening of healthy body"; no "false social life" and no more work. Into 1955, he vowed not to eat any "rich or espensive foods"; and from 1955 into 1960, no more "writing for communication& after sketchbooks, or wilds no more writing or I art-ego of any kind, finally no I-Self, or Name; no shaving of beard." By 1970, Jack would have given up any possessions, but for "wilderness robe, no hut, no mirror, begging at houses of village"; and no communication with the world or family. Finally, by the year 2000, he would have attained his first Dhyana ("untemptation ecstasy") and Nirvana ("willed death beyond death").[14] By the time he reached 1955, he would have broken all of these and continue doing so for the rest of his life.

Jack charted how he would accomplish his asceticism in his "Elements of the Basic Deceit." On a practical level, he wanted to nail down his goal and detail how he would do it. He had to decide where he wanted to settle. Would it be Mexico? California? North Carolina? Lowell? New York or the woods? What were the disadvantages of each of these places? Mexico was an "alien scorpion land" and too far away. California was too expensive and it had its dry seasons. North Carolina meant no sex because he was under the scrutiny of his sister and mother. It was a "strange snake land." Lowell was a "dreary return," cold and expensive. New York and Long Island were overcrowded, expensive, sinister, cruel, and suffered from "TVitis." Finally, to retire to the woods, Jack feared poisonous plants and his inexperience.[15]

What were his means of saving money (railroad, seaman, writing, others)? What were his fears that got in the way? Changing his mind; having no patience or stamina; inability to work well; art ego anxiety; loneliness; basic insanity; cowardice; the dominance of his appetites. How would he search for love? He listed "Indian whores, Mexico woods, and New York girls." What were his disadvantages? No sleep, money, not enough money, bribes, work, men, war, art, compromise. Forever it seemed, Kerouac was a man without a country. An exile at home. Though he wrote about life, he did not know how to live it. He was always restlessly searching.

Bill was no different. He was living in "Interzone" (his name for Tangier) near Place Amrah in the Native Quarter. He was so close to Paul Bowles's residence, Bill wrote Jack, that he could spit on his roof. Jack had no interest in Bowles or his writings, crudely noting in his journal that the writer was a pederast. Bill wanted Allen or Jack to bring order to the chaos of pages rapidly piling on his writing table. Like Jack, Bill was penniless; at one point, he went thirty-six hours without food. In desperation, he sold his typewriter and could not do the work he requested from his writer friends. Allen owed Bill money, and until it arrived, Bill had to make do with what he could scrounge together for sustenance (mostly fried apple peels and fatty pieces of pork). Bill had no appreciation for Jack's Buddhist beliefs, so he found no solace in that direction.

Caroline offered to help her brother get one of his many manuscripts published. She was impatient with Jack because she bore the brunt of Gabe's welfare after her marriage started to flounder. There was no "Lake of Light" in Rocky Mount. Jack wrote to Allen for $25 to hitchhike to Salt Lake City, Utah. From there, he would take the Southern Pacific until he got to California. Jack did not want to deal with agents and editors. Sterling Lord deeply discouraged him after he questioned whether *Buddha Tells Us* was good. Allen was the only one who truly corresponded as a friend and confidant.

Despite his melancholy, Jack was slowly gaining recognition in the media. "Jazz of the Beat Generation" was published by *New Directions* in April. "Jazz of the Beat Generation" became tied to Kerouac as his penultimate statement before *On the Road* was published, concluding with, "We find it, we lose, we wrestle for it, we find it again, we laugh, we moan. Go moan for man. It's the pathos of people that gets us down, all the lovers in this dream." Readers contacted *New Directions* editor Arabelle Porter in praise of Kerouac's writing. Critic and jazz scholar Stanford Whitmore requested an explanation from the writer of his technique. Whitmore intuitively perceived the link between Kerouac's prose and bop. Jack responded with "Belief and Technique for Modern Prose," which comprised twenty-seven principles (later expanded to thirty) to be published in 1957. Scribbling in secret notebooks and wild typewritten pages for one's own joy headed the list of revolutionary techniques that in time would prove that what he had written wasn't drunken gibberish or stoned spewings, but that they were laid down aforethought with meditative intent. He wrote a new list for disbelieving critics and readers who took stabs at all of the books published in the wake of *On the Road*, the "Essentials of Spontaneous Prose" (published in 1959 by *Evergreen Review*), which further explicated Kerouac's technique with graphic instructions on how to accomplish what he had done. They serve as a skeleton key to deciphering his peculiar universe. Jack had been running with time through the laws of time, emphatically bashing his fist to the table with every breathing dash between swinging volleys of prose. In time, Kerouac became wearied at explaining his techniques and defining the word *beat* for the media. It very well may have exhausted all of his post-1957 energies.

* * *

In Rocky Mount, Jack staved off another phlebitis attack with a penicillin shot. It didn't slow him down. He was confident he could receive a $200 stipend from the National Academy of Arts and Letters. This was not good enough for his sister and brother-in-law. Gabe was getting old, and she could not be expected to continue working for Jack's sake. The American South was throttled with a vicious heat wave. It was time to leave. Encouraged by the prospects of receiving grant relief, Jack left southwest for Victoria, Texas. He packed his "Mazatlán" suitcase: blanket, bag, raincoat, lantern, camp kit, a Peruvian jackknife, Levis, crepe sole shoes, pencils and notebooks, toilet kit, iodine, Anacin, swim shorts, work gloves and cap, mackinaws, Buddhist books, fishing hook and line, harmonica, a rope with a loop, matches and Bull Durhams, and food: salt pork, salt, Nescafe, peanut butter, sugar, and figs. Barely saying goodbye to anybody, he left the house and was relieved as soon as he was on the road.

He barely slept after passing through Gainesville, Georgia. He wanted to hitchhike straight to San Francisco to meet Allen (who ended up financing the trip), but his legs were too sore. The world flew by in cascading colors. A dream already ended. He knew that what he saw would not be there in "seven million million million aeons," and so it was worth preserving for posterity. He sketched out, page after page, the devil's work. The pages ruffled in the wind. The Devil would always work against God for as long as Mind Essence created its ignorance.

He decided to go to Mexico City for free penicillin before turning north. He could not do anything if his legs failed him. By July 29, he was in Monterrey, Mexico. He needed to save his few dollars, so he wandered the streets as a transient and slept on a park bench.

In Mexico City, Jack slept at Bill Garver's pad at 212 Orizaba Street. Garver was clean now, and so Jack had to buy drugs from the street. Whatever he found, it made him instantly sick. It wearied him tremendously. Mexico was different now: Burroughs had left, his friend Dave Tesorero had died, and the creative overdrive that dominated Jack's last stay was a challenge to duplicate.

Then he got dysentery. The Word became his shelter. It was his sole solace:

Two sides of the same Mind
Are existence and non-existence
Two sides of the same Mind
Are life and death.[16]

Jack fell in love with Tesorero's widow, or at least he thought he was. She was a morphine junkie, Esperanza Villanueva Tesorero (nicknamed "Saragossa" on the streets). Jack had met her during his previous visit, but she was married. Esperanza was sixteen years old when Tesorero, twenty-five years her senior, took her in. Later, he married her. Through Tesorero, she became addicted to opiates. Tesorero was Burroughs's junk connection. After Tesorero's death in November 1954, Esperanza took over supplying Bill with heroin. In her junk-sick misery, Esperanza turned to the streets to sell her body. She lived with her ailing sister, Josephine. Among the slums, Esperanza had a reputation for violent attacks upon other women. They feared her as a real threat.

However, Jack saw something else in her. To him, she had the complexion of the Virgin Mary with the eyes of a dove. He saw through her flaws because he knew that nobody was perfect. All were cast off from Samsara's wheel. All beneficent of the same suffering. All mothers and fathers were guilty of their children's birth just as their parents were. They were all "equally different forms of the same holy gold."[17] The world stank of death. Purity could only be found in the eyes of a dove or in the chuckle of a hen.

Jack's Mexico City days became a morphine blur enhanced further with Canada Dry and bourbon hi-balls. In his pencil-driven pages, Jack's eye seized on what he felt and saw, his senses burning to transmute all through Buddhist insight. Junkies, slums, prostitutes, and sickly animals (a rooster, dove, flea-infested cats, and Chihuahua) were projections of the same emptiness. He wondered, "How can things be empty yet full of shit?—must be that emptiness indeed is shit."[18]

Esperanza had cream-colored thighs. She tugged at her nylon stockings. She sat demurely upon her sister's bed. She reminded him of Billie Holiday. He detailed her every move. He projected his vision of her through his voyeurism: "I'm riding along with Esperanza in the cab, drunk, with big bottle of Juarez Bourbon Whiskey in the till-bag railroad lootbag they'd accused me of holding in railroad 1952."[19] His prose is direct. It is spontaneously lifted from the eye to the page. She was no soft pale Carolyn tempting him under Neal's domineering shadow. Esperanza was dangerous and dark. Mysterious. Her jet-black hair and moist brown eyes made him sad. To Jack, she was not *esperanza* (hope), but *tristessa* (sadness).

Jack fought back his lust much as Peter Martin did in "The City and the Path"; at this rate, he would never make Buddha in his lifetime. To conquer it, he continued to get high. He walked through the ghetto dimly under a mountain of dark clouds. The rain fell. Brown water chugged down the gutters that were clogged with trash. The city stank. Yet, it was life itself. Were these Daydreams or Blues? A Sketch or a Vision? An Ecstasy or a Flash? A Gloomy Bookmovie? A TIC, dream, or haiku? For now, it was straight spontaneous prose.

A phantom rose from the spectral dust. Leopards of lust. There was no life in the streets of "come-hither" whores by the hundreds seeking men of quiet desperation. Yet, he lists in a chart of sexual encounters that he had had sex with "several" women in Mexico City. After he had them, Jack was disgusted. He felt like an old lecher (and what did he write in his notebook? that sex was like "gathering branches" without knowing where their roots are). Whitman stated that "sex is the root of

it all"; Jack believed that the "root of all these cocks & cunts of people &
animals" grew in the "sea of rebirth."[20] He was destroyed by conflict. Mara
the Tempter and the Holy Sea of Compassion. Dark-lidded voluptuous
Indian women captured his attention with regularity.

Their relationship was doomed from the outset. She was too far gone
in her addiction. Jack felt awkward when he held her: "I feel we are two
empty phantoms of light or like ghosts in old haunted-house stories,
diaphanous and precious and white and not-there." By late August, she
was covered in cysts and temporarily paralyzed. She had always been
sickly. For Jack to continue with her, she would have been twice the
burden he already bore by himself. Furthermore, he could never bring
her home. She would be exiled from Gabe's kitchen without question.
He would not have sex with Esperanza until the following year when he
returned to Mexico.

In mid-August, Jack wrote, "On the Path."

All life is suffering.
The cause of suffering is ignorant craving.
The suppression of suffering can be achieved.
The Way is the Noble Eightfold Path.

Jack's burst of creativity coincided with the "lowest beat ebb" of his
depression. By repurposing the suffering and misery he faced, he also
revealed startling truths through his writing. He began the first of 150
spontaneous choruses per notebook page. He corresponded with several
people about *Mexico City Blues*, which along with essays and reading
notes ultimately filled six notebooks. To Allen, he wrote, "I have just
knocked off 150 bloody poetic masterpieces."[21] To Sterling Lord, "I
wrote a big volume of poetry (150 poems) the past week, MEXICO
CITY BLUES which will do for poetry what my prose has done, eventually change it into a medium for Lingual Spontaneity."[22] Jack realized
that this literature had no commercial value. It wasn't for contemporary
audiences. It was for eternity.

Jack had avoided "crafty" revision in his last two years of writing. He
maintained that spontaneity tapped into the sound of the mind. He had

gone to Mexico primarily to get high on pot and write. He came away with two major works that would redefine American poetry. He found that he could, at last, write without being hampered. Malcolm Cowley had succeeded in getting him a $2,000 Academy of Arts and Letters grant. For $50, he sold a short story, "The Mexican Girl," to *Paris Review*.

It wasn't the same for *On the Road*, still facing uphill challenges with Viking. Cowley wrote that it was stalled. Jack's usage of real names for his characters remained a problem. The publisher was not willing to risk its publication unless changes were made. They postponed any further work. Despite all of the spectacular writing accomplished since *On the Road* in 1951, none of it would be reflected in the one book that an editor was willing to publish. He had moved on. Nonetheless, Jack relented in September 1955 to the changes. He consented to change the names, locations, and dates to prevent libel charges.

That same month, Jack left Mexico for Berkeley. He flushed his remaining pot down the toilet to avoid border hassles. The previous week, he had been arrested at the border for possessing mescaline. He was suffering from phlebitis. It had continued unabated despite the penicillin he was injecting. Allen was still there, so Jack was to meet up with him at 1610 Milvia Street.

He took a train to Santa Ana and a bus to Mexicali. He hitchhiked to Los Angeles and hopped a Zipper to Frisco. There was no stopping him. Jack had written Cowley high on his accomplishments, even if he knew the editor was not on board with his visionary trips. He had fulfilled a good portion of his projected Duluoz Legend, even titling the twenty-five-thousand-word *Tristessa* as part of it at the head of the notebook page whenever he picked back up on the story. "I am so glad that I self-taught myself (with some help from Messrs. Joyce & Faulkner) to write SPONTANEOUS PROSE so that the eventual LEGEND will run into millions of words, they'll all be spontaneous and therefore pure and therefore interesting and at the same time what rejoices me most: RHYTHMIC. . . . "[23]

By Cowley's assessment, most of it was drug-influenced rubbish. He was only interested in selling *Beat Generation* (*On the Road*) and was willing to write an introduction for Viking to publish.

When Jack's marijuana use rendered his penicillin treatment worthless, he endured the pain in his legs and moved on. The bus pointed northwest to Allen's Berkeley cottage. It rolled along the highway past "dry cracked ravelled arroyos at the base of vein bleeding mountains of sand, rock, and rustle."[24] The landscape was stark and pale. He scanned the "sad brown twilight of it all" jotting his fresh impressions into his notebook.

In September, Kerouac wrote two new pieces in a notebook devoted primarily to *Mexico City Blues*. The first was "Brakeman on the Railroad": "I'm standing in the crossroads waiting for my freight train to stop rolling so I can cut the train in half and take the matter past. Two AM its nothing but lovers in the car, shyly watching the brakeman in the night."

The other was based on the short life and death of Gerard. He had already attempted this in San Luis Obispo in 1953 with a short story, "Death of Gerard": "There is a memory so deep, so beautiful, in the memory of this world, right or wrong." Kerouac attempted it again at his sister's kitchen table. By his estimate, in the late summer of 1955, he had completed seven volumes of the Duluoz Legend. He felt that all of these books justified his hardscrabble years. His life's work was shaping up at last.

In October, Kerouac hiked the Sawtooth Range with his new friends, Gary Snyder and John Montgomery. Snyder was a Buddhist scholar and poet who, like Jack, possessed an intuitive knowledge of much of the Buddhist canon. Montgomery was a librarian. The climb was both athletic and spiritually stimulating. The silence of Matterhorn Peak was far different from the rabble of North Beach. Kerouac was grateful for the time spent with Snyder and later wrote about this period in *The Dharma Bums* (1958).

He also recorded his dreams, sometimes even seeing the face of his dead brother:

"Visions of Gerard can be traced in part to a dream: One awful central scene, it's in the parlor brown and funeral and coffin-like, Gerard is dead in his coffin and all my writings are racked like candle flickers in a file box by the stuffed sofa in the suffocant gloom dark, literally writing in my brother's tomb—but it's the awful silence, the solemn ceremony of my papers. . . . "[25]

In Kerouac's journal, this dream included an incestuous episode involving Nin. It was not the incestuous act but the "understanding all night long that there had been incest and we should be punished soon." It was the guilty aftermath of having committed the act. Jack, much like Allen, borrowed actively from his dreams for his fiction. Combined with conversations with his mother, these dreams permitted Kerouac to transport the reader back to the tragic decade of 1920s Lowell.

Jack translated some French notes. He was on a train to a San Jose racetrack. It was December. He knew the novel's centerpiece would reveal Gerard to the reader as Kerouac saw him: "pure, tranquil, and sad." To execute this project, Kerouac relied on his prose method and a steady intake of tea, wine, and Benzedrine. Starting each writing session "fast," he would "blow" the words out alternately in spontaneous bursts and long, "slow" sentences. To facilitate these momentary flashes of insight and memory, Kerouac planned to incorporate "pops, tics, flashes" and "blues" within each chapter to create an experimental novel to match *Doctor Sax* in scope and ambition. (As defined by Kerouac, a "pop" is an American haiku consisting of short three-line poems, a "tic" is a "vision sudden of memory," a "blues" is one complete poem a notebook page in length, and "flashes" are "short sleepdreams or drowse daydreams of an enlightened nature describable in a few words." None of these methods were used to write the novel.) After making these preliminary notes, he put the book aside until he reached the East that Christmas.

Cowley responded to Jack's September 1955 letter later that month. He suggested that Jack discard the title *Beat Generation* and use *On the Road*. Kerouac agreed, knowing he could use the former title for another related work. Later that fall, Cowley wrote again to Kerouac, concerned with the libel issues of *On the Road*.

"We are still thinking very seriously about publishing *On the Road*. The difficulties are still the ones I mentioned in my last letter, and the principal difficulty is the danger of libel. For the last two weeks the manuscript has been in the hands of the Viking lawyer, who will mark the dangerous passages and submit a brief to us."

It wasn't just a matter of changing names and locations. What mattered to Viking's legal department was Jack's depiction of some of the characters' actions and the repercussions it could create for the company if Kerouac's portrayal sparked "shame or ridicule." Viking's attorney informed Cowley that the best resolution was to have Jack obtain signed waivers from Neal and Allen who figured prominently throughout the book. Malcolm was optimistic that the issues could be resolved and they could soon finalize a contract. On November 8, Malcolm wrote Jack, repeating attorney Nathaniel Whitehorn's advice:

"You must remember that in a book of this type every character starts out with two fixed points of reference and identification. Each of them is a friend of the author or has had some contact with him in the manner reflected in the book, and each is also a friend or acquaintance of Dean. In addition, each of them is a friend of one or more of the other characters. As a result, identifying any particular character takes but a little more definite reference."[26]

The lawyer was especially troubled by *On the Road*'s "Denver" section because it depicted the lives of many "respectable" people. Jack got the necessary waivers from Allen and Neal and mailed them to Cowley.

The three months in California were the best time in Jack's adult life thus far. The wine flowed freely, he had friends and acquaintances with similar passions, and another book was on its way to bookshelves across America. For once, Kerouac could enjoy the prospects of potential commercial success from *On the Road*. If the novel were successful, the rest of his unpublished work would finally see the light of day. Kerouac also imagined selling film rights for $150,000 with Marlon Brando as Dean Moriarty and Montgomery Clift as Sal Paradise.[27]

Kerouac's freedom to hitchhike and hop freights between cities on a whim especially thrilled him. He resorted more often to the railroad, particularly since the average American tourist had become increasingly paranoid about picking up dusty hitchhikers. Once, Kerouac lucked out. He caught a ride to San Francisco from a lithesome young blonde in a strapless white bathing suit. She drove a 1955 Mercury Montclair:

"I am bloody well afraid to look at her, the curl of her milk armpits, the flesh of her cream legs, the cream, legs, curls, love, milk, wow, did I love that, not looking, but giggling, hearing she has been driving all the way from Fort Worth Texas without sleep I say 'O how would you like some Mexican Benzedrine?' (which I have in big battered pack that I just been sleepin on beach in cold night of sea fog coast with, sad, talking to old sad Greeks at noon, the old Greek taking his annual vacation wanders up and down the sands looking at driftwood)—'Crazy!' she yells, I whip out my Benzedrine, yanking out all my dirty underwear and unspeakable Mexican raggedy junks and give her, she takes two, very much, we stop at a coke station and she mumps out jumping, the sweetest little perfect everything you know."[28]

She dropped him roadside. They made a date to see each other again. Although he never did, he wrote of her in a short prose piece later published in *Playboy* (January 1965) and titled "Good Blonde."

With a final monthly stipend of $50, Jack bought a new poncho and a down-insulated sleeping bag. When he visited the Cassadys, he slept in their yard, in his sleeping bag, before leaving for the East Coast. Toward the end of his visit, Jack drank wine with Neal and went to the race track. As usual, Neal lost money. He coerced his latest girlfriend, Natalie Jackson, into forging Carolyn's signature on $10,000 worth of savings bonds (compensation from the railroad after his accident). Soon afterward, Natalie leaped off a roof and killed herself. Jack was shaken by the news having been the last to speak with her. He wrote:

"About this time Natalie Jackson committed suicide—I tried to tell her everything was empty, including her paranoic idea that the cops were after her & all of us—she said O YOU DON'T KNOW! then the next day she was found dazed on the roof and when a cop tried to catch her she jumped, off Neal's tenement roof."[29]

Distressed and visibly shaken, Neal returned to his family to restore normalcy. He prayed to save Natalie's soul from limbo. During the day, the Cassady children took turns reading one of Jack's poems back to him. On his last day, Neal wanted Jack to return to the track with $300 in cash Jack had wired to him. Thinking better of it, Jack told Carolyn that he had to leave before he was penniless again.

In San Jose, Jack went into a train yard. He was cautious of guards vigilant for vagrants breaking the boxcar seals, shattering the windows, and leaving broken bottles around the tracks. The sun had set. Jack was chilled to the bone. Still, he waited until he learned that the train wasn't going to show. He lit a fire by the rails and heated a can of macaroni. He spoke with some on-duty switchmen. They advised him to move to the other side of the yard to elude the night watchman. Later that night, Jack boarded a flatbed, unrolled his sleeping bag, and slept twelve hours through the Diablo Range. When the train stopped in Watsonville, north of Salinas, Jack saw flashlights playing along the sides of the cars. He jumped off and hid in a lettuce field. When the *Zephyr* blew its whistle to leave, Jack ran under cover of darkness and boarded. He rode until eight o'clock the following day when he reached Los Angeles.

Jack hated Los Angeles. The smog burned his eyes. It hurt his sinuses. Huddling by a highway, he watched the Yuma *Zephyr* as it prepared to go to Arizona. He expected it at four but did not show up until 8:40 p.m. Jack was almost injured this time: when he hopped it, the train was moving at 15 miles per hour. He ran with a pack on his back. He tried to tie the pack onto the catwalk by its strap clip. The train picked up steam faster than Jack expected and threw him off balance. He jumped off before the train picked up more speed and landed in a ditch. There he stayed. After a dinner of beans and macaroni, he unrolled his bag and slept fitfully.

The next day, December 14, Jack went to an L.A. bus terminal to catch a bus to Riverside. While waiting, he went into a coffee shop on South Main Street. His restless imagination took over. He wrote a poem:

Los Angeles
Original name of Our Lady
The Queen of the Angels
Synus in me Mynus
Mizruble,
Tried — Waited —
The Yuma Zipper
    was a bloody no-good
18-car scaled somnumbitch.[30]

On the next day when his bus arrived in Riverside, Jack went to a dried-out river bed to sleep. He lit a small fire, drank tea, and ate a supper of beans. He took out his notebook, recorded the date, and wrote a poem, "Little Pureland Blues." He was suspicious of the law busting in on his serenity. Fires weren't allowed. A man told him he wasn't safe, so Jack waited until dusk to light a fire and heat his food. Despite this warning, he stayed until the next day before hitchhiking to Beaumont. Amid a group of high schoolers, he ate as carefree as they did: a hot dog, hamburger, french fries, and a strawberry shake. In Calexico, a watchman on patrol nearly arrested him for trying to piss at a construction site. He searched out another river bottom for the night. A deaf and hard-of-hearing Mexican gestured to him that he would be robbed or murdered if he stayed.

Gesturing to the mountains south, the deaf man indicated that that location was safer. Jack took his advice and left. Later that day, he reached the border between California and Mexico. He crossed into Mexicali and walked around, ogling the women: "Thank you O Lord for returning me my zest for life, for thy ever recurring forms in Thy Womb of Exuberant Fertility!"[31]

Jack bought sixty codienattas[32] and fifty Benzedrine inhalers for $3.50 at a drugstore. When he returned to the border, an American border patrol guard searched his bag, narrowly missing the flap pocket where he stashed his wares. They also missed a batch of goofballs[33] he had concealed within.

Jack tried to catch the Zipper out of town in El Centro, California, at the southern border of Imperial Valley. However, a train conductor told him he would have to jump a freight train through Mexico instead. Jack opted for the road and flagged down a truck driver named Charley Burchette. Burchette promised to give him a ride to Springfield, Ohio, if he showed him a good time in Mexicali that night. They parked the truck in Calexico, crossed the border, got drunk on tequila, and consorted with some "sultry" Mexican whores. On December 20, four nights later, Charley dropped him off in Springfield. Jack boarded a bus to North Carolina for $12.31.

To his mother, Jack continued to express his forlorn state, that he was lonely and missed her while he was away. Gabe "read between the lines" of his last letter and had tried to dissuade him from going to Mexico, feeling that he could never really accomplish anything out there besides sleeping on the road and eating "scanty" foods. For Gabe, such aimless travels were a waste of money. She called him "Garbo"[34] for wanting to be isolated away from his family. Gabe implored him to leave Mexico and return home for Christmas. Caroline offered up her porch for him to sleep. She even installed an oil burner to keep him warm during the winter nights.

Gabe still nursed a hatred for Allen, and she guessed that Jack was "probably spending all your money to feed him." She was controlling and able to utilize her son's sensitive nature to manipulate his feelings toward his friends. She advised him not to live off of the Cassadys' charity: "don't wear out your welcome out there." She played Jack and Caroline off of each other, by turns begging them to get along, and secretly talking about each behind their backs. Her restless nature turned Jack away from any stability he may have yearned for. She pined to Jack a litany of complaints:

"I'm so tired of all this mess, its too hot or too damp and too damn much bugs you cant enjoy sittin out doors for the mosquitoes eat you up even in the day time. Its a damn round of scratches all day all night.[35] What good is it if I have to stay behind closed doors all the time, see nobody or go for a decent walk on a good hard sidewalk. All I can see ahead of me is make beds, wash clothes, iron and wash dishes and cook and take care of children, and to top it all no place to go but to start this routine day after day, why did I get myself into this Ill never know, its crazy, and I could kick myself good and hard."[36]

Her ploy of "letting off steam" fed into Jack's guilt and sense of obligation. On the one hand, she implored him to return to North Carolina, on the other, she complained of having to live there.

Two days before Christmas, Jack was standing outside Caroline's home in the woods. He had walked three frozen miles along Route 64 under the winter moon to her home. When he reached the yard, he stood in the dark watching his mother wash dishes.

I'll never hurt you again.

They were expecting him. He apologized to his mother for being late. Caroline prepared the couch. However, Jack opted for the back porch and his sleeping bag despite the cold. There was no promised heater. The frost shone in the moonlit yard. After the family retired to bed, Jack shrugged on his poncho and stepped outside with Bob, the family hunting dog: "I sighed because I didn't have to think any more and felt my whole body sink into a blessedness surely to be believed."[37]

On Christmas Eve, Jack drank from a wine bottle while watching the televised Christmas mass at New York's St. Patrick's Cathedral. Afterward, he read from his Bible and wrote "Drinking Pomes"—

You blest me
      sweet cat
With yr arrival
      on my lap

—and scribbled notations.[38]

After the excitement of the Christmas holiday, the Blake household went quiet. Gabe left for New York to attend her stepmother Amanda Dube's funeral. Nin and Paul were at work. Jack sat at the kitchen table to write. He swallowed Bennies, lit a candle, and wrote: "O Lord, reveal to me My Buddhawork and give me the great intense eager ecstatic excitement of the Holy Words, amen."

The temptation, it would seem, would be for him to write of his latest West Coast travels. There was a fresh influx of artists and Buddhists. There was the San Francisco Renaissance, which he acknowledged as an emerging literary movement. Instead, he reached into early childhood and tapped the rich reserve of memories he stored there. His Catholic sensibility reasserted itself, sometimes overwhelming his Buddhist learning. References from St. Paul's letters to the Corinthians resided alongside quotes from Visuddhi-Magga. He spent the first days of 1956 "drunk with Shakespeare's power" after reading *Henry IV*.

By January 7, he was six thousand words in, writing confessional and schoolyard scenes. A fresh reading of parts of *Finnegans Wake* contributed to his verbal experimentation. His speed-whacked mind grew nauseated.

On January 10, Jack finished the "Christmas Eve" chapter after spending a "Long Night of Suffering" during its composition. Twelve pages completed on January 12 went to waste when Kerouac crossed out all of the work. He decided to take a three-day break. The scene he planned to write next was the most daunting of all: Gerard's funeral. On the 16th, shortly after midnight, Kerouac wrote the novel's closing lines. He considered it a "modest" closing: a gravedigger poised above the open grave with a shovelful of freshly turned soil. In his journal, he jotted: "O rainy bleary face of graves! Wont they get sick of me for this one?" In his assessment, the novel was important. He wrote to Gary Snyder (now in Japan) that it was his "best most serious sad & true book yet." After finishing, Kerouac prayed to "St. Gerard" to "protect" him from getting drunk again.

Despite his misgivings over his sobriety, Jack left for New York two days later to retrieve Gabe. Once there, he saw "The Mexican Girl" in the *Paris Review*. He stayed two weeks before returning to North Carolina with his mother. Kerouac was miserable in New York. Nin rebuked him for their mother having to work to support him instead of the opposite. When Jack claimed that he had given Gabe $50 of his stipend, Gabe denied it. He was coming down from Bennies, which left him depressed. Wine sickened him. He felt old and futile mixing with the Village poets that he perceived as "enthusiastic fools of the future." Miserably, he watched Alene Lee kissing other men through a tavern window. He ended the night sleeping on a cold bench.

Jack was paranoid after losing contact with Cowley. He wrote his agent expressing a fear that Viking had totally forgotten about *On the Road* after he verbally agreed to the manuscript. Jack had two more pencil-written drafts typed for Sterling to send to Viking: *Visions of Gerard* and *Tristessa*.

Jack's family conflicts had gotten worse. He complained to Allen that he was constantly babysitting and washing dishes, though he was hopeful by writing *Wake Up*. He had tentative plans to return to New York and bring back with him "100 pounds" of his manuscripts and his mother using Paul Blake's pickup truck. In July, he would leave his mother behind and hitchhike and freight hop to Texas with his backpack, sleeping bag, and the *Diamond Sutra*. There was the white-hot desert where he planned to stay before hopping the Zipper to Frisco in September. He implored Allen not to leave before he got there.[39]

After completing *Wake Up*, Jack handwrote a "spontaneous study" of Burroughs titled *Visions of Bill* which he intended to write in the same vein as *Visions of Neal*. It would be greater, in Jack's estimate, than Laurence Sterne's *Tristram Shandy*[40] (1759): "I intend to be the greatest writer in the world and then in the name of Buddha I shall convert thousands, maybe millions: 'Ye shall be Buddhas, rejoice!'"[41] He used a notebook bought in Mexico City, wrote "Visions of Bill" in black marker on the front cover, and flipped to the first page where he drew a likeness of Burroughs in eyeglasses and fedora hat. Then he began writing:

"Ever onward the Faustian soul, so especially about Bill. I dont have to wait till he dies to complete his story, he above all's best left marching in with that aggressive swing of his arms thru the Medinas of Arabic Africa when he's not well dressed in tie & white shirt & coat to look like a businessman so he can connect for junk in rainy Greenwich Village. . . . "[42]

Through every page, Jack wrote without crossing out in spontaneous prose, outlining the Burroughsian world as Kerouac saw it in his time. Jack's history of his friendship with Bill extends to his very first impressions of him before meeting him one fateful day: "What was the beginning for me was 1944, summer, when I first heard about him thru Lucien & Dave —'Bill Burroughs' made me picture a stocky dark haired person of peculiar intensity because of the reports about him, the peculiar directedness of his actions but here he comes walking into our pad dull and bespectacled and thin in a seersucker suit as tho he's just returned from a compound in Equatorial Africa when he'd sit at dusk with a martini discussing the peculiarities of the natives. . . . "

Though it is a completed novella, Jack did not retype it for publication.[43]

Though Jack wrote Allen that he "loved everybody" and saw himself as an "imaginary blossom," his family was not having it.[44] In protest of Caroline putting him to work, Jack "banished" himself to Big Easonburg woods to meditate his family woes in fitful anguish. Paul refused to offer Jack his cot or porch. The Blakes were sick of their tight quarters. Paul

Jr. had to sleep with Gabe. The agreement, Gabe reminded Caroline, was that her investment in Paul's television business would cover her and Jack's room and board. Soon, Gabe tired of Nin and decided to leave with Jack. Tentatively, Jack planned to go to San Francisco and rent an apartment for them both before leaving for his fire-lookout job in June. Months later, Kerouac would write about the "cold eyed sister / that made a bum outa me."[45]

Jack worked through March typing *Some of the Dharma* and completed it shortly after his thirty-fourth birthday. He planned a sequel to *The Town and the City* titled *The Martin Family*; it was never finished beyond eight short chapters. The next day, he wrote Carolyn that he was going west to meet with Malcolm Cowley in Palo Alto. He would try to see her afterward.

He was ready to return west. His trek brought him through the drenching humidity of the American South where he got lost in Georgia. "I'm in hell again!" he proclaimed in *The Dharma Bums*. Dreading an equally treacherous pass through Texas, he opted to buy a bus ticket to El Paso and, from there, hop a boxcar freight. However, Kerouac, after a night of delicious sleep, opted to hitchhike to Las Cruces, New Mexico.

Then Jack hitchhiked to Mill Valley, California (about forty minutes from San Francisco). For several weeks, he cohabited with poets Gary Snyder and Philip Whalen, who were sharing a friend's "unfinished shack" (as described by poet Michael McClure and owned by Locke McCorkle) within a perfumy cluster of eucalyptus and evergreen trees. In this rustic setting, all of them reposed in the serenity that Kerouac had been seeking.

Gary Snyder left for Japan in May 1956. Before leaving on April 1, Jack wrote "Emptiness Prayer":

"What does it mean that I am in the endless universe, thinking that I'm a man sitting under the stars on the terrace of the earth, but actually empty & awake throughout the emptiness and awakedness of everything? It means that I am empty and awake, knowing that I am empty, awake, and that there's no difference between me and anything else."[46]

This notebook was added to during his Mill Valley stay, loaded with precise scriptures and some "doodling with an endless automatic writing piece" titled "Old Lucien Midnight." This new writing, he explained to John Clellon Holmes in a letter, "raves on and on with no direction and no story and surely that wont do tho I'll finish it anyway while doing other things. . . . " It was the opposite of scripture writing. One and the other shared the same notebook, two stylistic opposites.

Jack was insulted by Sterling Lord among others who asked Kerouac if his Buddhist writings were any good, in particular his "Lake of Light" Buddhist book, *Buddha Tells Us*.[47] Lord, for Jack, was taking too long. In frustration, Caroline volunteered herself as Jack's business manager of his manuscripts, stated that he ought to get rid of Lord in favor of somebody who could work more expeditiously on his behalf. He implored to Allen for any new ideas which Ginsberg could pass through Nin for her unprofessional consideration.

Jack relished his isolation, reading haikus and sponge baths in the sunny yard. At night, he slept under the moon thinking, "Why?" His eyes were on the immediate future, the mountain sixty-three hundred feet above the world and, later, another foray to Mexico, and then, possibly, his road novel would finally see the light of day. He was far away in spirit from the Cassadys, whom he felt were "crazy" over their Cayce preoccupations.[48]

On April 10, he scribbled in pencil another piece of scripture, "Dharma 10."

"Did I create that sky? Yes, for, if it was anything other than a conception in my mind I wouldn't have said 'Sky'—That is why I am t.g.e. There are not two of us here, reader & writer, but one, one g.e., One-Which-It-Is, That-Which-Is-Everything-Is. (For the thatness of the emptiness of all things is the same.)"[49]

Why then, if he was under such pretenses of bliss, did he still feel the need to binge on alcohol? He blew $10 meant to buy a pair of jeans on whiskey. Remorseful, he tried to make his way to Laurel Dell "to purify me" but lost his track on the Sierra Trail. He built a bonfire and sat naked, eating from a tin of beans. Exhausted, he fell asleep under the moon after listening to the hooves of deer cavorting through the clearing. When he woke, a bull had taken his shirt off a stick and was playfully tossing it around before joining the rest of the cows. Then Jack had breakfast, a sacred ritual he especially enjoyed because it brought him the satisfaction of independence. He filled Snyder's tea tin with a stewed mixture of black-eyed peas and port and some oatmeal, bacon, apricots, and corn-cake batter. In two hours he returned, presumably purified, to the cabin and promptly fell asleep.

Much as he did when writing *Visions of Gerard,* Jack lit a candle and wrote in pencil. As he wrote, he shared pages with McClure, who was a regular visitor at the shack. McClure was impressed by Kerouac's wordplay, that he could tap his sensorium and wrote without regard for convention:

"The Mill Valley trees, the pines with green mint look and there's a tangled eucalyptus hulk stick fallen thru the late sunlight tangle of those needles, hanging from it like a live wire connecting it to the ground—just below, the notches where little Fred sought to fell sad pine—not bleeding much—just a lot of crystal sap the ants are mining in, motionless like cows on the grass & so they must be aphyds percolatin up a steam to store provender in their bottomless bellies that for all I know are bigger than the bellies of the Universe beyond."[50]

On June 18, Jack left McCorckle's cabin and walked to Marble-mount, California. He was scheduled to begin his new job in late June. He was given instructions by friends for a faster route to the Cascades, suggesting that he stick to the coastline before turning northeast toward the mountains. At the start, he bought a supply of rye crackers, dates, peanuts, and four pints of beer and put it all deep into his rucksack. He had $14.57 left.

In the flap of his rucksack was a black 5 & dime notebook which on its small pages Kerouac typed out the words of the *Diamond Sutra.* He also wrote into the notebook the *Maha Prajna Paramita Hridaya* and Snyder's translation of Han Shan's *Cold Mountain.*

By noon he arrived at Geyserville's Russian River Bridge and hitched a much-shorter ride with a farmer and his family. Another offered a truck ride to Eureka, driving 280 miles through slanting gray rain. The driver, Ray, spoke a cadence that syncopated with the beat of the windshield blades. Ray told Kerouac of his father who was dead ten years now. It made Jack want to weep. When they reached Humboldt Redwood

Forest, Ray bought Jack a shrimp dinner, strawberry pie with ice cream, and four cups of rich black coffee. Since they couldn't find a motel, they slept by the beach in the truck cab.

The following morning, after eating a big breakfast, Jack saluted his driver off and started walking. He also stopped to replenish his strength with a noonday nap. A fear of poison oak made him sleep restlessly. He woke, ate his lunch, smoked his pipe, and wondered where to go next. He turned northeast toward the old gold-mining town of Kerby, Oregon. There he got another ride—lasting a single mile—and then another by a lumberjack who reminded him of Neal Cassady. The lumberjack's truck swept across the valley toward the distant hazy mountains until passing through Eugene, fifty miles east of the Pacific coastline. By this time dusk had tea-steeped the sky into blood-red remnants. Kerouac admired the driver's independence and fearlessness, and that he, too, harbored a fanaticism for sports matching his own.

Under a pine tree, Kerouac ate and napped for twelve hours. He lathered up insect repellent to ward off the angry mosquito swarms that rose in clouds. When he woke the next morning, he counted his money—$14.03—and set his sights for Portland, Oregon. Portland was another 110 miles if he chose to follow straight up Route 99. Two brothers delivered him just outside Junction City, where, after having coffee with them, he walked two miles to a restaurant, ate eggs and hash browns, and wondered, perhaps bleakly, about his future. Yet, he realized, the "road is life," and so he continued.

What if *On the Road* failed? It was also possible he could experience a reversal of fortune: respectability and money and fame. Unfazed, he composed a poem about walking along the highway as cars indifferently zipped by, another day—another era; of lunchroom flowers and ghostly mountains lingering mirage-like over the horizon; of a Chinese woman and her pet Chow; of murmuring lunchtime conversations; a glass of water with a protruding phallic spoon, its smooth sheen beaded with perspiration. No detail was too trite for poetry.

The following morning, Jack reached Seattle, Washington, and read the *Diamond Sutra* in a skid-row room. He hitched out the next morning with a lonely Okie. Jack was grateful for his company. The driver continued picking up other hitchers: another Okie and a sailor from Montana bursting with intelligent talk. They kept Kerouac's ear occupied for eighty miles until reaching Olympia, Washington. At the dock of a ferry, Kerouac paid his fare and, just as he did on the SS *Dorchester*, climbed the stairs to the top deck and stood in the drizzly rain and watched the restless green waters. Beneath a soggy issue of *Time* he found an abandoned half-pint of vodka and drank it as the bracing wind slapped his face and ruffled his hair.

At Puget Sound, he caught a glimpse of his final destination on the horizon: the North Cascades.

Another skid-row room; money was running low and it cost him $1.75. He had a regimen in place: a meditative read from the *Sutra*, a steamy bath, and sleep. By morning he shaved to make himself more acceptable to drivers and then walked along 1st Avenue looking for a Goodwill. He bought a new belt, jockstrap, shirt, handkerchief, and bandana. At the Public Market, he fueled his body on breakfast and coffee and calculated another 150 miles to Rainier Station with only $8.60 to his name. The skies improved: cool, clear, and sunny: "O my Karma luck fantastic," he wrote. He walked up Alaskan Way to Aurora Street to "hit the final wilderness road to my Complete Rejoicement in the Wisdom & Be Compassion of the Talahasta." By 4:00 p.m., he reached Burlington, Washington. He had thirty miles to go. A lumberman drove him for a stretch and then Ken Nordstrom driving a 240 horsepower Olds '66 fresh from the San Jose car races took him the rest of the way north before Kerouac turned east through Sedro-Wooley's Main Street of five-and-dimes, hardware, and grain stores until the land abandoned civilization altogether until reaching Concrete. The mountains were upon him. He was riverside, with fallen logs and hermit clouds skirting timbered peaks.

Over the choppy waters of Ross Lake, Kerouac, a muleskinner guide named Andy, assistant ranger Marty Gohlke, and some horses and mules crossed on a tugboat during a pelting rain storm. "Well, boy," Andy told Kerouac, "now we're gonna put you away where we can't reach ya—you better get ready."

The tugboat disembarked its human and animal cargo. One mule, strapped down with batteries and canned goods, trod through the downpour. The steep terrain gave way to alpine meadows and then the first intimations of the mountaintop proper. A gray fog moved in ghostly tendrils until the world, at last, succumbed to a forest of clouds.

And then darkness fell.

Dismayed, Jack realized he would be without alcohol and was afraid that he could not endure abstinence. His sleep was fitful; a dream of his father dying in his chair and his mother sent to an insane asylum marked one long night spent staring into the dark abyss. In his fire tower, he spent hours in a canvas chair facing the north, where Mount Hozomeen loomed before him in its natural splendor. Taking in the whole panorama of the Hozomeen terrain, the landscape was stark and spooky. Inside the lookout tower, Jack had a stove on which to cook his food. At night, lying awake in his sleeping bag, he could hear the sounds of mice in the cabin and of deer foraging within the perimeter of the campsite. He spent some of his time listening to the "big event in the loneliness" which started at eight o'clock. It was radio chatter crackling between fire towers scattered throughout Mount Baker National Forest. When he wasn't playing his fantasy-baseball game or doing his job, Kerouac wrote by the light of his kerosene lamp. His accumulated spiral notebooks (numbering roughly 615 pages) contained an array of different works he attempted to write simultaneously. Some of the material would later be included in the first half of his novel *Desolation Angels* (1965). Another never-completed novel is about his Ozone Park years of the mid-1940s.

By the end of July, the novelty of fire-watching became routine drudgery. There were, thus far, no fires. He dourly noted; "O I looked forward to come up here, why don't I eat my own dreary enthusiasms." His dream of living like Thoreau had failed. There was no revelation. There was nothing to stare at anymore but the great mountain vistas, which humbled him to insignificance. To Kerouac, Mount Hozomeen appeared as a "Chinese mountain" spiked with pointed firs and burdened by huge gray boulders of basalt:

"[M]y God look at Hozomeen, is he worried or tearful? Does he bend before storms or snarl when the sun shines or sigh in the late day drowse? Does he smile? Was he not born out of madbrained turmoils and upheavals of raining fire . . . ?"[51]

By night, the distant glowing lamp lights of the other lookouts sparkled from the engulfing darkness of the mountain valleys. At night, after standing on his head, a self-prescribed exercise to ward off phlebitis, Kerouac wrote "thousands of words." The next morning, after making his breakfast and washing up, he returned to fire-watching. Staring at the same views began to weary him.

While at Desolation Peak, he recalled and recorded football board games with his father during winter blizzards; warm June evenings on Pawtucketville's Phebe Avenue; the "marshmallow lips" and "silk thighs" of Mary Carney; and his final surrender to eternity.

Jack also wrote blues poems and "Ozone Park" that he intended to add to the Duluoz Legend. His notebook was forming into a work in and of itself. It was scattered with haiku and prayers, quotes from the *Sutra*, detailed expenses for his stay, and commentary on his everyday activities. He meditated on the Essence, the Tathagata, beyond all coming and going. The big Nothingness. Long walks on logging roads took him to a place of dead trees. He sang into the silence despite the plague of mosquitoes biting him. At night, the mice kept him awake. He had to set up a water trap to reduce their numbers, guilty because he felt that he had abandoned his Buddhist principles. One time, he found a mouse in a basket of food hung from the rafter. It was chewing through a packet of dried pea soup. Jack stabbed the creature through the packet and wounded it. He felt its eyes looking through him. He knocked it on the head with his flashlight. Its eyes popped out. Horrified, Jack sat down and trembled. Heartsick. He tossed a baby mouse down off a cliff. To the sky, he proclaimed, "If there's a hell and bad karma, send me hell and give me bad karma for doing this and may I be reborn a mouse." If it came down to it, he didn't care if there was a God, a Buddha, or even a Heaven. He finalized this sorry chain of events with one of his most enduring aphorisms: "I don't know, I don't care, and it doesn't matter."

Jack had everything to look forward to, especially a September trip to Mexico. He had $300 in traveler's checks. The days grew longer. He felt himself a failure in his writing. Looking out in contemplation at a sea of shining clouds, he continued working on "Ozone Park." The mouse-killing business had moved him to open the story with his father drowning mice when Jack was a child. After fifteen thousand words, he thought it wasn't enough. By mid-July, he was frustrated. The endless hordes of insects drove him insane. It was hot; the sun blazed in the cloudless sky. The air was thin: "for the fuck of me I'd like to get the fuck out of here!" He was out of cigarettes. He fought boredom. His Thoreau fantasy had gone bust. He stood on his head in the moonlight and saw that the earth was truly upside-down in the void. Mountains became "hanging bubbles." And what was a man but a "weird vain beetle full of strange ideas walking around upside-down and boasting."

Jack came down from the mountain on September 5. He had a new body of work he could begin to transform into finished books. He completed a transliteration of the *Diamond Sutra*. He paid his store bill and mailed Gabe $100. Then, to San Francisco, where he met up with poet Gregory Corso, Neal, Peter Orlovsky's brother, Lafcadio, and Allen. They were photographed together by *Mademoiselle* magazine. *Howl and Other Poems* was about to be published by City Lights. Allen's poetry prompted *Mademoiselle*'s photos and article of the "Flaming Cool Youth of San Francisco Poetry." In the photo, a tired and drawn Kerouac, silver crucifix dangling from his neck, poses among a motley group of invigorated poets. Buzzing on the attention given to Allen, Jack suggested to Sterling Lord that he should submit excerpts from *The Subterraneans* to magazines and journals. Robert Creeley chose two of Kerouac's writings for the *Black Mountain Review*. Jack then hopped the *Zephyr* and a bus to Tucson, Arizona. As he hiked through Arizona on the way to Mexico City, he was stopped for vagrancy. What puzzled the cops was that Jack had a pack of $5 traveler's checks in his possession.

"I'm 34, regular looking, but in my jeans and eerie outfits people are scared to look at me because I really look like an escaped mental patient with enough physical strength and innate dog-sense to manage outside of an institution to feed myself and go from place to place in a world growing gradually narrower in its views about eccentricity every day— Walking thru towns in the middle of America I got stared at weirdly—I was bound to live my own way."[52]

And then a hitchhike traipse through the moonlit morning hours straight to Nogales for a bus to Mexico City. It was a long exhausting trek. He fell into a sound sleep, relieved to at last be at rest, the best kind, when the journey has ended.

* * *

October 1956: On his arrival, Jack took a bang of morphine offered by Bill Garver and slept in his rented rooftop apartment at 212 Orizaba Street. Garver had two rooms that cost Jack 140 pesos a month ($11.76 USD at that time). Back in the States, things were slowly turning in Jack's favor. *Evergreen Review* wanted *The Subterraneans* for their first paperback publication. Potentially, he wrote Allen, he could earn $500 at a penny a word (fifty thousand words). Jack also intended on finishing *Tristessa* and beginning *Desolation Angels*, documenting his fire-watching experience. Another notebook of poems (Jack claimed they surpassed *Mexico City Blues* in a letter to Ginsberg) was lost to a thief who pocketed his notebook and wouldn't give it back.

Bill Garver was an old associate of Herbert Huncke when they stole overcoats in New York. He was a junkie associate of Burroughs's in Mexico. He had been living in Mexico City on a trust fund of $150 per month. In Jack's company, Garver behaved much like Burroughs. He was a splendid talker, orating at length on books they mutually enjoyed. Garver's monologue fed into "Orizaba 210 Blues" where Jack transcribed his monologue directly through choruses 31 to 41. Through all of the other choruses, Jack swam into a language sea, letting words wash over him with renewed confidence.

Jack met up with Esperanza, but she was out of her mind on goof-balls. He made it with her once but regretted it afterward. She had written Spanish letters, telling Jack that he was "sweet." She implored him to write back. Jack had visions of her warm arms embracing him. Now, he was here and he saw that she was not what he had remembered of her, or what he imagined. Garver warned Jack that she had changed in the last two weeks. She had been punching him. Had struck him with objects. One morning, Garver brought Esperanza into their room. He was holding her up. She had recently suffered partial paralysis down one of her legs. Her body was covered with cysts. She meekly smiled at Jack.

At once, Jack felt it was his duty to save her. However, he was conflicted, once he saved her, then what would he do with her?

And then, Esperanza was tearing the room apart causing Garver to sleep on the rooftop bed. She had fallen on the floor and struck her head. Too many Secanols. She was taking the risk of respiratory failure or even death should she ingest too many. She was unhappy with Jack and ordered him out of Garver's room. She tried to strike him with a bottle. Then she sat on the floor in an idiotic stupor.

On the rooftop, Garver was also high on Secanols. He feared that she would kill them both. They hid the bread knife. Jack slept on the stone floor fitfully with the skittering vermin.

By the next day, she had recovered. Jack felt like he was in love with her, projecting upon her the same ideals that he had written about when he began *Tristessa*. In a cab, he told her that he loved her. She did not reply but told Garver that he had hit on her. Jack told Garver that she was lying. It seemed that along with her addiction, she had changed into a dishonest junkie like the rest of them. Disappointed, he gave up on her. He describes her in *Tristessa* as "the sad mutilated blue Madonna."

"Orizaba 210 Blues" drifts from wordplay to free-associative imagery. He incorporated within the work eleven verses transcribing Bill Garver, who lived beneath Jack's rooftop room. The verses are a word-for-word accounting of Garver's New York City exploits as a thief trying to satisfy his drug dependency. By the forty-second chorus, Jack switched to French. The sixty-ninth chorus is a prayer, almost a plea for a Higher Power to intercede on his behalf. Interestingly, the poem is entirely devoid of Buddhist references.

One morning, after a late night of "scribbling poems and blues" by candlelight, Jack was awakened by Allen, Peter, Lafcadio Orlovsky, and Gregory Corso. They walked through the Thieves Market and the Tenochtitlán pyramids. Although the history and mythology of Mexico impressed Allen, Gregory couldn't understand why anybody would want to be among a people so oppressed by poverty and sickness. Corso decided to leave.

* * *

By November 1956, Jack, still in Mexico City, awaited word from Malcolm Cowley. He felt that he had given Viking enough time to consider. However, not only was *On the Road* under consideration, but Cowley's interests also extended to *Maggie Cassidy* and *Doctor Sax*, which he wanted to merge into a single book. Jack refused and stood firm: "I've been through every conceivable disgrace now, and no rejection or acceptance by publishers can alter that awful final feeling of death-of-life-which-is-death."[53]

Viking finally accepted *On the Road* in the autumn of 1956. Proudly, Jack signed the contract before leaving for Tangier.

* * *

In January 1957, Jack had come off a good run of furious composition that cooked on the embers of a fire fueled by narcotics, alcohol, and a diminishing reserve of mental coercion.

Then it was mid-February. The worst of New York's savage winter had yet to pass. Jack would not wait for spring. He was leaving for Tangier.[54]

It was a slow-going freighter he embarked on—the SS *Slovenia*—docked in Brooklyn and Perth Amboy, New Jersey. On board, flannel-shirted Jack ate at an expansive table draped with white linen. A street pigeon at a peacock soirée. A German woman joined as they supped on soup, chicken, and a dessert smothered in raisin sauce. The night before, he had worked up a drunk. A dreadful hangover followed like an ever-lingering cloud. He suffered despair. Writing no longer brought joy. Nor religion. Reading Kierkegaard, he came into accord with the anxiety that he endured. It was a spiritual death vacillating from Christianity to Buddhism. He was in a vicious cycle: he had money to burn and it was spent on all-night drinking binges and food. When he was broke, he repented to Jesus and Buddha. He was guilt-haunted. He was guilty of his mother, now an older woman, still working to support him.

He had a daughter he refused to acknowledge. The past ran like a black river through his heart. Gabe was his best companion. She was the only woman that ever mattered. No other came close. Other women were for sexual gratification. His mother was his true intimate.

Warding off drink in an effort to stay dry for as long as possible, he sat in the ship's cabin and read the *Diamond Sutra*. He favored the isolation of a small room. To be cloistered from the teeming world meant that he could be caught up in creation when it came to him. He envisioned a secret Parisian garret for himself.

Slovenia rocked in the stormy Atlantic seas. The decks were awash with flecks of sea foam. Jack maintained his resolve. To keep his cool for as long as possible. He abandoned Kierkegaard and turned to world history: Augustus, Horace, Cicero, Virgil. He watched the full moon rise over far-off Africa. Two cats squared off on the evening deck: the Golden Eternity of God. The Unborn Light.

On February 23, *Slovenia* arrived. Jack found Bill had gone completely "mad." A comic genius, even. He imagined Bill to be cackling prophecies. They walked the Arab quarters in search of notebooks. They smoked marijuana in public. No hangups, no laws or rules. Jack became enamored with Morocco for the same reasons as Burroughs: its apparent lawlessness and exotic allure. Jack's tiny room was in his favor. It was maintained daily by a Chinese maid and a French landlady.

He wandered through the Casbah. At a Spanish restaurant, he bought a 35-cent glass of port, shrimp soup, and noodles, pork with tomato sauce, bread, a fried egg, an unpeeled orange, and a cup of espresso. This was more to his liking. He had a limited budget, and though he had a windfall he didn't want to spend it all. He still needed to buy a portable stove (which he found for 50 cents), alcohol, and coffee. He also wanted a new pair of pants for a blue suitcoat borrowed from Bill. This was to visit an underaged Arab whore that he came to frequent in the coming weeks.

Then he was high on hash before combining Diason (codeine), Secanol, Soneryl (for his hay fever), and the savagely addicting Sympatina (a form of Benzedrine) to get him moving. This was embellished by Burroughs's offerings of opium and red wine. When all of this seeped through his system, all Jack could do was to do nothing at all. He sat in a chair in a drooling stupor.

On the first of March, Jack received some letters. Sterling Lord informed him that his prospective publisher, Grove Press, had cut *The Subterraneans* in half. He had photostats of their changes. It was worked over so much that it threw Jack into despair. His precious spontaneous prose was riddled with newly added commas. His paragraphs were broken into traditional formatting. His first impulse was to leave. With money from *On the Road*, he could buy a piece of land and build a shack in Marin County, California. He required no running water. No electricity. Just an oil lamp, firewood, and a clean pair of overalls. And then he would write as he pleased, without editorial interventions, "aim on into the inner life of work."[55]

Kerouac wrote a cablegram at once:

"Photostats show common halting namblypambly changes that will decisively damage my repute as a natural prose writer—Tell them return ms. & I give back money—After they will have Tristessa as is, or 3 or 4 excerpts as is."[56]

It drove Jack mad. He indulged at once in an array of narcotics and drinks. The next day he was sick. He had overdosed on opium. He drank an entire bottle of Moroccan red wine and swallowed three Sympatinas. Bill tried consoling him: "Just collect your scratch from your publishers and forget their shit." He distracted Jack with a steak and mushroom dinner at the Panama. Afterward, Jack revisited his dollar whore. He could debauch in relative obscurity with nobody to judge him except his own conscience. He harbored no guilt in appeasing his sexual appetite. He favored dark-haired, brown-eyed Moors trafficked in from Spain. He obtained them from a pimp named Paco (one of "Bill's boys," Kerouac wrote in his diary) who took him past various houses of prostitution clustered between the Continental Hotel and along the main street. These places were plainly marked by means of a light burning in vestibules and open doors.

The girls required no papers to be legally registered. All one had to do was declare that she wanted to do business. Age made no difference, as long as she was over fourteen. However, some were twelve years of age. They catered chiefly to tourists. However, it would not be long before the girls bought and paid for began to frustrate him. Jack, though he thought them cute and sweet, felt them to be too jaded and impatient. Besides, his respite was now cut off as his money dwindled. He would rather eat and drink than fuck.

Now that Kerouac had canceled *The Subterraneans*, he vowed that he would rather die than be a hack. Debt before dishonor. He wrote "fuck Malcolm Cowley" after he told Jack that he "didn't know how to write." Kerouac's sacred vows of compassion had limits: "fuck this unnatural business of universal kindness!—I like to be kind to those who humbly deserve it, not to arrogant idiots—I KNOW WHERE I AM."[57]

Isolated, depressed, and non-communicative, Jack ate supper in his room. He couldn't even talk to Bill; his writing conjured vivid nightmares of slimy plasma dripping from his mouth. Beach air was the antidote. Jack found it easier to "rough it" outdoors than stay in his hotel room. The Moroccan countryside was beautiful, almost as grand as Mexico. He walked through its green hills. He pitied the old burros with listless fly-harried eyes. These people were grounded to the earth from which they were born. An old man read the Koran to some children. A woman in white hung bright clothes on a wash-line.

Where was his source?

Dismayed, he returned to Bill who medicated his friend with hashish and brandy. They went to eat and meet some acquaintances. When they returned, Jack ingested majoun, a pastry ball of nuts, honey, dried fruits, opium, hemp, and datura seeds (a species of poisonous nightshade). Fucked up beyond belief, he was determined to write short stories about "cunt, beer, and the swelling cock." But even this effort went nowhere. After the first week of March 1957, he felt like he was going to die. He suffered from nightmares. By the afternoon of the next day, he roamed the river bottom as the tide flowed in. It reminded him of Salisbury Beach, a Massachusetts sea resort he visited as a boy. He plucked shells for Burroughs's fish bowl. He chugged from a bottle of Los Mosqueteros Malaga wine. Pleasantly buzzed, he ran out of money and so resorted to the New Testament and the *Diamond Sutra* to nourish him. Outside his window, he witnessed a boy beating his burro with a stick right out of *Crime and Punishment*.

This was the Golden Eternity.

He began fading fast. After rowing in the bay to look for the Yugo-slavian freighter due to arrive with Allen and Peter, Jack got deathly ill. He had a fever. A chest cold. He collapsed into his bed. Bill medicated him again with codeine-infused Diosans. The room was cold and dank.

He was on the verge of turning thirty-five years old.

He craved to become newly born.

This Existential Dream. The Golden Eternity of God's Mind.

Who was he and where had he been? His entire life whirled before him. All of the country criss-crossing, hitchhiking, sleeping in river bottoms, starvations, hopelessly moving his family, funerals, young man "anguishings," go-nowhere love affairs with "unsympathetic girls," "stupid" marriages, "idiot" drunks, smiles frozen in clay, the growing wreck of his face . . . what did it serve him?

It was no wonder he was sick. He was already tired of Tangier. It made him depressed. To drown his anguish, he ingested more hashish. However, it was poisoned, and he and Bill (and two other men) got sick. He took more Diosans and aspirin. Bill told Jack that he was dying because he still lived with his mother. Horrified, Jack got drunk and high in a flamenco bar. He passed out and woke up even more ill. He peeled and ate seven oranges in a vain attempt to get better. He fell asleep and had a vision of God who told him not to drink anymore. He then saw the second half of his life which was only days away. It told him to get himself together or else.

Kerouac's birthday: March 12. Bill attempted alcoholic intervention. He read Jack the "Doctor Dent" method of treating acute alcoholism. This method, initiated by Doctor John Y. Dent, was treated by way of apomorphine, then utilized to treat Parkinson's disease. For alcoholism, it was used to battle and suppress cravings. It sometimes worked for Bill who was a stoic advocate of the program. Jack listened. In his diary, he wrote that it was the beginning of a new life. If he relapsed, then he would seek free treatment in Geneva, Switzerland, from Doctor Friedman.

And then he forgot all about it.

By the next day, he wanted to return to America. Gabe was depressed and lonely. He wanted to take her with him to California and find themselves a rustic shack. He wrote Neal about his idea. Several months later,

Carolyn wrote back to inform him that she thought he was a bad influence on Neal. Jack was mortified.

He wanted to camp in the desert. Brood at campfires. Meditate on the highway and watch the western horizon. In California, he was a "free child." He and his mother could possibly subsist in Berkeley for $50 a month. However, as of now, he lacked the money to leave. Somehow, all of it was gone. Maybe by June he could enlist on a merchant ship out of France and return to New York. Before then, he could pass through London, Paris, Brittany, and Dublin.

He was tired of freezing in his room. Bill, to compensate Jack for his typing chores, bought him a 225-peseta kerosene stove for heating his garret. Jack dreamed that he was yanking from his throat long great gobs of undigested food and cold-jellied fat. He blamed it on Bill's "evil ugly old" influence. He was freaking Jack out. He found Bill to be telepathic and insane. His sinister vibe, the "dreary" Arabs, and their hateful atmosphere drove Jack mad.

Jack read the *Diamond Sutra*. High on Benzedrine, he rearranged it in his mind. The next day, he took a long walk with Bill through a field strewn with white flowers. They had long conversations, smoked hashish, and swallowed majoun. The call of a Muslim man praying to Mecca rang over the countryside. Lambs and goats with their shepherds traversed strangely flowing fields. The call of a bell rung by a priest echoed through the countryside. Jack brought up a Buddhist koan. Bill had his own: "Which is more holy, the priest reverently saying his rosaries or the old queen reverently studying his dirty pictures one by one?" He told Jack that the answer was that the priest got his rocks off on the feel of rosary beads on his fingertips.

They were still waiting for Allen and Peter. They were marked overdue by March 18. Jack continued typing for Bill. As he did, he pondered another idea for a book, a one-thousand-page novel to be titled *Beat Generation*. It would begin in 1951 when Jack fell sick with phlebitis in a VA hospital bed; to the shooting of Joan Burroughs in Mexico; to 1952, when Jack typed *Visions of Neal* from his notebooks in Cassady's attic; and then the road trips through Nogales and Culiacán before ending up in Mexico City with Burroughs. Kerouac's Buddhist phase of 1953 would carry *Beat Generation* through present-day Morocco. There was another he wanted to write: *The Story of an Alcoholic*. Neither book transpired. For as long as Jack needed money, he could no longer lavish the world with his experimental prose-slinging.

He was too burnt out.

Then Ginsberg and Orlovsky arrived. They all went to the Casbah. Since Jack could no longer see the world through fresh eyes, he relished it through theirs. They smoked tea at Arabic hangouts. Allen and Bill seemed to enjoy the dark young boys that hovered among them. They were looking for cash for sexual favors. This perturbed Jack and he labeled Bill and Allen as "ignorant pederasts" and became "disgusted with the scene of queers."

Jack and Peter took two prostitutes to bed with them. By dawn, Jack woke. He was disgusted at "uncompassionate nowhere stinking bitches." He was getting no writing done. He was drunk again. He was sicker.

Fuck it all.

Jack longed for the romantic optimism of Paris, but he would always be miserable. He was physically and psychically poisoned. He wondered if metabolism had more to do with his alcoholism than a desire to kill himself slowly. He fought it back with long nighttime walks. He swam on a lonely stretch of beach. He wanted purity. Anything was better than his old raunchy life of drugs and drink.

Two days later, he was given good news. *On the Road* would also be published by Andre Deutsch. This meant an advance payment of $400, which he could pick up by going to London if the terms were agreeable. This would be his ticket out of Tangier. His optimism was temporarily recovered. He again sketched out a floor plan for a cabin in California. He could be like Thoreau. He could find himself at last.

If only Neal would answer his letter.

Jack stood on his midnight rooftop and listened to the city come alive. It was Ramadan. He heard a flute and the beating of drums. He made himself fast from 3:00 to 7:00 a.m. He heard the wind, the sea crash, and the rattle of drums.

He argued with Bill about the age of the universe. Jack did not like Bill discussing murder. Bill felt that he didn't kill enough. He pretended to torture a cat in front of a roomful of men. He called himself a religious leader as he did it. Jack was tired of Bill's routines. He loathed how Bill "whimpered" when he was "fucked up the ass." Jack felt that if Bill ever led a new movement, it would be one of bloodshed, homosexuality, and castration among "adolescent pubertal morons." However, he remained on good enough terms with Bill, in that he agreed to bring the work he was typing, now titled *Word Hoard*, to Jean Genet's translator in Paris. There Jack would meet Gregory Corso, who agreed to let Jack stay with him. He bought a ticket to sail fourth class to Marseilles for 8,500 francs ($21.25) and saved money by hitchhiking through Provence and Burgundy.

Jack wandered through the French rail yards with a full backpack. Taxicabs indifferently zipped past him. France's gay colors starkly contrasted with Morocco's dark quarters. He found hitchhiking too difficult and gave up after thumbing for five miles. Unlike Morocco, it was expensive in France. By the end of the day, he squabbled at the prices and was sharply critical. He called the French citizens "dishonest."

He wanted to go home.

By the time he reached Paris, Jack failed to find a room. After getting drunk in a St. Germain cafe, he made a phone call to Bernard Frechtman to deliver the *Word Hoard* typescript (known as "Word" in *Interzone* [1989]). When he at last found Corso that evening, Jack got drunk with him and his girlfriend, Nicole. Drunkenly, Jack had it in his head that he could sleep with Nicole. He told Gregory that he loved her. Corso reneged on his offer after helping to spend 5,000 francs of Jack's money. He gave Jack a single night.

That night, Jack complained of having to sleep on the floor while Nicole "whimpered" under Gregory. He slipped out and found a cheap room in a Paris slum. As he walked along the Seine, he drank a pint of cold milk and prayed to Buddha to free him from worldly attachments (once again). He wrote in his notebook that he failed to observe people passing by. When he did notice them, he dismissed them as a "sad flashy dream" because there was actually no world. The next morning, after shaving to look presentable, he trekked with his one-hundred-pound

pack up Avenue de l'Opéra to deliver *Word Hoard* to Frechtman. He
hoped Frechtman would offer him a bed. He would even take his floor.

"No."

Kerouac called another acquaintance of his that he knew from
Greenwich Village, novelist James Baldwin. Kerouac implored that he
had nowhere to sleep.

"Can I sleep on your floor?"

"No."

Kerouac's reputation from the Village had already preceded him,
and Baldwin was not willing to entertain a parade of days ending in a
soul-crushing debauch. Furthermore, he was as poor as Kerouac and only
had limited resources to survive as a Left Bank writer. Jack was left in a
quandary.

Should he leave Paris and go to London? Jack made a phone call
to his London publisher. He hated the city. He needed money. Where
would he go once he reached London? When would they be expecting
him to sign the contract? He had 6,000 francs left and another 4,000 in
traveler's checks. He saw Parisian sex workers that he wanted to sleep
with, but they refused to look at him when he asked them how much. He
drank coffee and ate pastries at a cafe on Boulé St. Germain, trying to
figure out what to do next. Discouraged, he returned to his "beat" 75-cent
skid-row room at The Relais on Christine Street. It was a cold room. A
narrow bed. Restlessly, he walked the boulevards that offered little respite.
They only led to further suffering. Its quaint bistros and ornate cafes in
this gilded lily city were for "sadfaced" diners.

He bought a ticket to London. Before leaving, Jack was tempted to
patronize the "whore beauties" of Rue St. Denis. He paid for the first
woman he met, a tall bosomy brunette in slacks that cost him 800 francs.
He kissed her with each lunge, and after he came from his "gay fast bang,"
he reminded himself that she was worth it. Afterward, he cashed his last
traveler's check at the Gare du Nord and splurged on a glass of port and
gruyere cheese. Repenting from his lack of physical restraint, he sought
forgiveness at the 6:30 p.m. Notre Dame mass.

It was time to leave.

The city was a stab in the heart. It was too hectic, like New York. With one day left, Jack walked through the Louvre. He was most absorbed by Rubens and Van Gogh (before the Musée d'Orsay acquired all of the Louvre's Van Goghs in 1986), and felt a clearer affinity with the latter. Van Gogh's suffering and devotion to his art inspired Jack to acquire his own paints once he returned to California. He drank more red wine and bought gruyere, pâté, and a head of cheese to make a batch of sandwiches for his train ride to London.

And then he left.

* * *

Kerouac felt different, like he was decaying before his eyes. In front of a mirror, he looked old at thirty-five. Only one week before, he was told that he appeared to be twenty-five years old. What happened? Rings formed beneath his eyes. Creases deepened his face. He was unshaven. He felt ugly. A ghoul. Did he too change in as little as a few weeks just like Esperanza?

In London, Jack was temporarily detained by customs officials. He sat to the side as the passengers disembarked. After proving that he was an American writer picking up a royalty check, he was set free to the streets with only 14 shillings left in his pocket.

At Victoria Station, Jack drank a huge glass of stout at the Shakespeare bar. His head swam with fresh impressions as he walked down Buckingham Palace Road in the city of Blake and Shakespeare. He strolled past the Palace, St. James Park, the Strand, Trafalgar Square, and Fleet Street toward St. Paul's Cathedral. At Westminster Abbey, he paused in reverence at the graves of Dickens, Spenser, and Chaucer. At St. Paul's Cathedral, he listened, stunned, to Bach's "St. Matthew's Passion." He cried after envisioning an angel in his mother's kitchen. In front of him, a bas-relief of Christ and three Roman soldiers made him recall Luke 3:14–18: "And the soldiers demanded of him, saying, And what shall we do? And he said unto them, Do violence to no man, neither accuse any falsely and be content with your wages."

His mission occurred to him at last. Through a haze of booze, drugs, sex, and self-abasement, it was time to stand still. Become contemplative.

Seek solitude in the woods. Teach patience and compassion. Holiness. He paused in the hushing dusk and observed the ruins of Hitler's blitzkrieg among the overgrown weeds at St. Paul Cathedral's circumference. Hitler had given orders not to bomb the holy structure. Among the weeded stonework, a single yellow flower grew. In a little over five months, Jack Kerouac's entire life would change. *On the Road* was to be published, and then he would have to start all over again to his peril.

ACKNOWLEDGMENTS

This book would not be possible without Rick Rinehart of Rowman & Littlefield, who was most helpful in making possible this updated incarnation of my original biography of Kerouac published in 2004. Thank you, Rick, for this opportunity. Also, my sincere thanks to Lynn Zelem, project manager for *Becoming Kerouac*, and copyeditor Joshua Rosenberg for making this an undoubtedly better book.

Also, I must thank Jim Sampas, literary executor of the Estate of Jack & Stella Kerouac, for his enthusiastic reception of this book along with ushering in the idea of a companion text to fully flesh out what I was attempting herein. I thank Sylvia Cunha for her gracious assistance and enthusiasm for all things Kerouac and her hand in ushering in a new era of Kerouac studies.

Thank you to my longtime friend and Kerouac research assistant Steve Roux for his hard work collecting some of the material I used for this book. Steve has been instrumental in every stage of my research and to him I am indebted always. Thank you to Erin Monahan, Archive Curator at UMass Lowell, for her assistance in gathering unpublished Kerouac texts for *Becoming Kerouac* and its companion book, *Self-Portrait: Unpublished Writings of Jack Kerouac* (Sal Paradise Press/Rare Bird Books, 2024). She was a vital time saver in helping me locate key archival texts. I also thank Kerouac scholar Charles Shuttleworth for permitting me to take advantage of his ongoing research, particularly in Kerouac's spiritual writings as well as a sundry assortment of letters, notebooks, and typescripts done in Kerouac's hand.

I thank my daughters, Chloe and Rachel, for their love and support of my interests. They are my golden beacons.

Lastly, I thank my wife, Caitlin Stuart, for always being there to support my interests, and lifting my spirits when they were down. Through Caitlin I am able to realize most things in my life, and to her I am forever indebted.

NOTES

CHAPTER ONE

1. "Untitled scroll," 1959 (Berg Collection, New York Public Library).

2. A psychedelic vine he had acquired in Lima, Peru. In January 1953, William Burroughs initiated a seven-month expedition into the jungles of South America in search of yage, the fabled hallucinogen of the Amazon. Burroughs kept notebooks and wrote letters to Ginsberg about his search. Burroughs and Ginsberg later edited *The Yage Letters* for City Lights Publishing in 1963 and later issued a "redux" version in 2006.

3. Michael Schumacher, *Dharma Lion: A Biography of Allen Ginsberg* (University of Minnesota Press, 2016), 328.

4. Ted Morgan, *Literary Outlaw: The Life and Times of William Burroughs* (Norton, 2012), 338–39.

5. Leo Alcide Kerouac had died on May 17, 1946, in Queens, New York.

6. Kerouac explained to Ginsberg that the form of mescaline he took was a pill as opposed to a peyote button because of "Compensatory chemical laboratory arrangements to cut out unnecessary puke nausea—altho there was much of that. . . . " Kerouac, *Selected Letters: 1957–1969* (Viking, 2000), 252.

7. Kerouac later typed a "clean" version, removing the sexual references to his mother and other associates.

8. "Mescaline" (Berg, NYPL).

9. Kerouac to Allen Ginsberg, October 19, 1959, *Selected Letters*, 252.

10. Jack Kerouac, *Some of the Dharma* (Penguin, 1997), 151.

11. Jung writes, "At the moment of the dream, this event may still lie in the future. But just as our conscious thoughts often occur themselves with the future and its possibilities, so do the unconscious and its dreams. There has long been a general belief that the chief function of dreams is prognostication of the future." C. G. Jung, *Man and His Symbols* (Doubleday, 1964), 78.

CHAPTER TWO

1. Journal, 1939 (Berg Collection, New York Public Library).

2. Kerouac complained to Navy psychiatrists that he had a sexual experience with a thirty-two-year-old woman at age fourteen. An obsession with sex during adolescence

plays out in autobiographical references to his life in Pawtucketville and Lowell, in *Doctor Sax.*

3. C. G. Jung, *Aspects of the Feminine*, trans. by E. E. C. Hull (MJF Books, 1982), 113.

4. Journal, 1939 (Berg, NYPL).

5. At the header of a holograph manuscript by Kerouac, titled "Rasping Smoke in a Dry Throat," he writes in pencil, "Jack Kerouac Age 18, Summer-1940—First lines of 'modernistic' period" (Berg, NYPL).

6. "Rasping Smoke in a Dry Throat" (Berg, NYPL).

7. Ibid.

8. "Nothing," in Jack Kerouac, *Atop an Underwood: Early Stories and Other Writings* (Viking, 1999), 26–27.

9. *Atop an Underwood*, 24–25.

10. Ibid., 25.

11. The existing correspondence between Jack and his family is extensive, especially so with Gabrielle who was an inveterate letter writer to Jack despite previous biographies suggesting that she spoke and wrote poor English.

12. Lowell by this time was in rapid decline. Mills were closing and the downtown stores were failing. One-third of its citizens were on government relief as Lowell was losing the textile industry that had come to define it in the previous century.

13. Fifty-one-year-old Leo Kerouac's problematic employment prospects stemmed from New York City printer unions' unwillingness to hire applicants living outside the city because they favored a local labor pool. Leo's persistence to keep himself employed sometimes broadened his chances. He acquired a traveler's permit to work in any section of the country, which brought him little advantage. These circumstances account for Jack's constant money concerns; he had to cover his living expenses without having to defray his parents' limited income. Somewhat presciently, Leo gave himself five years to stick it out, after which he felt he would be finally finished. He would die in 1946. Until then, writing Jack, he assumed the worst and hoped for the best: "strictly between you and I—there's a nigger behind the woodpile [Note: regional saying for when one suspects that somebody is trying to deceive you, or that something is going on behind your back]—but don't take it to heart, I'll get along as usual." (Leo Kerouac to Jack Kerouac, February 6, 1941: Berg, NYPL).

14. A player reserved for when needed to score points, which may be why Kerouac complained of sitting on the bench for most of the Columbia games.

15. Jack Kerouac, *Vanity of Duluoz* (Viking, 1994).

16. "Journal of an Egotist" (Berg, NYPL).

17. Fyodor Dostoevsky, *Notes from the Underground* (Open Road Media, 2014), e-book.

18. "Journal of an Egotist" (Berg, NYPL).

19. Ibid.

20. Ibid.

21. Ibid.

22. Ibid.

23. *Columbia Spectator*, April 7, 1941.

24. "The Stupid Journal," June 1, 1941 (Berg, NYPL).

25. "The "father never found" is a concept Kerouac drafted as a theme for *On the Road.*

26. Moody Street ran from City Hall clear to a truss bridge crossing the Merrimack River into Pawtucketville, where several of Kerouac's former homes were located.

27. Caroline Kerouac was treated for a burst appendix there.

28. Journal, 1941 (Berg, NYPL).

29. Likely their dalliance was with a woman Jack called "Mary Filthy" who was an usherette at a Lowell theater. According to his "sex list," Kerouac had sex with her three times. He was also seeing another local woman, Jean Belanger, with whom he engaged with once.

30. Journal, Summer 1941 (Berg, NYPL).

31. "Most men lead lives of quiet desperation," from Thoreau's *Walden* (1854).

32. Journal, Summer 1941 (Berg, NYPL).

33. Burton Stollmack.

34. "Farewell Song, Sweet from My Trees" (Berg, NYPL).

35. I have paraphrased from a letter by Herman Melville to Nathaniel Hawthorne.

36. Journal, Summer 1941 (Berg, NYPL).

37. Jack Kerouac to Caroline Kerouac, undated 1941 (Kerouac Archive, University of Massachusetts Lowell).

38. Kerouac to Sebastian Sampas, mid-September 1941, as published in Kerouac's *Selected Letters: 1940–1956* (Viking, 1995), 16.

39. "Here I Am At Last with a Typewrite," in *Atop an Underwood*, 130.

40. Ralph Waldo Emerson, "Self-Reliance," in *Essays—First Series* (1841).

41. "Washington in 1941" (Berg, NYPL).

42. Ibid.

43. Walt Whitman, "Song of Myself," in *Leaves of Grass* (1882).

44. *Atop an Underwood*, 18.

CHAPTER THREE

1. *Atop an Underwood: Early Stories and Other Writings* (Viking, 1999), 19.

2. "No Connection: A Novel That I Don't Intend To Finish," in *Atop an Underwood*, 93.

3. Ibid.

4. "Joyce and Saroyan" (Berg Collection, New York Public Library).

5. "Self-Analysis of a Youth," entry in "The Stupid Journal," 1942 (Berg, NYPL).

6. This sixty-thousand-word draft of *Vanity of Duluoz* (Viking, 1994) seems missing from Kerouac's existing archive. He later re-wrote *Vanity of Duluoz* in 1944 as *Michael Daoulas*, which morphed into *Galloway* and then *The Town and the City*, published in 1950.

7. "Liverpool Testament" (Berg, NYPL).

8. Typescript introduction to *The Joy of Duluoz* (Berg, NYPL).

9. Sebastian Sampas to Kerouac, November 6–8, 1941 (*The Sea Is My Brother*, ed. Dawn M. Ward [Da Capo, 2011]).

10. "The Stupid Journal" (Berg, NYPL).

11. According to Kerouac's "sex list," he had over two dozen sexual encounters in Washington, DC, involving three different women.

12. Leo Kerouac to Jack Kerouac, circa 1942 (Berg, NYPL).

13. Ibid.

14. Kerouac lost his academic scholarship due to poor grades and desertion.

15. Jack Kerouac to Norma Blickfelt, July 15, 1942 (Catalog of Peter Harrington).

16. Ibid.

17. A person who performs menial kitchen tasks.

18. The misspelling appears on his birth certificate. Kerouac went with it to save time instead of applying for an amended document.

19. Leo Kerouac to Jack Kerouac, dated July 6, 1942 (Berg, NYPL).

20. Ibid.

21. "Voyage to Greenland / 1942 / Growing Pains or A Monument to Adolescence" (Berg, NYPL).

22. *Vanity of Duluoz*, 121.

23. Emerson, "The Scholar" (1876).

24. U-223 (*Wachter*) on February 3, 1943. The sinking happened 150 miles west of Cape Farewell, Greenland. En route from St. John's, Newfoundland, to Narsarssuak, Greenland, and holding 751 passengers, general cargo, lumber, and sixty bags of mail, the ship went down. Only 229 survived.

25. *New York World Telegram*, October 21, 1942.

26. Alex Oberweger, "Who Was Lou Little?" (September 20, 2017), Columbia Lions web page.

27. Little and Dwight D. Eisenhower met in 1924, when Little's Georgetown team played a service squad coached by the future president. It was in 1947 that Eisenhower convinced Little to stay in Morningside Heights, rather than accept Yale University's offer to become their athletics director.

28. *Vanity of Duluoz*, 252 (e-book).

29. Leo Kerouac to Gabrielle Kerouac, October 23, 1942 (Berg, NYPL).

30. Ibid.

31. Gabrielle Kerouac to Jack Kerouac, late October 1942 (Berg, NYPL).

32. Leo was referring to the Navy V-12 program.

33. Leo Kerouac to Jack Kerouac, November 5, 1942 (Berg, NYPL).

34. Ibid.

35. Kerouac to Sebastian Sampas, November 1942 (Berg, NYPL).

36. In Kerouac's one-page autobiographical short story, "The Wastrel," he describes this period as one of "wild debauchery," including sex orgies and long experiments of endurance when he stayed up for forty hours at a time wandering around in futility. This is highly plausible given his tendencies to do the same in the years to come.

37. James described "centre of consciousness" as when the narrator is looking from the rear of the character's head to see what he sees, though it is described from a vaster experience of the invisible narrator. The invisible narrator combines the virtues of an omnipotent narrator with a first-person narrator.

38. Leo Kerouac to Jack Kerouac, circa November 1942 (Berg, NYPL).

39. Ibid.

40. Ibid.

41. 1942.

42. "The New Romanticism," December 31, 1942 (Berg, NYPL).

43. Ibid.

44. Oswald Spengler, *The Decline of the West: Vol. I: Form and Actuality*; *Vol. II: Perspectives of World-History*, trans. Charles Francis Atkinson (New York: Alfred A. Knopf, 1926 and 1928), I, 106.

45. Kerouac's reading of Spengler predates the often quoted anecdote that William Burroughs had introduced him to *The Decline of the West* in 1944. By then, Kerouac had not only read *The Decline of the West*, but had begun assimilating it into his writing.

46. Michael D'Orso, "Kerouac, Spengler, and the 'Faustian Soul'" (master's thesis, William & Mary, 1981).

47. "Brother," February 15, 1943 (Berg, NYPL).

48. "Morning with Brothers" (Berg, NYPL).

49. "The Story of Wesley Martin" (Berg, NYPL).

CHAPTER FOUR

1. The March 1943 pencil-written draft of 143 pages was titled *Merchant Mariner*. Kerouac later retitled it *The Sea Is My Brother*.

2. "Preface to the Will," March 4, 1943, 1 (Berg Collection, New York Public Library).

3. Ibid.

4. Caroline Kerouac to Jack Kerouac, April 8, 1943 (Berg, NYPL).

5. Kerouac records a total of twenty sexual encounters with Coffey, a fact he avoids in his depiction of her as "Pauline (Moe) Cole" in *Maggie Cassidy*. She was also known as "Peggy" in local Lowell circles.

6. Kerouac to Sebastian Sampas, March 21, 1943 (Berg, NYPL).

7. March 4, 1943, is Kerouac's recorded date of arrival at Newport, Rhode Island, Naval Training Base.

8. Kerouac and biographers have uniformly stated that he had brought with him his manuscript for *The Sea Is My Brother*, which examining physicians were permitted to read. If he had indeed brought it with him, it would have been returned to his home address with the rest of his personal belongings. It could be that his parents brought it with them to the hospital upon Jack's request.

9. Though Kerouac himself had explained that he was sent to Bethesda for knocking a hat off or slugging an officer after wanting an unauthorized smoke break (or some such variant), or putting down his rifle to go to the base library, military records reveal that he was not sent to sick bay "due to misconduct" but because of headaches.

10. The term *dementia praecox* was a psychiatric diagnosis for people who appeared to have dementia before they were advanced in age. It was also known as "precocious madness" which indicated that the patient was suffering premature dementia. It was also regarded as a form of schizophrenia. There was no cure, which accounts for Kerouac's honorable discharge for medical reasons.

11. K. S. Kendler, "The Genealogy of Dementia Praecox I: Signs and Symptoms of Delusional Psychoses from 1880 to 1900," *Schizophrenia Bulletin* 45(2), March 7, 2019, 296–304. Erratum in: *Schizophrenia Bulletin* 45(6), October 24, 2019, 1382.

12. This and other details are taken from Kerouac's naval medical records archived in the Library of Congress.

13. The Converse Publishing Company was a print shop initially located at 140 State Street, however, in 1888, the company moved into a small two-story building at 159 Pratt Street (later renumbered as 169 Pratt Street, currently 163 Pratt Street). Leo's return address pinpoints this plant as his place of occupation.

14. Leo Kerouac to Jack Kerouac, May 3, 1943 (Berg, NYPL).

15. Leo Kerouac to Jack Kerouac, May 13, 1943 (Berg, NYPL).

16. A Verbal IQ score of 133 is classified as "Very Superior" and is applicable to 2.1 percent of the world population. If Kerouac would have picked a typical occupation in this league, he would have been among lawyers, physicians, (civil and mechanical) engineers, and surgeons.

17. ""My Generation, My World," in Jack Kerouac, *Atop an Underwood: Early Stories and Other Writings* (Viking, 1999), 228–29.

18. "The Wound Of Living," in *Atop an Underwood*, 230–31.

19. Barry Miles, *Call Me Burroughs: A Life* (Hachette, 2013), 99–100.

20. Adams was drafted overseas through 1945.

21. It is tempting to fully flesh out Joan Vollmer as a vital bright star of the Beat Generation, but she did not leave enough of a trace to amount to anything tangible. She emerges as a fascinating cipher but remains perhaps the most significant enigma to this history.

22. Kerouac documented a single sexual liason with Joan Vollmer in 1945.

23. Holograph notes, "Supreme Reality" (Berg, NYPL).

24. "Outline of Position," August 1943 (Berg, NYPL).

25. "Edna Porter Martin Tate," 1943 (Berg, NYPL).

26. Jim Perrizo, "Frankie and Johnny: A New York Memoir" (undated). Most of my details about Edie and Jack are sourced from Perrizo's text.

27. Sebastian Sampas to Jack Kerouac, August 29, 1943 (Berg, NYPL).

28. Also called "Big Slim" in the draft notes.

29. "Notes for The Brothers" (Berg, NYPL).

30. Though Kerouac envisioned *Galloway* as a novel in his notes, it exists in its only extant form as a forty-two-page novella.

31. Though Jack did not keep a dream record for the period he wished to write about, he would do so in the future.

32. Kerouac believed he was afflicted with psychological maladies as he was influenced by the Navy doctors and their findings. Since their methods were archaic, and diagnoses outdated, it is difficult to take Kerouac at his word, other than what he believed or felt was eventually poured into his writing, especially in novels like *Doctor Sax* which indeed take on a hallucinatory bent.

33. "Outline of Position," August 1943 (Berg, NYPL).

34. Ibid.

35. Ibid.

36. "The Problem of Myself," December 1943–January 1944 Journal (Berg, NYPL).

37. 1943–1944 Journals (Berg, NYPL).

38. "The Problem of Myself," December 1943–January 1944 Journal (Berg, NYPL).

39. Published in *Selected Letters: 1940–1956*, commencing December 28, 1950, to January 8, 1951.

40. This anecdote, initiated by Kerouac, has no reality in medical science. This author cannot find a single case where a patient's teeth fell out from grief. If this is in fact true, it stands to believe that this may have more to do with oral hygiene than Gerard's death. Later, in 1942, Gabrielle will tap Jack's savings to repair two upper front teeth that she had broken or lost. This documented evidence suggests this oft-repeated anecdote is Jack's exaggeration.

41. Alfred Adler, *The Case of Miss R.: The Interpretation of a Life Story* (George Allen & Lunwin Lmtd., 1929), 30.

42. 1943–1944 Journals (Berg, NYPL).

43. Journal entry, January 1944, in *Orpheus Emerged* (iBooks, 2000), 355.

44. "The Problem of Myself," 1943–1944 Notebook (Berg, NYPL).

45. Diary 1944–1945 (Berg, NYPL).

46. Ibid.

47. Ibid.

48. "The Problem of Myself," from Part 2, "Art and Personality" (Berg, NYPL).

49. "Supreme Reality" Notebook, March 1944 (Berg, NYPL).

50. Jack Kerouac, *The Haunted Life and Other Writings* (Da Capo, 2014), 117–18.

51. Ibid.

52. "A Dissertation on Style," October 8, 1944 (Berg, NYPL).

53. Barnard College Mortarboard Yearbook (1944), 66.

54. Allen Ginsberg, *The Book of Martyrdom and Artifice* (Da Capo Press, 2006), 47.

55. Ibid., 50.

56. Ibid., 47–50.

57. Quite frankly, I see no other way to put it. The truth of it is murky, disappearing down a dark well of time that cannot be illuminated without sources. We have to go with the surface appearance that Carr was significantly younger than Kammerer, and that something quite nefarious had gone awry.

58. Published in *The Haunted Life* as "The Odyssey of Peter Martin" (1943).

59. Ibid., 106.

60. Jack Kerouac, *The Town and the City* (Harcourt Brace, 1950).

61. Notebook entry, 1944 (Berg, NYPL).

62. As accounted by Caleb Carr to journalist Mark Judge, February 24, 2014. Carr had replied to Judge's article, "Son of Famous Beat Murderer Lucien Carr Disputes 'Kill Your Darlings' film's version of events" on Daily Caller.

63. "I Bid You Lose Me" Notebook, November 10, 1944 (Berg, NYPL).

64. Catherine De Leon, "Beat Surrender: Reclaiming the Legacy of Lucien Carr" (PleaseKillMe.com, October 5, 2020). De Leon must be given credit for most of the research about Lucien Carr and his New Vision.

65. Nietzsche, *Unpublished Fragments from the Period of Thus Spoke Zarathustra*—from *The Complete Works of Friedrich Nietzsche: Vol. 14*, 239 (Stanford University Press, 2019).

66. Dustin Griffin, "The St. Louis Clique: Burroughs, Kammerer, and Carr," *Journal of Beat Studies* III, 2014.

67. "The Definition of Art for the Layman," from "Jail Notes," August 1944 (Berg, NYPL).

68. "Jail Notes," August 1944 (Berg, NYPL).

69. Jack Kerouac to Allen Ginsberg, ca. September 1944.

70. "A Dissertation on Style" (Berg, NYPL).

71. Ginsberg, *Book of Martyrdom and Artifice*, 88.

72. Nietzsche, *The Birth of Tragedy* (Modern Library, 1937), 950.

73. Possibly, he was borrowing Lucien Carr's motive for killing Kammerer as an excuse to leave his duties.

74. Ginsberg, *Book of Martyrdom and Artifice*, 92.

75. "Fuck it then!"

76. "Dialogs in Introspection" (Berg, NYPL).

77. "Ralph Waldo Emerson, "The Poet," from *Essays* (Second Series) (1844).

78. "Dialogs in Introspection" (Berg, NYPL).

79. Ginsberg, *Book of Martyrdom and Artifice*, 92.

80. Translated from French text from "The Neurotic Personality of Our Time," in Ginsberg, *Book of Martyrdom and Artifice*, 92.

81. "Waiting for Celene" (Berg, NYPL).

82. Celine Young, after graduating from Barnard College and a complete split from Kerouac and Carr, went on to work as a copy girl for the *New York World-Telegram* and another position at the American Broadcasting Company as of 1945.

83. "Waiting for Celene."

84. "Beat Surrender," De Leon.

85. Nietzsche, Part 1, Chapter 22 of *Thus Spake Zarathustra.*

86. Berg, NYPL.

87. Title page of "I Bid You Lose Me" (Berg, NYPL).

88. A diary entry dated November 16, 1944, as reprinted in Kerouac's *Selected Letters: 1940–1956*, 81.

89. "The Dark Corridor" (Berg, NYPL).

90. Ibid.

91. Nietzsche, "Foreword to 'A Case of Wagner,' 3, in *The Complete Works of Friedrich Nietzsche: Vol. 9* (Stanford University Press, 2021).

92. Diary entry, November 16, 1944 (Berg, NYPL).

93. "Ah! I'm finished."

94. "Notes Gleaned from a Voyage to Morphina, 21 January 1945," from 1943 to 1945 Journal (Berg, NYPL).

95. Ibid.

96. Celine Young was an English Literature student, and so Ginsberg meant that she longed to be within the vicinity of writers without having to partake in their excesses.

97. Blaise Pascal and Roger Ariew, *Pensées* (Hackett Publishing Company, 2005).

98. Jack Kerouac, *The Portable Jack Kerouac* (Penguin Books, 1995).

CHAPTER FIVE

1. Johann Peter Eckermann, *Conversations of Goethe* (Penguin Classics, 2022).

2. "I Am My Mother's Son," in Jack Kerouac, *Atop an Underwood: Early Stories and Other Writings* (Viking, 1999), 162.

3. Typescript "October had come again and he was leaving once more" with "conversation piece" between "Bill" and "Joan." 1945 (Berg Collection, New York Public Library).

4. Excerpt from *Vanity of Duluoz* in Jack Kerouac, *The Portable Kerouac* (Viking, 1995), 135.

5. Leo Kerouac to Caroline Kerouac Blake, March 24, 1945.

6. Details of Leo Kerouac and his sickness are drawn from Jack Kerouac, *The Haunted Life and Other Writings* (Da Capo, 2014).

7. Ibid., 185.

8. Predominantly, in works such as *Tristessa* and *Desolation Angels* when he writes of the Mexican-Indians of Mexico and the Berbers of Morocco.

9. Jack Kerouac, *Orpheus Emerged* (iBooks, 2000), 85.

10. "Book of Symbols" Journal (Berg, NYPL).

11. Kerouac applied in July 1945, and given his marks and absences from Columbia, he was disqualified despite the availability of his veteran's benefits.

12. Posthumously published in *The Unknown Kerouac* (Library of America, 2016), 334–419.

13. Allen Ginsberg to Jack Kerouac, July 1945 (Columbia University Library).

14. "Ozone Park Notes," July 27, 1945 (Berg, NYPL).

15. Ibid.

16. *Galloway*, second draft, 1944 (Berg, NYPL).

17. "Allan MacKenzie" section of *Galloway* (Berg, NYPL).

18. "Part II" of *Galloway*, second draft, 1944 (Berg, NYPL).

19. "The Plan for the Novel Galloway" (Berg, NYPL).

20. 1945 Journal (Berg, NYPL).

21. "My Dying City," November 25, 1945 (Berg, NYPL).

22. Ibid.

23. Although Kerouac claims in *Vanity of Duluoz* that excessive Benzedrine intake was the cause, phlebitis can also be hereditary. Also, inactivity (such as prolonged bed rest and long periods of travel in a confined space) or a traumatic injury to the legs (such as his football injury in October 1940) can exacerbate it.

24. 1946 Journal (Berg, NYPL).

25. Jack Kerouac, *The Town and the City* (Open Road Media, 2016).

26. Carolyn Cassady, *Off the Road: Twenty Years with Neal Cassady, Jack Kerouac, and Allen Ginsberg* (Overlook Press, 2008).

27. Douglas Brinkley, ed. *Windblown World: The Journals of Jack Kerouac, 1947–1954* (Viking, 2004), 67.

28. Journal entry, April 17, 1948 (Berg, NYPL).

29. Journal entry, January 27, 1948 (Berg, NYPL).

30. Journal entry, April 12, 1948 (Berg, NYPL).

31. Journal entry, April 17, 1948 (Berg, NYPL).

32. Ibid.

33. Ibid.

34. Kerouac to Allen Ginsberg, September 18, 1948, from *Jack Kerouac - Allen Ginsberg: The Letters* (Viking, 2010), 44.

CHAPTER SIX

1. Jack Kerouac to Allen Ginsberg, January 2, 1948, *Selected Letters: 1940–1956*, 140.

2. Kerouac to Neal Cassady, June 27, 1948, *Selected Letters*, 155.

3. Neal Cassady to Allen Ginsberg, May 1948, as published in *As Ever: The Collected Correspondence of Allen Ginsberg & Neal Cassady* (Creative Arts, 1977), 35.

4. Ibid.

5. Ibid.

6. Kerouac to Neal Cassady, October 18, 1948 (Berg Collection, New York Public Library).

7. Walt Whitman, "Specimen Days," in *Prose Works—1892: Volume 1* from *The Collected Writings of Walt Whitman* (New York University Press, 1963), 71.

8. Ibid.

9. Jack Kerouac, *On the Road* (Penguin, 2016), 15.

10. Neal Cassady to Kerouac, June 16, 1948, as published in *Neal Cassady: Collected Letters, 1944–1967* (Penguin Books, 2004), 80.

11. *Windblown World: The Journals of Jack Kerouac, 1947–1954* (Viking, 2004), 238.

12. Ibid., 138.

13. Neal Cassady to Kerouac, *Neal Cassady: Collected Letters*, 109–10.

14. "Whitman: A Prophet of the Sexual Revolution" (Berg, NYPL).

15. Ibid.

16. Pauline to Kerouac, January 12, 1949 (Berg, NYPL). Pauline is "Lucille" in *On the Road*.

17. John Clellon Holmes, "This Is the Beat Generation," *New York Times* (November 16, 1952).

CHAPTER SEVEN

1. Readers interested in the details of this trip will find them in Douglas Brinkley's edited *Windblown World: The Journals of Jack Kerouac 1947–1954* (Penguin, 2004).

2. Ibid., 409.

3. "Shades of the prison-house begin to close / Upon the growing Boy, / But he beholds the light, and whence it flows, / He sees it in his joy; / The Youth, who daily farther from the east / Must travel, still is Nature's priest, / And by the vision splendid / Is on his way attended; / At length the Man perceives it die away, / And fade into the light of common day." (Wordsworth, "Ode," lines 68–77).

4. "Shades of the Prison House," August 25, 1949 (Berg Collection, New York Public Library), 49.

5. Ibid., 53–54.

6. *Selected Letters: Volume I: 1940–1956* (Penguin, 1996).

7. Jack Kerouac to Elbert Lenrow, June 28, 1949, as printed in *Kerouac Ascending: Memorabilia of the Decade of On the Road* (Cambridge Scholars Pub., 2010), 36.

8. Kerouac to Neal Cassady, *Selected Letters* (July 28, 1949), 211–17.

9. Ibid.

10. Jack Kerouac to John Clellon Holmes, June 24, 1949, *Selected Letters*, 195–200.

11. Ibid., 200.

12. Jack Kerouac to Allen Ginsberg, July 26, 1949, *Selected Letters*, 209.

13. Jack Kerouac to Elbert Lenrow, June 28, 1949, *Selected Letters*, 201–8.

14. Jack Kerouac to Neal Cassady, July 28, 1949, *Selected Letters*, 214.

15. Kerouac was afraid that Ginsberg may have had letters to or from him and the manuscript in Priscilla Arminger's (Vicki Russell's) possession.

16. "Of Growth and Decay," *New York Times*, March 5, 1950.

17. Jack Kerouac to Frank Morley, July 27, 1950, *Selected Letters*, 226–27.

18. William S. Burroughs to Jack Kerouac, March 10, 1950.

CHAPTER EIGHT

1. The title of an excerpt from *On the Road* published in *New Directions 16* two months before the novel's publication in September 1957.

2. Jack Kerouac, *On the Road*, 331.

3. Neal Cassady to Jack Kerouac, October 22, 1950, *Cassady—Collected Letters, 1944–1967* (Penguin Books, 2004).

4. Michael Schumacher, *Dharma Lion: A Biography of Allen Ginsberg* (University of Minnesota Press, 2016).

5. Lawrence Lee and Barry Gifford, *Jack's Book: An Oral Biography of Jack Kerouac* (Penguin, 2012).

6. "Gone on the Road" (Berg Collection, New York Public Library).

7. John Leland, *Why Kerouac Matters: The Lessons of On the Road (They're Not What You Think)* (Viking, 2007), 163.

8. Jack Kerouac to Neal Cassady, October 6, 1950, *Selected Letters: 1940–1956*, 230–34.

9. "American Times," October 2, 1950 (Berg, NYPL).

10. Ibid.

11. Jack Kerouac to Neal Cassady, October 5, 1950, *Selected Letters*, 212–13.

12. Neal Cassady to Jack Kerouac, November 5, 1950, *Cassady—Collected Letters*, 184–91.

CHAPTER NINE

1. Alfred G. Aronowitz, "The New Greenwich Village," *New York Post*, October 8, 1961.

2. Michael Schumacher, *Dharma Lion: A Biography of Allen Ginsberg* (University of Minnesota Press, 2016), 129–31.

3. Joan Haverty, *Nobody's Wife: The Smart Aleck and the King of the Beats* (Creative Arts, 2000), 71.

4. Ibid.

5. Ibid.

6. Gabrielle Kerouac to Jack and Joan Kerouac, April 1951 (Berg Collection, New York Public Library).

7. Jack Kerouac to Neal Cassady, December 27, 1950, *Selected Letters: 1940–1956*, 242–45.

8. Jack Kerouac to Neal Cassady, December 28, 1950, *Selected Letters*, 246–63.

9. Jack Kerouac to Neal Cassady, January 9, 1951, *Selected Letters*, 281–93.

10. "The Power of the Subconscious Mind," September 1, 1943 (Berg, NYPL).

CHAPTER TEN

1. The surname "Boncoeur" translates in English to "good heart."

2. "Ben Boncoeur" (Berg Collection, New York Public Library).

3. Ibid.

4. A Vacation Club account was a way to save for one's summer or holiday expenses. This offered an affordable savings method that could be contributed to over time usually paid in weekly or monthly deposits from a company payroll.

5. Gabrielle Kerouac to Jack and Joan Kerouac, February 7, 1951 (Berg, NYPL).

6. Joan Haverty, *Nobody's Wife: The Smart Aleck and the King of Beats* (Creative Arts, 2000).

7. Ibid.

8. Kinston, North Carolina, is about one hour south of Rocky Mount. What he was doing there when he was presumably in New York for this month is unknown. However, this location is what he wrote on the front page of this untitled essay. A letter from Caroline Kerouac to Gabrielle Kerouac (dated February 1952) suggests that at some point, Jack and Gabe were interested in moving there.

9. "Holograph Essay," March 13, 1951 (Berg, NYPL).

10. Kerouac had placed an asterisk for a footnote here: "just as is the electronic airborne signal."

11. Untitled essay, March 13, 1951 (Berg, NYPL).

12. *The Letters of John Keats*, ed. H. E. Rollins, 2 vols. (Cambridge University Press, 1958), i, 193–94.

13. Li Ou, *Keats and Negative Capability* (Bloomsbury Publishing, 2011).

14. Kerouac to Ed White, April 1951, *Missouri Review* 17, no. 3 (1994): 141.

15. Sade's book was written in miniscule writing on a narrow twelve-meter-long strip of parchment in just thirty-seven days during his imprisonment in the Bastille. Sade concealed the illicit manuscript in his cell. It was later found when the prison was stormed during the French Revolution.

16. Holograph manuscript, "Beat Generation—Tangier," March 26, 1957 (Berg, NYPL).

17. Dialogue is taken from Kerouac's holograph manuscript titled "Beat Generation," March 26, 1957. This text was to be a follow-up to *On the Road*.

18. Kerouac to Neal Cassady, June 10, 1951 (Berg, NYPL).

19. "Desolation Peak" Notebook of 1956 (Berg, NYPL).

20. "Potboiler 'Hip,'" August 25–29, 1951 (Berg, NYPL).

21. Though Kerouac did once again attempt to rewrite "Hip" in one of the notebooks for *Visions of Cody* on July 25–26, 1952, according to Jean-Christophe Cloutier in his book of Kerouac's French texts, *La vie est d'hommage* (*Les Éditions du Boréal*, 2016).

22. Herman Melville, *Pierre* (Hendricks House, 1956), xiii ("Introduction by Henry Murray").

23. Journal, Fall 1951 (Berg, NYPL).

24. Ibid.

25. "On the Road with Dean Pomeray," October 1951 (Berg, NYPL).

26. Journal, Fall 1951 (Berg, NYPL).

27. *Visions of Neal* Notebook, October 1951 (Berg, NYPL).

28. Ibid.

29. Jack Kerouac to Neal Cassady, October 9, 1951, *Selected Letters: 1940–1956*, 326–27.

30. Kerouac was earning about $25 per week.

31. *Lonesome Traveler* (Library of America, 2007), 656.

32. Allen Ginsberg to Neal Cassady, July 3, 1952, *The Letters of Allen Ginsberg* (Hachette Books, 2008).

33. Allen Ginsberg to William Burroughs and Jack Kerouac, June 12, 1952, *Letters of Allen Ginsberg*.

34. Jack Kerouac to John Clellon Holmes, June 5, 1951 (Berg, NYPL).

35. William S. Burroughs to Allen Ginsberg, July 13, 1952, *The Letters of William S. Burroughs: 1945–1959* (Viking, 1993).

36. Santa María la Redonda is a traditional barrio located in the Cuauhtémoc municipality of Mexico City.

37. "The Statue of Christ," *Tristessa* Notebook, 1952 (Berg, NYPL).

38. Allen Ginsberg to Jack Kerouac, June 6, 1952 (Columbia University Library).

39. Jack Kerouac to Allen Ginsberg, October 8, 1952, *Selected Letters*, 377–80.

40. Caroline Kerouac Blake to Gabrielle Kerouac, May 16, 1952 (Berg, NYPL).

41. Jack Kerouac to John Clellon Holmes, June 17, 1952 (Berg, NYPL).

42. Jack Kerouac to John Clellon Holmes, June 1952, *Selected Letters*, 375.

43. Carolyn Cassady to Jack Kerouac, June 5, 1952 (Berg, NYPL).

44. Ibid.

45. Jack Kerouac to Carolyn Cassady, June 3, 1952, *Selected Letters*, 362–64.

46. Jack Kerouac to Stella Sampas, December 10, 1952, *Selected Letters*, 390.

47. Jack Kerouac to Allen Ginsberg, October 8, 1952, *Selected Letters*, 378.

48. Neal Cassady to J. C. Clements, August 21, 1952, *Collected Letters, 1944–1967* (Penguin, 2004), 330–31.

CHAPTER ELEVEN

1. Caroline Kerouac Blake to Gabrielle Kerouac, September 11, 1952 (Berg Collection, New York Public Library).

2. Ibid.

3. Neal Cassady to Allen Ginsberg, October 4, 1952, *Neal Cassady: Collected Letters, 1944–1967* (Penguin Books, 2004), 337–38.

4. Jack Kerouac to John Clellon Holmes, October 12, 1952, *Selected Letters*, 381.

5. Ibid., 381–82.
6. Untitled poem, October 1952 Notebook (Berg, NYPL).
7. "The Railroad Earth," *Lonesome Traveler*, 80.
8. Neal Cassady to Carolyn Cassady, December 2, 1952, *Collected Letters, 1944–1967*.
9. "Benzedrine Vision," 1952 (Berg, NYPL).
10. Ibid.
11. Ibid.
12. Ben Giamo, *Kerouac; The Word and the Way* (Southern Illinois University Press, 2000), 99.
13. "The Blessedness Surely to Be Believed" (Berg, NYPL).
14. Ibid.
15. "Maggie Cassidy" Notebooks I through V (Berg, NYPL).
16. 1954 Notebook (Berg, NYPL).
17. Ibid.
18. Ibid.
19. Ibid.
20. Ibid.
21. "Book of Daydreams," May 11, 1953 (Berg, NYPL).
22. 1954 Notebook (Berg, NYPL).
23. "Off the Coast of Mexico," June 5, 1953 (Berg, NYPL).
24. Ibid.
25. Ibid.
26. Later collected in Kerouac's *Lonesome Traveler* (Grove Press, 1960). None of the prose found in this autobiographical story can be found in his notebook of this time, which indicates he wrote it all spontaneously at a later date.
27. Described by Kerouac in his "Editorial Explanation of Various Techniques of the Duluoz Legend" included in *Some of the Dharma* (Penguin, 1997).
28. "TICS," June 28, 1953 (Berg, NYPL).
29. "Sisters" by Alene Lee, first published in *Beatdom* (February 17, 2010).
30. William S. Burroughs and Allen Ginsberg, *The Yage Letters* (City Lights, 1963).
31. As recounted in *Jack's Book*, ed. by Barry Gifford and Lawrence Lee (Penguin, 1973).
32. Ibid.
33. Jack Kerouac, *Book of Dreams* (City Lights, 1960), 165.
34. "The Power of the Subconscious Mind," as written in 1943 SS *Weems* Journal (Berg, NYPL).
35. On the Path," August 19, 1955 (Berg, NYPL).
36. Ibid.
37. Ibid.
38. Ibid.
39. Helen K. Taylor to Malcolm Cowley, October 22, 1953 (Malcolm Cowley Archive, Newberry Library).

40. Kerouac claimed that he had Schmorl's nodes, a common spinal disc herniation in which the soft tissue of the intervertebral disc bulges out into the adjacent vertebrae through an endplate defect.

41. "On the Path" (Berg, NYPL).

42. Ibid.

43. At this point, Kerouac has been following what is roughly modern-day Interstate 95, which begins in Maine and extends southerly to Miami, Florida.

44. "On the Path" (Berg, NYPL).

45. Kerouac, *Some of the Dharma*, 83.

46. Carolyn Cassady, *Off the Road: My Years with Cassady, Kerouac and Ginsberg* (Penguin, 1991), 108.

47. *Some of the Dharma*, 38.

48. Ibid., iii.

49. "Bus East," *Pomes All Sizes* (City Lights, 1992), 377–81.

50. Jack Kerouac to Carolyn Cassady, April 22, 1954, *Selected Letters*, 408.

51. Jack Kerouac to Allen Ginsberg, late May 1954, *The Letters* (Viking, 2010), 218–19.

52. Mary Ackerman did recover. She married in 1955.

53. Interview with Ramblin' Jack Elliott, *Guitar Player* (August 8, 2022), Martin McQuade.

54. Jack Kerouac to Allen Ginsberg, after June 18, 1954, *The Letters* (Viking, 2010), 224–25.

55. *A Buddhist Bible* (Beacon Press, 1994), 112.

56. Jack Kerouac to Carolyn Cassady, May 17, 1954, *Selected Letters*, 418–23.

57. Jack Kerouac to Carolyn Cassady, July 2, 1947, *Selected Letters*, 427.

58. *Some of the Dharma*, 61.

59. "Lowell Sketches"—SK 13 for *Book of Sketches*, October 1954 (Berg, NYPL).

60. *Book of Sketches* (Penguin, 2006), 67.

61. *Some of the Dharma*, 140.

62. "The Origins of the Beat Generation," *Playboy* (January 1959).

CHAPTER TWELVE

1. Jack Kerouac, *The Portable Kerouac* (Viking, 1995), 222–23.

2. Ibid., 84.

3. Ibid., 89.

4. Ibid., 103.

5. Jack Kerouac to Alfred Kazin, October 27, 1954, *Selected Letters: 1940–1956* (Viking, 1995), 450.

6. Kerouac wanted to capitalize on the success of John Clellon Holmes's essay, "This Is the Beat Generation," so he retitled *On the Road* to *The Beat Generation*. It would later be returned to *On the Road*.

7. Jack Kerouac, *Some of the Dharma* (Penguin, 1997), 186–87.

8. Jack Kerouac, *Wake Up* (Viking, 2008), 7.

9. Ibid., 36.

10. "Bowery Blues," in *Jack Kerouac: Collected Poems* (Library of America, 2012), 254.

11. Ibid., 254–64.

12. "The City and the Path," April 21, 1955, "Dharma (10)" Notebook (Berg Collection, New York Public Library).

13. "The Scripture of the Golden Eternity" Notebook (Berg, NYPL).

14. "Modified Ascetic Life" (Berg, NYPL).

15. "Elements of the Basic Deceit" (Berg, NYPL).

16. "Mexico City Blues" Notebook, August 22, 1955 (Berg, NYPL).

17. "Scripture of the Golden Eternity" Notebook (Berg, NYPL).

18. "Mexico City Blues" Notebook, August 22, 1955 (Berg, NYPL).

19. Jack Kerouac, *Tristessa* (Library of America, 2007), 563.

20. Ibid.

21. Jack Kerouac to Allen Ginsberg, August 19, 1955, *Selected Letters*, 507.

22. Jack Kerouac to Sterling Lord, August 19, 1955, *Selected Letters*, 510.

23. Jack Kerouac to Malcolm Cowley, September 11, 1955, *Selected Letters*, 515.

24. Kerouac, *Some of the Dharma*, 339.

25. Jack Kerouac, *Book of Dreams* (City Lights, 1960), 116.

26. Malcolm Cowley to Jack Kerouac, November 8, 1955, Newberry Library, Malcolm Cowley Collection.

27. Eventually, this daydream came true. Film director Francis Ford Coppola optioned the film rights for *On the Road* on April 1, 1978. On March 4, 1980, the famed director of *The Godfather* and *Apocalypse Now* purchased the film rights for $95,000. Various payments and extensions of rights would be paid out in part to Jan Kerouac.

28. Jack Kerouac to John Clellon Holmes, October 12, 1955, *Selected Letters*, 522–23.

29. Kerouac, *Some of the Dharma*, 268.

30. "Dharma (10)" Notebook (Berg, NYPL).

31. *Some of the Dharma*, 365.

32. Codeine.

33. "Goofballs" are slang for either a tranquilizing drug or barbiturates.

34. Actress Greta Garbo (1905–1990) was notorious for her reclusive nature: "As early as I can remember, I have wanted to be alone. I detest crowds, don't like many people." Ruth Biery, "The Story of Greta Garbo As Told by Her to Ruth Biery, Chapter III," *Photoplay*, June 1928c.

35. Gabrielle was petrified of insects yet had a reservation toward killing anything no matter how small according to a letter from her to Jack.

36. Gabrielle Kerouac to Jack Kerouac, December 5, 1955 (Berg, NYPL).

37. Jack Kerouac, *The Dharma Bums* (Viking, 1958), 134.

38. *Some of the Dharma*, 366.

39. Jack Kerouac to Allen Ginsberg, March 4, 1955, Columbia University Library.

40. Kerouac may have intended the comparison to include the picaresque and stream-of-consciousness elements of *Tristram Shandy* to be incorporated in *Visions of Bill*.

41. Jack Kerouac to Allen Ginsberg, March 4, 1955, Columbia University Library.

42. "Visions of Bill" Notebook (Berg, NYPL).

43. Published in *Self-Portrait: Unpublished Writings of Jack Kerouac*, ed. Paul Maher Jr. and Charles Shuttleworth (Sal Paradise Press/Rare Bird Books, 2024).

44. Ibid.
45. "Desolation Blues," in *Desolation Peak* (Sal Paradise Press, 2022), 222.
46. Kerouac, *Dharma Bums.*
47. The alternate title of *Wake Up* written in March 1955.
48. Jack Kerouac to Allen Ginsberg, May 27, 1955, Columbia University Library.
49. "Dharma 10" (Berg, NYPL).
50. Old Angel Midnight, #8 (Library of America, 2012), 486.
51. Jack Kerouac, *Desolation Angels* (Penguin, 2003), 5.
52. Ibid., 255.
53. Jack Kerouac to Sterling Lord, October 7, 1956, *Selected Letters*, 588.
54. All details of Kerouac's trip and stay in Tangier were sourced from Diaries #2 and #3, January 7 to May 27, 1957 (Berg, NYPL).
55. "Diary #2" (Holograph diary), "Feb. '57 / Bila Kayf," January 7, 1957–February 21, 1957.
56. Ibid.
57. Ibid.

WORKS CITED

Note: All works cited are done so within the scope of fair use. All writings of Jack Kerouac are quoted by permission of Jim Sampas, literary executor of the Estate of Jack & Stella Kerouac.

Burroughs, William S.
    Queer (Viking, 1985)
    Naked Lunch (Grove Press, 2001)
Burroughs, William S. / Jack Kerouac
    And the Hippos Were Boiled in Their Tanks (Grove, 2008)
Cassady, Carolyn
    Off the Road: My Years with Cassady, Kerouac, and Ginsberg (William Morrow, 1990)
Cassady, Neal
    The First Third (City Lights, 1971)
    Collected Letters, 1944–1967 (Penguin, 2004)
Ginsberg, Allen
    The Book of Martydom and Artifice (Da Capo Press, 2006)
    Jack Kerouac/Allen Ginsberg: The Letters (Viking, 2010)
    As Ever: Collected Letters of Allen Ginsberg and Neal Cassady (Creative Arts, 1977)
    The Best Minds of My Generation (Grove Press, 2017)
Goddard, Dwight
    A Buddhist Bible (Beacon Press, 1994)
Kerouac, Jack
    Doctor Sax (Grove Press, 1959)
    Maggie Cassidy (Penguin, 1993)
    Desolation Angels (Penguin, 1993)
    The Portable Kerouac (Viking, 1995)
    Selected Letters: 1940–1956 (Viking, 1995)
    Selected Letters: 1957–1969 (Viking, 2000)
    Some of the Dharma (Penguin, 1999)
    Atop an Underwood: Early Stories and Other Writings (Viking, 1999)

Orpheus Emerged (iBooks, 2000)

Book of Dreams (City Lights, 2001)

Windblown World: The Journals of Jack Kerouac 1947–1954 (Viking, 2004)

Book of Sketches (Penguin, 2006)

On the Road: The Original Scroll (Viking, 2007)

Wake Up—A Life of the Buddha (Viking, 2008)

The Sea Is My Brother (Da Capo Press, 2011)

The Haunted Life and Other Stories (Da Capo Press, 2014)

Desolation Peak: Collected Writings (Sal Paradise Press/Rare Bird Books, 2022)

Library of America (*Road Novels* [2007], *Collected Poems* [2012], *The Unknown Kerouac* [2016])

Self-Portrait: Unpublished Writings of Jack Kerouac (Sal Paradise Press/Rare Bird Books, 2024)

Lin, Yutang

The Wisdom of China and India (Random House, 1942)

Melville, Herman

Pierre (Hendricks House, 1949) and Introduction by Henry A. Murray

Miles, Barry

Call Me Burroughs: A Life (Twelve, 2013)

Morgan, Ted

Literary Outlaw: The Life and Times of William S. Burroughs (W.W. Norton & Co., 2012)

Parker, Edie

You'll Be Okay: My Life with Jack Kerouac (City Lights, 2007)

Schumacher, Michael

Dharma Lion: A Biography of Allen Ginsberg (U. of Minn. Press, 2016)

Spengler, Oswald

The Decline of the West (Volumes I and II) (Arktos, 2021)

Wolfe, Thomas

You Can't Go Home Again (Scribner, 2011)

Index

Christianity, 258. *See also*
Catholicism
Clements, J. C., 189
Coast Guard, 99
Cocteau, Jean, 87
codeine, 137
Coffey, Margaret, 47
Columbia University: breaks
from, 16; disenrollment from,
66; education at, 10–11, 34;
failures at, 35–37; football at,
14; Ginsberg, A., at, 66–67;
Navy and, 38; re-registration at,
28–29, 32–33
confessionals, 245–46
Conrad, Joseph, 120
consciousness, 2, 25
Corso, Gregory, 4, 205, 255,
257, 265
Cowley, Malcolm: advice from,
239–40; Jennison and, 228;
Lord and, 222; publishers and,
197–98; relationship with, 246,
248; resentment with, 261;
support from, 237, 258; Taylor
and, 209
creativity: of artists, 78–79;
characters and, 106–7, 175–76;
depression and, 236; music and,
177–79; for poetry, 242–43;
psychology of, 5; writing and,
228–30
Creeley, Robert, 255
Crime and Punishment
(Dostoevsky), 79, 261

Crime and the Human Mind
(Abrahamsen), 87
Cru, Henri: assistance from, 57,
181; relationship with, 33–34,
36–38, 40
culture: to artists, 73–74; of Beat
Generation, 2; hitchhiking,
186, 216; narcotics in, 132;
religion and, 68–69, 74–75,
97; television, 117–18; of U.S.,
62–63, 139, 152–53

"The Dark Corridor" (Kerouac,
Jack), 78–79, 82–84
death: in family, 206; fear of,
5, 114, 173–74; of Kerouac,
Gerard, 8–9, 60–61, 64, 125,
238–39; of Kerouac, L.,
2–3, 57, 104–5; to Kerouac,
Gabrielle, 45; philosophy of,
30; psychology of, 2, 9, 96; of
Sampas, Sammy, 64, 66, 69,
220; of Vollmer, 2, 174, 183,
263; writing about, 196
The Decline of the West (Spengler),
40, 96
Delilah (Goodrich), 188
Dementia Praecox, 49
Denver, Colorado. *See specific topics*
"Deposition" (Burroughs, W. S.), 2
depression: alcohol and,
201–2; creativity and, 236;
hallucinations and, 194–95;
travel and, 260
De Sade, Marquis, 167

prostitution, 92, 145, 187, 215,
243, 259–61, 264, 266
pseudonyms, 92
psychedelics, 2–5
psychology: Adler on, 60–62;
of alcohol, 86, 100, 113;
anxiety, 41, 61, 120, 126–27,
231, 258; of artists, 71–72; of
Benzedrine, 126–27, 202–3,
240–41, 263; of creativity, 5;
of death, 2, 9, 96; Dementia
Praecox, 49; of dreams, 206–7;
Eastern philosophy and,
207–8; of education, 22–23;
ennui, 63–64; of family, 1–2,
20–21; in hospitalization,
170–71, 174–75; illness and,
103–4; of injuries, 11–12;
of Jung, 8; of loneliness, 36,
50–51; of narcotics, 260; of
Navy, 47–48; philosophy and,
258–59; of psychedelics, 3–4;
psychoanalysis, 24, 51–52, 88;
of rejection, 27, 205–6; of self-
awareness, 25, 60–62; of travel,
30–31, 255–56; of work, 17,
21; of World War II, 131–32;
writing and, 56–57, 173–74,
254–55
publishers: Ace, 198; Brown, 121,
128; contact with, 180–81;
Cowley and, 197–98; Deutsch,
264; Dodd Mead, 228;
Harcourt, Brace, 135–36, 150;
Little, 121, 128; Macmillan,

121; power of attorney with,
201; queries with, 120–21,
150–51; rejection from, 128,
133; success with, 209, 256; for
The Town and the City, 135–36;
Viking, 197–98, 209, 228,
237, 239–40, 246; writing and,
186–87

Queer (Burroughs, W. S.), 183–85

Racine, Jean, 137
racism, 204–5
Random House, 121, 228
rejection: encouragement and,
22; from Giroux, 150–51, 168;
from Knopf, 224; psychology
of, 27, 205–6; from publishers,
128, 133; from Random
House, 228
relationship: with Apostolos, 17,
27; with Burroughs, W. S.,
85–86, 97–98, 100, 182–83,
185, 193–94, 231–32, 262; with
Cowley, 246, 248; with Cru,
33–34, 36–38, 40; with Garver,
194, 196, 234, 256–57; with
Ginsberg, A., 75–76, 79–80,
103, 112–13, 119–20, 189,
200–201, 230; with Holmes,
192, 249; with Kerouac, C.,
19, 23, 34, 61, 94–95, 129–31,
241, 243–45; with Kerouac,
Gabrielle, 1–3, 10–11, 34, 86,
96, 116, 126; with Kerouac,

outlines, 180–81; output, 85, 86–87, 90–92; philosophy and, 13–14, 71–72, 96–97, 103–4, 195–96; in poverty, 192–93; process, 3–5, 16–17, 22, 69–70, 76–77, 90, 116, 140, 250; pseudonyms, 92; psychology and, 56–57, 173–74, 254–55; publishers and, 186–87; about religion, 97–98; as sacred, 13, 172; to Sampas, Sammy, 42–43, 47; at sea, 202–3; self-awareness and, 55–56; sexual identity and, 153–54; sober, 200; from stream of consciousness, 25; from stream-perception, 163–65; success with, 232–33;

themes in, 37–38; TICS, 203–4; travel and, 14–15, 110–11, 241–43; typewriters for, 175; about Washington, DC, 20; as work, 22–23; about World War II, 69–70
Wyn, Aaron A., 180
Wyse, Seymour, 63–65

yage, 2
You Can't Go Home Again (Wolfe), 11
Young, Celine, 67, 70, 72; Ginsberg, A., and, 76, 80–81, 86–97; to Kerouac, Jack, 77–78, 80–81, 90
Young, Lester, 59